SPRAWL

SPRAWL

a compact history

ROBERT BRUEGMANN

THE UNIVERSITY OF CHICAGO PRESS | CHICAGO AND LONDON

The University of Chicago Press, Chicago 60637
The University of Chicago Press, Ltd., London
© 2005 by The University of Chicago
All rights reserved. Published 2005
Paperback edition 2006
Printed in the United States of America

14 13 12 11 10 09 08 07 06   2 3 4 5
ISBN: 0-226-07690-3 (cloth)
ISBN-13: 978-0-226-07691-1 (paper)
ISBN-10: 0-226-07691-1 (paper)

Library of Congress Cataloging-in-Publication Data

Bruegmann, Robert.
  Sprawl : a compact history / Robert Bruegmann.
    p. cm.
  Includes bibliographical references and index.
  ISBN 0-226-07690-3 (cloth : alk. paper)
    1. Cities and towns—Growth.   2. Land use.   3. Urban policy.
4. City planning.   5. Metropolitan areas.   I. Title.
HT371.B74 2005
307.76—dc22

                                                    2005007591

♾ The paper used in this publication meets the minimum requirements of the
American National Standard for Information Sciences—Permanence of Paper
for Printed Library Materials, ANSI Z39.48–1992.

CONTENTS

INTRODUCTION

When the plane banks sharply to the left about an hour and a half into the flight from Chicago, I know that we are starting our long descent into New York's LaGuardia airport. Looking down, I can see long, wooded ridges running diagonally from the southwest to the northeast, alternating with wide stream valleys between them. This part of western New Jersey is beautiful from the air. In summer the deep green of the oaks and maples on the ridge tops forms a striking contrast with the lighter greens that make up the patchwork quilt of fields in the valleys. At first glance, this landscape of cropland, farmhouses, roads, and streams seems timeless, little changed over the centuries.

Of course, the landscape is not natural but almost entirely manmade, and it was created relatively recently, mostly within the past one hundred years. Even from 15,000 feet, moreover, it is clear, if you look carefully, that a great deal has changed very recently. There are many more houses in the valleys than the small number of people who still farm there could possibly occupy, and it is possible to make out through the dense tree cover of the hillsides many other houses that clearly have no connection with agricultural production. This is not at all the completely rural scene that it might appear to be. All the evidence suggests that most of the people living here have little to do with farming or any other traditional rural activities.

It is difficult, at least at first glance, to imagine what all the people living in these houses do, where they work, shop, and play since there are no office buildings, shopping centers, or movie theaters in sight. It is possible that some of them work from their home, relying heavily on the phone, Internet, and express delivery services to keep them connected to the urban world, and it is possible that others drive to jobs in small towns nearby. The substantial number of houses, however, suggests that the majority must commute some distance to work, perhaps to nearby corporate facilities tucked discreetly into the rolling hills or, further afield, to large business centers along highways like the Route 1 strip near Princeton. Others probably make their way daily into downtown Trenton or Center City Philadelphia, twenty and forty miles to the southwest, respectively, or into downtown New Brunswick, Newark, or even Manhattan, thirty, forty and sixty miles, respectively, to the northeast. In virtually every case, however, no matter how rural the view from the living room window, these residents are more closely tied economically and socially to the urban world than they are to the apparently rural one they can see out their windows.

Indeed, the connection to the urban world is confirmed visually from the plane window within a few minutes, as the first subdivisions come into view, first one, then dozens of them, each neatly filling the land once occupied by a single farm or small group of farms. Then a freeway edges into sight, then an office park, then more subdivisions until the urban uses are dominant and are interrupted only occasionally by a patch of green—an agricultural hold-out, a golf course, or a public park. As the urban rhythm quickens, this landscape soon fills the horizon, a vast crazy quilt of nearly continuous suburbia, with subdivisions, shopping centers, and industrial parks crisscrossed by roads and railroads and dotted with parks and open spaces.

Sprawl! By almost anyone's definition this part of central New Jersey would qualify as sprawl. Once an arcane term used primarily by city planners and academics, "sprawl" has recently emerged as a part of everyday speech. Most often described as unplanned, scattered, low-density, automobile-dependent development at the urban periphery, sprawl now shares space on the covers of national news magazines with perennial "big" issues like health care and race relations, and it has become a prominent issue on talk shows and campaign trails. From every direction, Americans are bombarded by the message of anti-sprawl reformers. They are told that sprawl threatens to destroy open space, consume agricultural land, drive up utility costs, undermine urban social life, heighten inequalities, deplete natural resources, and damage the environment. And, by the way, it is ugly.

The sprawl of central New Jersey, according to these critics, represents an expensive and unsustainable pattern of development. The widely dispersed nature of this development makes everyone dependent on the automobile, which in turn, uses excessive amounts of energy, creates pollution, and contributes to global warming. Moreover, anti-sprawl activists claim, the sprawl being built today will inevitably harm the older communities that are outflanked by it.

They hold the landscape I have just described responsible for the deterioration of many of the older neighborhoods that come into view as the plane continues eastward across New Jersey, northward across Staten Island, and then across western Brooklyn and Queens into LaGuardia. Large numbers of once flourishing shops along the commercial streets of Bayonne and Jersey City disappeared when new suburban shopping centers appeared further out, they will say. In many of the tightly packed neighborhoods of Brooklyn and Queens, house prices stagnated or fell as affluent middle-class residents left for newer and more spacious houses further out in Long Island. In some cases the result was racial turmoil, abandonment, and the concentration of poor and minority residents in the oldest, least desirable housing.

According to its critics, sprawl hurts everyone and must be stopped. Instead of the unplanned, wasteful patterns visible at the edge of the New York region, they advocate new, carefully planned "smart growth," including denser urban infill and, where green-field construction is necessary, more compact "sustainable" communities, less dependent on automobiles, and more in tune with traditional urban patterns. Many of these critics hail anti-sprawl efforts underway in states like Oregon and Maryland or in communities like Boulder, Colorado.

Most of what has been written about sprawl to date has been devoted to complaints. The usual questions asked are exactly how damaging sprawl is and what are the most appropriate ways to stop it. What I decided to do instead, in this book, was to look at this issue from a historic perspective and to examine the way the concept of sprawl was invented and how it has been used over time. After all, sprawl, like "urban blight," the "slum," or many other terms connected with urban development, is not so much an objective reality as a cultural concept, a term born at a specific time and place and used over the years by a wide range of individuals and groups for specific purposes. In the process, it has accumulated around it an entire body of ideas and assumptions.

One of the most striking things revealed by even the most cursory study of the way "sprawl" has been used over the years is the difficulty of pinning down a common definition or linking it to realities on the ground. For example, which of the various landscapes in central New Jersey I have just described ought to be called sprawl? Is it the outmost band of development we saw from the window of the plane, an area perhaps best described as "exurbia," the very low-density urban penumbra that lies beyond the regularly built-up suburbs and their urban services? Or is it the newly emerging suburban band of conventional subdivisions, golf courses, schools, and strip malls located closer in toward the city? If the latter is sprawl, is it logical to exclude older suburbs? Certainly at one time these older communities, even many of the most densely packed inner neighborhoods in Brooklyn and Manhattan, were themselves relatively low in density and suburban in character compared to what was then the core of the city. Why wouldn't they be considered historic sprawl?

Or what about the neighborhoods like the Lower East Side of Manhattan, places whose central location and intensely urban character make them, in the opinion of many people writing about this subject, the opposite of sprawl? Isn't it possible to see areas like this as both cause and effect of sprawl? Certainly, given the way the Lower East Side has decanted outward large numbers of people, it would make sense to say that this neighborhood helped fuel sprawl. Or, looked at from the other side of the equation, both the depopulation of the Lower East Side and its current repopulation by a new set of inhabitants can be seen as the effect of sprawl, the end of the long chain of reactions that followed in the wake of the construction of new housing on the periphery. As new houses were built, they attracted families from existing neighborhoods who, in turn, sold their houses to people who lived still closer to the center. At the end of this chain were many very poor residents of the Lower East Side desperate to move. At a certain point, after most of the poorest families departed, the area became attractive to a new, more affluent population that appreciated the depressed prices, the central location, the "traditional" feel of an urban neighborhood, even the disreputable aura of the place. The result was gentrification—meaning a rise in social and economic profile.

Gentrification at the center and sprawl at the edge have been flipsides of the same coin. In a typically paradoxical situation, no matter how much the new, more affluent residents profess to like the "gritty" urban character of the place, so different in their minds from the subdivisions of the far suburbs, what makes the neighborhood attractive today are less the things that are actually traditionally urban but those that are not. The most important of these are sharply lowered population densities, fewer poor residents, less manufacturing activity, and the things that the Lower East Side finally shares with the suburbs: reliable plumbing, supermarkets with good produce, and a substantial cohort of middle-class residents.

In short, I believe that the individuals and groups using the word "sprawl" have actually been describing several quite different landscapes, and they have neglected others that might logically be included under this rubric. Far from being a defect, I will argue, the difficulty in defining sprawl has been one of the chief reasons the term has proved so useful to reformers. It has allowed for the creation of a large coalition of individuals who agree that they are against sprawl but who don't actually agree on much else.

Many of the things that critics of sprawl appear to agree on, moreover, are based on out-of-date or insufficient evidence. Despite a common belief that suburban sprawl is accelerating and that the most affluent people are moving constantly outward to areas of ever-lower density, in fact the suburbs of American cities are, if anything, becoming denser. Suburban lot sizes, after peaking in the 1950s, have been declining, and the number of square feet of land used by the average house in new developments at the suburban edge has fallen sharply in the past ten years even as the houses themselves have grown in size. A surprising amount of the new housing at the very edge of most American cities consists of row housing and garden apartments for working-class Americans. This phenomenon is quite visible from the plane flying over the suburban edge in New Jersey but is even more conspicuous on the ground at the edge of the fastest growing cities of the American South and West, which are the very ones that have usually been described as the most sprawling.

The notion that Phoenix and Las Vegas and Los Angeles are among the country's most sprawling places is also problematic at best. Los Angeles, for example, often taken to be the epitome of sprawl, has become so much denser over the past fifty years that it is now America's most densely populated urbanized area, as measured by the census bureau. It is considerably denser than the New York or Chicago urbanized areas, for example. Although this might seem preposterous since Los Angeles has no neighborhoods with densities anything like parts of Manhattan, Los Angeles has a relatively high density spread over an extremely large area. Los Angeles also has none of the very low-density exurban peripheral growth seen in the New York region. In fact, quite unlike Eastern cities, Los Angeles has almost no exurban sprawl at all because the high cost of supplying water makes relatively compact development almost inevitable.

Turning from suburban sprawl to exurban sprawl, the picture is quite different. Exurban sprawl is apparently in the process of accelerating, with more people occupying more land at lower densities, but we know very little about exurban sprawl. It is also difficult to know what part of exurban development should be called sprawl at all. Certainly a group of four houses in central New Jersey sitting on two-acre lots behind long driveways and carefully mowed front lawns would be sprawl by most people's definition. But what about the houses visible from the airplane window over New Jersey that clearly aren't new but, instead, old farmhouses taken over by urban residents who no longer farm the land? Would this still be sprawl? And, finally, what about the houses on very large acreage, nestled into the trees in such a way that that they are all but invisible from the air or surrounding roads? Would it make any sense to use the term for this area, which might well serve as an important wildlife sanctuary?

I used to think it ironic that my interest in sprawl started as a by-product of research on central Paris. In more recent years, I have come to realize that this is actually quite a characteristic progression whenever individuals try to make sense of anything as complicated as cities and urban systems. In my case, during the period I was working on my dissertation and flying back and forth from Paris, I was forcefully struck by the tiny size of my object of study, the historical core of Paris, compared to the vast suburban and exurban areas that surrounded it. How different was this little island of tall, tightly packed apartment blocks from the large expanses of low-density housing, industrial parks, open spaces and superhighways that made up most of the rest of the urban region. Much of the recent development at the edge of the Parisian metropolitan area, in fact, looked remarkably similar to the landscape I saw from the plane window touching down at Cincinnati or Philadelphia.

After finishing my dissertation and moving to Chicago in the late 1970s, my interest in these outer urban landscapes grew, fueled by a desire to understand the vast changes I saw happening on my frequent trips out to the suburbs. Although I had been familiar with American cities and their suburbs all my life, I realized that neither my previous experience nor the existing literature was of much help in describing, let alone explaining, the vast transformations that were taking place all around me. In the Chicago area in the mid-1980s, for example, thousands of acres of agricultural countryside as far as sixty miles from the Loop, Chicago's central business district, in a great arc from Kenosha County, Wisconsin, to Lake County, Indiana, were being converted to subdivisions and industrial parks. Glossy office buildings were creating a kind of linear Main Street along the Interstate 88 tollway corridor near Naperville and Aurora, some twenty to thirty miles west of the Loop. The enormous Woodfield business district in Schaumburg, twenty-five miles northwest of the center of Chicago, already the second most important business district in the state, was starting to obtain a high-rise skyline that visitors flying into O'Hare could easily mistake for that of Chicago's Loop.

Much of what I saw contradicted the usual stereotypes about cities and suburbs. In the supposedly homogeneous suburbs, a Buddhist temple rose in a cornfield outside Aurora and a Japanese shopping center opened in northwest suburban Arlington Heights. The closing of a regional shopping mall in Harvey signaled economic woes and racial change across large areas of the south suburbs. These changes were not confined to the suburbs, moreover. The same big-box retail establishments and row houses visible in far suburban Gurnee or Tinley Park, forty or fifty miles from Chicago were sprouting in my own neighborhood, originally a German working-class community but now in the process of rapid gentrification. As an older working-class population left the area in the wake of the departure of manufacturing firms, they were replaced by new residents driving Volvos with license plate frames advertising suburban automobile dealerships. As an increasingly affluent population moved in, densities plummeted and automobile usage soared. Increasingly, although my neighborhood looked like a traditional city neighborhood—in fact more traditional by the year as the newcomers razed small frame houses with asphalt shingles and aluminum siding and replaced them with great stone-fronted houses that appeared older and certainly much grander—it started to function in ways that made it similar to any suburb, and it gradually obtained a comparable demographic profile. In short, little of what I saw happening around me was compatible with the usual stereotypes about city and suburb. How to make sense of the whole thing?

I went to the library to see if history books, guidebooks, sociological studies, or geographic analyses could help me understand these landscapes. I found that while there were endless publications that dealt with American city centers, there was little of any substance on the suburbs and almost nothing on the much more dispersed regions beyond that. Much of the literature seemed to be a continuation of a tradition popular in the 1960s and 1970s of urban intellectuals bashing the "burbs" and then others rushing to their defense. True, by the end of the 1980s a more substantial literature had started to appear on the early history of suburban development. A few substantial articles on exurbia had appeared as well.

However, this remained a rather thin literature, given the fact that more American and Europeans live in the suburbs and exurbs than in either the central city or the countryside. And when most scholars approached the present, they tended to fall back on old stereotypes. Starting in the early 1990s, I noticed that the focus on the suburbs was starting to switch to a focus on sprawl in the works of many authors. Despite the shift in terminology, the ideas were very similar. Most of the sprawl diagnoses were still based on assumptions codified in the late 1960s when American suburbs were booming and city centers seemed to be in grave danger of collapsing. The "inner city" was portrayed as poor and filled with minorities. The suburbs were described as being white and affluent. Whatever validity these generalizations might have had in the late 1960s—and even then they were far from adequate—they were completely inadequate to describe metropolitan areas by the 1990s. Areas like the South Bronx, emptied out during the postwar decades, had started to fill up again. Many of the city centers were roaring back. Densities were rising in subdivisions at the urban periphery, many of which were being swelled by working class and minority families. A considerable number of the most troubled areas of metropolitan America were located in the suburbs, often the far suburbs.

As far as I could see, the sprawl crusade had generated a great deal of heat but not much light and was primarily of interest to a small group of academics. Then, to my surprise, in the mid-1990s, after I had done considerable work on a book on the decentralization of the American city, the anti-sprawl crusade suddenly caught fire. Articles appeared in the airline magazines, and sprawl reached the cover of the news weeklies. Virtually overnight the anti-sprawl reformers' new catchphrase "smart growth" seemed to be everywhere. It appeared as though every right-minded individual and organization in the country was convinced that sprawl was economically inefficient, environmentally detrimental, socially deplorable, and aesthetically ugly—in short, an unmitigated disaster. In fact, so many "right-minded" people were so vociferous on the subject that I began to suspect that there must be something suspicious about the argument itself. Hence, I decided to shift my focus and concentrate on the construction of the concept of sprawl and the assumptions that have motivated the campaigns to combat it.

In this book, I have looked at sprawl and public policy devoted to it primarily through the lens of history. I do this in part because I was trained as a historian. I also do it because I believe that all policy analyses are based, consciously or not, on assumptions drawn from history, just as all history is based on assumptions drawn from an observation of present circumstances. I have tried to look seriously at sprawl as a cultural issue. Although objective issues—the cost of low-density settlements or the effect of sprawl on commuting times or global warming—are clearly important, these are not, I believe, what has really driven and continues to drive the anti-sprawl crusade. What is actually at stake are much larger questions about planning and democracy, aesthetics and metaphysics, and differing class-based assumptions about what makes a good urban by comparison, most residents of affluent metropolitan areas live in relatively low-density suburbs, areas that are much cleaner, greener, and safer than the neighborhoods their great-grandparents inhabited. They also have a great deal more affluence, privacy, mobility, and choice. At very least, it seems to me, our highly dispersed urban regions deserve some respectful attention before we jump to the conclusion that they are terrible places that need to be totally transformed.

PART 1

sprawl across the centuries

PART 1

sprawl across the centuries

1 Defining Sprawl

Most American anti-sprawl reformers today believe that sprawl is a recent and peculiarly American phenomenon caused by specific technological innovations like the automobile and by government policies like single-use zoning or the mortgage interest deduction on the federal income tax. It is important for them to believe this because if sprawl turned out to be a long-standing feature of urban development worldwide, it would suggest that stopping it involves something much more fundamental than correcting some poor American land-use policies. In the following chapters I will argue that the characteristics we associate today with sprawl have actually been visible in most prosperous cities throughout history. Sprawl has been as evident in Europe as in America and can now be said to be the preferred settlement pattern everywhere in the world where there is a certain measure of affluence and where citizens have some choice in how they live.

In some ways, the most difficult obstacle facing anyone trying to discuss the history of sprawl is defining it.[1] From the beginning, sprawl has been one of those words more useful in suggesting an attitude than in indicating any actual conditions. The attitude has almost always been negative. Even the look and sound of the word suggest something unpleasant. Asymmetrical, with the *p* thrusting below the baseline on one end and the *l* sticking up above the rest of the letters on the other and with that long, yawning diphthong in the middle, it is ungainly and unrefined.

As in the case of many negative terms, there is often a good deal of disagreement on the actual target of disapproval. As one person's noise can be another person's favorite musical expression, so too is one person's sprawl another's cherished neighborhood. The target, moreover, can change over time. Just as a weed in one era can easily become a prized native plant in the next, the sprawl of one era has often looked like traditional compact settlement to eyes accustomed to the development patterns of succeeding years. "Sprawl," moreover, like "conspicuous consumption" or "elitism," has always conveyed a not-so-subtle accusation against the way other people choose to live their lives. Most people don't believe that they live in sprawl. Sprawl is where other people live, the result of other people's poor choices. It implies that cities that sprawl and, by implication, the citizens living in them are self-indulgent and undisciplined.

I will further examine the history of the word, its shifting meanings, and its polemical uses in part 2. For the present, however, for the purposes of trying to understand the basic urban processes that have been described as sprawl, I have chosen to define it in the most basic and objective way possible, as low-density, scattered, urban development without systematic large-scale or regional public land-use planning.[2]

Using this definition, we can safely say that sprawl has been a persistent feature in cities since the beginning of urban history. Throughout this history, as cities have become economically mature and prosperous, they have tended to spread outward at decreasing densities. What was new in the twentieth century was that sprawl at last became a mass phenomenon. This decrease in density in affluent cities is perhaps the single most important fact in urban development of our era. There are few urban areas in the world today that exhibit densities anything like those that characterized most large cities from Mesopotamian times through the nineteenth century.[3] Where 150,000 people per square mile was once a standard urban density, it is rare to find densities of even 25,000 people per square mile in affluent cities today, and most urban dwellers live in densities much lower still.

Trying to describe this vast change, however, is complicated. Sprawl, like everything about the growth of cities, is infinitely complex. In any city at any given time some parts will be increasing in density as the density in others declines. Every change in one part of the urban region, moreover, will have ripple effects through every other part. Trying to understand the reciprocal relationships among city, suburbs, and exurbs is like trying to focus the eye simultaneously on numerous objects ricocheting wildly around a confined space. Over the years, however, geographers and others have devised a number of graphic means to suggest visually the order behind what is apparently a ran-

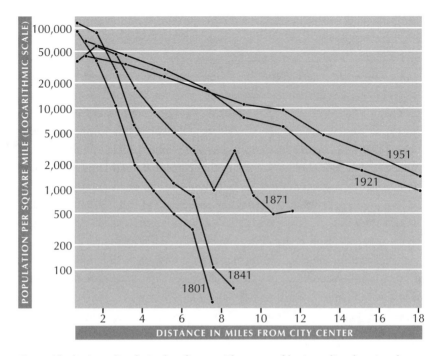

Figure 1. The density gradient for London, 1801–1951. The purpose of density gradient charts is to show the way density falls as one moves away from the center of a city. The vertical scale shows the density of population per square mile. The horizontal scale shows the distance from the center in miles. In the case of London, as in the case of virtually every economically mature city, the density gradient has become flatter over time as densities at the center have dropped and settlement has moved outward. The similarity in the movement of density gradients is one of the strongest indications of the essential similarity of decentralization and sprawl worldwide. (Redrawn by Dennis McClendon from a chart published by Colin Clark in "Transport: Maker and Breaker of Cities," *Town Planning Review* 28, no. 4 [1958], 237–50, chart on 247.)

dom set of patterns. One of these devices that I have found particularly useful in trying to visualize the effects of sprawl on urban development is the "density gradient" chart (fig. 1). On these charts, an urban area's residential or employment density is recorded in the vertical axis; distance from the city center on the horizontal axis.[4] As the technician plots the densities of the city at various distances from the center these dots typically form a line falling from left to right as densities fall when one moves outward from the city center.

Take, for example, the case of London in 1801 with its densely populated central core and less densely suburban ring surrounded by farm land. The line on the chart starts high at the left side of the chart showing densities of nearly

100,000 people per square mile at the center, declines through the part of the chart corresponding to the suburbs, and falls sharply almost to the baseline at the point about eight miles out where the fields begin. The city of Hong Kong would have a similar gradient today. Over the years though, London has lost population at the center and has grown prodigiously in its suburban ring, producing a much flatter density gradient. Many newer cities have pushed even further in this process. Phoenix is a good example of this pattern. The residential density of central Phoenix is extremely low compared to any older city, but its suburbs are scarcely less dense than its center. In fact, they are actually quite a bit denser than those in many older cities in the eastern United States or Europe. The resulting residential density gradient in Phoenix, like that of several other fast-growing cities in the American Southwest, is among the flattest ever recorded for a large city. Remarkably enough, though, it is possible that although the density gradient is still flattening in Phoenix and other cities of the Southwest and West, the line itself may be rising along most of its length, meaning that the era of decreasing density may be over. This is merely the latest chapter in a long and curious history.

2 Early Sprawl

One of the most important facts about cities from the beginning of recorded history until the fairly recent past was the sharp distinction between urban and rural ways of life. Within the city wall of most early cities, a visitor would see a dense mass of buildings, congested streets, and a rich and highly dynamic urban life offering many choices, at least for those able to afford them. A few miles outside the walls, however, the same visitor might see nothing but croplands and rural villages. The pace of daily activities would be slower, the environment less quick to change, and social and political life completely different.

In almost every era in urban history, however, there was a transitional zone between the two, a region just outside the city that housed activities and individuals that were still intimately connected with the social and economic life of the city but that couldn't be accommodated easily within the walls. This zone provided space for burial grounds, pottery works, or other industries that were either too space consuming or too noxious to be tolerated within the city itself. It also housed marginal social or political groups and families too poor to afford dwellings inside the walls. In a great many cities, however, this zone also supported activities of a very different sort. Here were the houses of affluent or powerful families who had the means to build and maintain working farms or villas or second houses where they could escape the congestion, noise, contagion, and social unrest that have characterized the center of large cities from the beginning of time until our own day. Sometimes these settlements were permanent, sometimes for seasonal or occasional use. Sometimes they were fairly compact, composed, for example, of small villas surrounded by gardens in a pattern we would today call suburban. In other cases they were very dispersed with imposing houses set on a large acreage, often with a conscious attempt to maintain a rural appearance. These we would call today exurban.

Although this pattern apparently characterized Babylon and Ur and many of the earliest large cities known to us, the best evidence we have comes from ancient Rome. At the beginning of the Christian era, this great city had an estimated population of about 1 million people piled up within city walls that enclosed a little more than six square miles. In other words it had a population of a city like Dallas today but in less than one-fiftieth of the space. This created densities of something like 150,000 per square mile. This kind of density, which would translate to more than two hundred people per acre, seems to have characterized most large, thriving cities up until the beginning of the twentieth century.[1] It is hard for us today even to imagine the consequences of crowding of this order in cities that had, by today's standards, primitive water delivery, waste removal, and transportation services.

In Rome, as in most other cities until quite recently, this crowding was even worse than the figures suggest because social and economic inequalities were much greater than they are today. A small group of wealthy Romans lived in splendor in spacious palaces that, together with nonresidential facilities, took up most of the space within the walls. This left relatively little acreage for the neighborhoods that housed the vast majority of families. In these neighborhoods apartment blocks were built so densely that they allowed little direct sunlight or ventilation into living quarters. Human wastes disgorged from the apartments into the streets contaminated the soil and water; a vast number of fires used for heating and industrial uses polluted the air. It is not surprising that periodic epidemics wiped out large segments of the urban population.[2] These urban plagues continued in the Western world until well into the twentieth century, and they continue to this day in some large cities in the developing world.

Despite the obvious problems, several factors made high densities in cities a necessary evil. One was the fact that most cities owed their existence to some specific geographical feature: a site along a trade route, a safe harbor, a good location for a bridge, a piece of ground that could be easily defended, a rapids that could be harnessed to provide water power. The cities that developed around these strategic points could not spread very far because of the limits of accessibility. For the wealthy, accessibility was usually not a problem because they had horses and carriages; for the poor there was only walking. This meant that until the widespread availability of inexpensive public transportation, which was a development of the late nineteenth century, most urban functions had to be located in close proximity to one another. Residential, commercial, and industrial facilities often mingled indiscriminately along the crowded streets with little consideration for the health or safety of the inhabitants. Crowding was reinforced by military considerations as well. Most large cities, at least until the nineteenth century, were walled for security reasons, and the crushing expense of building and maintaining the wall guaranteed that cities remained as compact as possible. They expanded only when the lack of space for essential urban activities became truly intolerable.

Outside the walls of Rome was what citizens called *suburbium,* meaning what was literally below or outside the walls. Here were land uses that couldn't be accommodated in the city. Along the roads that led out of town grew up settlements that clustered around industrial facilities, cemeteries, and businesses catering to travelers entering and leaving the city. For many suburbanites, the reason for living in the suburbs was a matter of cost. They could not afford to live in the city and so had to forgo urban services and the protection of the walls. These residents often lived in poorly built dwellings that could be even worse than those within the walls because of the lack of municipal services and the pollution generated by brick kilns, slaughterhouses, and other industries. At the opposite end of the spectrum were some of the wealthiest Romans, who could afford to maintain, in addition to their city residences, elegant villas near the sea or in the cool hills east of Rome near places like Tivoli and Frascati.

Sometimes these suburban or exurban dwellings served only as weekend houses, but for those who could afford to do so, these weekend houses often became much more than that. Ancient, medieval and early modern literature is filled with stories of the elegant life of a privileged aristocracy living for large parts of the year in villas and hunting lodges at the periphery of large cities. Nor was the preference for living quarters outside the center restricted to the Western world. Exactly the same sentiments in favor of low-density living outside the city were voiced by the gentry in China at least as early as the Ming dynasty.[3] High density, from the time of Babylon until recently, was the great urban evil, and many of the wealthiest or most powerful citizens found ways to escape it at least temporarily.

It appears that the forces that work toward increased concentration and those fueling a drive toward decentralization are, like so many other aspects of urban life, related to economic cycles.[4] Although little is known about these cycles, it appears that throughout history, at least until recently, as most cities went through their most intense phase of early economic growth, the process of concentration tended to dominate over that of decentralization as residents from outlying areas were drawn into the city center. Then, as the economy matured, the balance shifted as the number of residents who were able to move outward to the suburbs and exurbs exceeded the number coming from the agricultural hinterland to the center.

We can use modern London as a good exemplar of these processes. Because London was the largest and economically most dynamic city in the Western world in the early modern period, it was here that these trends were most apparent. In the seventeenth and eighteenth centuries, for example, there was a vast influx of new residents both because changes in agricultural production forced thousands of families off the land and because an expanding urban job market based on new modes of industrial production lured others in. The piling up of population and commercial activities at constantly higher densities in the center, however, tended to produce a countervailing move of people out to the urban periphery.

During this period an entire new class of Londoners, flush with the profits earned in an expanding economy, was able to build or lease houses well beyond the walls of the city of London. The most important direction for affluent suburban growth was to the west, stretching in the direction of the leafy gardens of the royal palaces at Westminster and Whitehall. In this area, in what is now London's Central West End, several of the great aristocratic families developed their land as private, sometimes gated, communities with townhouses laid out around landscaped squares. Life here would have been remarkably calm, quiet, and orderly compared to that along the teeming streets of the walled city of London a mile and a half to the east. For many residents it involved what was then a long-distance commute back into the city by private carriage.[5]

There was also suburban development to the east of the London walls but of a vastly different kind. This area accommodated large-scale warehouses and industrial facilities near the great London docklands. These industrial activities drew working-class families attached to them. The densities of these districts sometimes rivaled those within the walls. As a consequence they, like the least affluent quarters of the city of London itself, were congested, unpleasant, and unhealthy. Observers increasingly spoke of two entirely different Londons, the affluent, airy one to the west and the dark and congested one to the east. Clearly, from the beginning of modern urban history, and contrary to much accepted wisdom, suburban development was very diverse and catered to all kinds of people and activities.

Beyond suburbia there was also a significant development in what we would now call exurbia, in thinly settled areas beyond the regularly built-up city and suburbs. Although much of this exurban territory often looked purely rural and agricultural, this appearance, often maintained at great expense, belied the fact that the primary economic, social, and cultural ties of the inhabitants were back to the city.[6] Daniel Defoe, in his descriptions of Surrey in the early eighteenth century, was struck by the number of houses of "gentlemen of quality" in the villages around the city. These men were neither farmers nor members of the landed gentry. Instead their houses were "citizen's country houses whither they retire from the hurries of business and getting money, to draw their breath in a clear air, and to divert themselves and their families in the hot weather."[7]

This world, familiar to us from the works of authors like Jane Austen, represented a vast change in urban society. The amount of wealth required to build, staff, and maintain a country house in the Renaissance would have been beyond the reach of any but the wealthiest families in any society. These houses often required entire villages to house all of the workers needed to provide the necessities of everyday life. Already by the eighteenth century, in affluent countries like Britain, a highly developed transportation and communications system made it possible for a much larger group of citizens to enjoy the pleasures of living at different times in both city and country.

The exodus of families from central London to suburbia and exurbia was offset by the continued arrival of poor newcomers from the countryside. The result was a great churning of population as both centralization and decentralization exerted their influence. Already by the seventeenth century, however, the processes of decentralization were clearly the more important. As a result, London's density curve started to drop and flatten significantly as the center started to lose population and the periphery started to fill up (fig. 1). London had a long head start in this development over rivals like Paris or Naples not only because of its size and booming economy but because of the fact that England was an island and relatively peaceful. This had allowed it to dispense with the defensive walls that constrained outward development much earlier than most continental cities. As a result the London area soon boasted one of the lowest densities of any large cities in the world, a distinction it maintains to this day.

As cities throughout the Western world experienced the full impact of the industrial revolution in the nineteenth century they followed the lead of London

Figure 2. Nineteenth-century sprawl: speculative row houses in Camberwell, South London. In the nineteenth century, London exploded outward as developers threw up mile upon miles of brick terrace houses such as these. The resulting cityscape horrified highbrow British critics of the time, who considered the new districts to be vulgar, cheap, and monotonous. Nevertheless, the houses continued to be built because so many middle-class inhabitants of central London saw them as a vast step upward for their families. In the second half of the twentieth century, highbrow opinion finally came around, and today they are widely considered to be the very model of compact urban life. Ironically enough, they are today often considered the antithesis of sprawl. (Photograph by Robert Bruegmann, 1992.)

both in the process of piling up of density at the center and in the move of people and activities away from it (fig. 2). The two phenomena were, in fact, closely linked. The same factories that helped create wealth for a rapidly expanding middle class also created pollution and overcrowding. The same railroads that brought goods and people to the great factories also provided the means for the affluent to escape these industrial districts every evening.

Because of new building technologies and infrastructure in the nineteenth century, it was possible for real estate speculators to develop the industrial quarters of some large cities more densely than anything seen before. The central arrondissements of the city of Paris topped 200,000 people per square mile in the mid-nineteenth century. Cities in North America, because they reached the peak of industrial activity even later than their counterparts in Europe, attained even higher densities and did so somewhat later. New York City, for example, saw its apogee of density only in the early years of the twentieth century when parts of the Lower East Side of Manhattan peaked at more than 400,000 people per square mile or more than six hundred people per acre.[8] These were probably the highest densities recorded to that date and rival those of some of the densest districts in cities today, notably certain neighborhoods with vast numbers of new immigrants in Hong Kong, Manila, Cairo, or Mumbai (Bombay).

In the case of the affluent cities of the Western world, this crowding was short-lived. By the late nineteenth century, almost all affluent northern European cities were decanting rapidly.[9] A map of virtually any northern European city in the late nineteenth century would have shown a tightly knit pattern of streets in the historic core surrounded by broad boulevards where the outer walls had been removed, usually earlier in the century, then widely spaced villa districts to one side of the city and industrial suburbs to the other. Beyond were the small commuter suburbs and finally the exurban villages with their surrounding estates.

The process was even more rapid in American cities. The Lower East Side of New York, for example, began emptying out rapidly after 1900 as soon as immigrants accumulated enough money to allow them to get better housing in less dense neighborhoods farther afield. At first they walked over the East River bridges to nearby communities like Williamsburg and Greenpoint in Brooklyn. Eventually, inexpensive public transportation allowed them to live much farther from their place of employment, for example, in northern Manhattan and the outlying boroughs. After several decades of outward movement, there were not enough tenants left to fill the oldest and least sanitary tenements on the Lower East Side. In response to the outward migration, together with new, tighter building laws, many building owners boarded up their properties above the first floor or abandoned them altogether. Densities plummeted. Manufacturing firms dispersed along with the residents, sometimes in advance and sometimes trailing, as they required larger and more up-to-date facilities.[10] Along with the factories, many retail establishments dispersed as well. Both the residential and the employment density curves in the New York area flattened rapidly.

In American cities, as well as in European cities after their walls came down, there were two kinds of suburban development. The first involved outward expansion all along the urban periphery, creating a pattern of yearly growth like the annual rings on a tree. Despite the fairly small numbers of inhabitants, the suburban districts for the affluent took up a great deal of this space. Usually located on the other side of town and occupying much less space per capita were modest apartment blocks for the working classes and factories for industrial production. The other kind of suburban development appeared along railroad lines radiating outward from the city, creating small commuter suburban settlements that appeared on maps like the beads on a necklace.

Finally, at the edge of the urban galaxy could often be found large exurban regions. At first, in Europe, the largest amount of this land was occupied by the large estates of the landed aristocracy. Increasingly in the nineteenth century, in both North America and Europe, successful middle-class merchants sought to emulate the aristocracy by buying property and building country houses. These properties were often located outside small villages where there were urban services and good railroad connections back to the city center.

Even those who recognize that the general trend of decentralization has been essentially similar in Europe and North American sometimes say that American cities have followed a different social pattern. For example, it is often said that the wealthy have always lived in city centers in Europe with the poor at the periphery while in North America the reverse has been true. This formulation is quite misleading. In both cases there was a vast exodus of families of all kinds from the center. The difference was how quickly each left the center and how far each went. In Paris, for example, over the course of several centuries, the wealthiest families did exactly what their counterparts did in London or in New York or Boston. They kept moving from more congested districts at the center toward less dense districts in the periphery. In the case of European cities, this was often beyond existing city walls. Many place names in what is now central Paris record this exodus. The faubourg Saint Honoré or the faubourg Saint Germain, for example, were originally places outside the walls as the presence of the word "faubourg," meaning "suburb," reflects. As the city expanded and these walls came down, these settlements were eventually engulfed within the continuous fabric of the city.

The most affluent Parisians finally stopped their outward push in the early twentieth century at the far western edge of the city, in the elegant sixteenth arrondissement and the adjacent suburbs like Neuilly. The result was a large affluent enclave that still houses a great many of the wealthiest citizens of France. In a great many cities throughout continental Europe the most desirable quarter today is in a similar location, on the more affluent side of the city just within or outside the last city wall. The poor in Paris and elsewhere in Europe tended to congregate in the oldest and densest quarters near the center on the "wrong" side of town where they stayed until they were displaced by various renewal projects or by more affluent citizens attracted by the central location.

Although most American cities never had a wall, many of them, particularly
the older ones of the northeastern United States, show the same kind of pattern. The wealthy, on one side of town, moved quickly outward. As in Europe, a
great many of the wealthiest urban citizens in the older cities in North America
still live in areas where the wealthy found themselves at the end of the past
century. Sometimes this is within the city, for example, on the Upper East Side
of New York or the Back Bay in Boston. Sometimes it is in the near suburbs,
for example, in Brookline, located west of Boston, or in Evanston, Wilmette,
or Kenilworth, north of Chicago. The poor and the immigrants, who usually
lived near the center, on the other side of town, stayed longer because they
had less choice. Eventually, however, they moved outward, too, either because
they became more affluent and could afford greener, less congested quarters
or because their neighborhoods came to be desirable to more affluent families
and they were forced outward by rising housing costs.

In the matter of the dispersal of the population outward from the core, the
single most important variable was not whether the cities were European or
whether they were American but rather when these cities reached economic
maturity. The newer and more heavily industrialized cities of the nineteenth
century, Manchester or Liverpool in England, for example, behaved in ways
substantially similar to Chicago or Baltimore in the United States. Friedrich
Engels described the unbroken girdle of working-class neighborhoods in central Manchester that extended out from the commercial district for a mile and
a half in every direction and beyond as the quarters of the upper and middle
bourgeoisie.[11] He could just as easily have been describing an American industrial city in the late nineteenth century. It is true that American suburbs for the
very wealthy in the twentieth century were often located at long distances from
the central city, for example, in Lake Forest outside Chicago or Sewickley outside Pittsburgh. This did not tend to happen to the same extent in Europe but
perhaps only because American developments typically took place somewhat
later than those in Europe and at lower densities.

Finally, in both American and European cities, beyond the suburbs, which
had a very strong connection with the city, was a loose exurban band containing
widely spaced villas and country estates of the wealthiest residents of the city
as well as resort towns and, occasionally, industrial districts in the countryside.
This outermost band has always been an integral and significant part of the
urban system.[12] The area that is now the western suburbs of Paris, for example,
accommodated, in the seventeenth and eighteenth centuries, a large group of

chateaus and smaller estates clustered around the grandest estate of them all, at Versailles (fig. 3). Together they formed a vast aristocratic landscape carefully preserved to maintain its "rural" appearance. On maps of the era, this territory is often quite visible. Typically, the chateau would be located just outside a village. Around the chateau would be a formal garden and then a large hunting park with long, straight allées and *ronds* points carved through the forest for the easy passage of hunting horses and hounds. Starting about 1830, during the prosperity ushered in by the relatively peaceful years of the mid-nineteenth century, middle-class inhabitants were increasingly able to follow in the path of the landed aristocracy and the wealthiest members of the *grande bourgeoisie*.[13] Eventually many of the hunting parks were turned into middle-class suburbia.

The same pattern was visible around London where members of the landed aristocracy built their country houses. By the early twentieth century the advent of the railroad, private automobile, and labor-saving domestic devices made it possible for a considerable group of citizens to emulate the wealthy and to build and maintain country and weekend houses. Large areas outside London—for example, the "Cocktail Belt" or "Stockbrokers' Belt" in the Chiltern Hills and Surrey—were occupied by these weekend houses.[14] Even more remarkable were the seasonal exurban territories, often located at a substantial distance from the cities that provided their population. This was the case, for example, in the English Lakes District or along the French Riviera. On the Riviera, northern Europeans, particularly the British, started constructing villas near towns like Nice, Cannes, Hyères, and Menton as early as the late eighteenth century. By the end of the nineteenth century their villas and gardens occupied a vast acreage along the coastline, and the economy of Nice had become largely dependent on seasonal visitors and tourism.[15]

Most American cities had similar exurban regions. In the case of a city like Chicago, wealthy industrialists built country estates to the north and northwest of the city in places like Lake Forest and Libertyville. Much more modest resort communities grew up along the shore of Lake Michigan in Indiana or southwestern Michigan. Within the exurban band were also industrial satellite cities, such as Waukegan, Aurora, Elgin, and Joliet, which had their own downtowns, industrial areas, residential neighborhoods, and suburbs.

Among the best documented inhabitants of exurbia are a number of the early American prophets of what we now know as environmentalism. Henry David Thoreau, in his shack at Walden Pond just beyond suburban Boston, John Muir, in a house across the Berkeley hills from San Francisco, and Aldo

Figure 3. Historic exurban sprawl in the Paris region. This detail of a map, created by Abbé de la Rive in 1740, of the Paris region shows the way aristocratic landowners occupied very large parts of the territory west of Paris with country houses, gardens, and hunting parks, all of them serviced by the inhabitants of small villages in the immediate vicinity. The largest of all was the royal domain at Versailles, whose enormous garden with its symmetrical allées and canals is plainly visible in the lower left corner of the illustration. During the twentieth century, the spread of suburban development has engulfed this entire area. Whether in ancient Rome, Ming dynasty China, or the Napa Valley of California these affluent exurban regions have occupied vast areas of landscape.

Leopold, at his weekend retreat just north of Baraboo, near Madison, Wisconsin, were actually exurbanites, individuals who loved what they considered a rural life but who also wanted ready access to the city.

In short, whether residential or commercial, year-round or seasonal, contiguous with the settled area of the city or scattered across the hinterland, suburban or exurban, decentralization and sprawl were already widespread in large cities throughout the developed world by the end of the nineteenth century. In his remarkable 1902 work *Anticipations,* an attempt to predict future trends, British author H. G. Wells was able to prophesize with some confidence that by 2000 a citizen of London would have "a choice of nearly all of England and Wales south of Nottingham and east of Exeter as his suburb."[16] In the process, Wells believed, the city would diffuse itself to such a point that the old divisions between city and country would be eliminated. "There will be horticulture and agriculture going on within the urban regions and 'urbanity' without them," he wrote, stating that the network of roadways, wires, and railroads would make urban amenities available almost everywhere.[17] As strikingly prescient as this sounds today, in reality, like a great many successful predictions about the future, it was mostly an intelligent extrapolation from what Wells could see around him.

3 Sprawl in the Interwar Boom Years

The outward dispersion of people and businesses visible in the early twentieth century became even more conspicuous during the boom period of the 1920s. The basic processes were similar throughout the Western world but, as in the nineteenth century, with time lags due to the relative age of the city and the amount of economic and population growth taking place.

By the 1920s, in both northern Europe and America, the rush to the urban periphery was no longer confined primarily to the wealthy and powerful; it had become a mass movement.[1] In London in the interwar years, for example, tens of thousands of families of modest income were able to move out from congested central neighborhoods to row houses, single-family detached houses, or, most conspicuously, "semidetached" or double houses on the periphery (fig. 4).[2] A great deal of this housing was built at densities from six to ten units per acre, which was extremely low by historic British urban standards. Along with the residential population came a major outward movement of industry of all kinds.[3]

The result was an explosion of growth in urban land area. Although the population of the London urbanized area grew only by about 10 percent in the years 1921–31, from about 7.5 million to 8.2 million, the area developed for urban uses grew nearly 200 percent.[4] By the end of the interwar era, the London area displayed many of the traits that we associate with postwar suburbs. New industrial complexes had sprung up along the major highways out of the city, and mile after mile of new houses marched across what had been open

Figure 4. Sprawl in the interwar years. During the 1920s the population of the greater London area increased about 10 percent. The built-up area, in contrast, doubled, creating an outward sprawl at least as great as anything seen in late twentieth-century America. Much of the growth consisted of rows of semidetached houses like these in Merton Park in South London. These sturdy houses, like the row houses of the nineteenth century, were deprecated by much of the British cultural elite, but they were highly appreciated by ordinary Londoners. (Photograph by Robert Bruegmann, 2002.)

countryside. Half of all journeys to work were suburb-to-suburb rather than suburb-to-center.[5] The same kind of development could be seen in Hamburg, Stockholm, and many other affluent northern European cities. Maps showing the built-up areas of these cities often look like Rorschach test patterns with perforated extrusions extending in a highly irregular pattern far out into the adjacent countryside. Outward dispersal was also visible in the cities of southern Europe but to a much lesser extent, partly because of cultural and political conditions but mostly because these cities were less affluent and had a much smaller middle class. In every case, the outward movement of affluent and middle-class families left major concentrations of poor people in the oldest and densest parts of the inner city and the inner suburbs.

Beyond the suburban fringe, exurban development continued to flourish. While some of this continued to be due to wealthy city dwellers building villas and weekend houses in the country, there were growing numbers of middle-class and even working-class families who found that they could afford homes only far from the city where land prices were lower, particularly if they were willing to do some of the construction themselves and to forgo many public services. Other families took the same route to obtain weekend houses. In Britain this trend was quite conspicuous in scenic areas in the southeast of England where shacks and shanties sprouted up in areas that were called "plot-lands." The large seaside settlement of Peacehaven in Britain became the most conspicuous and most bitterly attacked example of this trend.[6]

There was another powerful decentralizing force at work, but at the center rather than at the periphery. As early as the middle of the nineteenth century, in cities like Vienna or Paris, public authorities had undertaken massive efforts to redevelop and upgrade parts of the inner city. The new luxury apartment blocks facing tree-lined boulevards built during the reign of Napoléon III in Paris and the massive apartment buildings along the *ringstrasse* in Vienna fueled a major trend toward "gentrification" or the replacement of the existing population by one enjoying a higher economic and social position in society. Although the word "gentrification" has often been used in a polemical way, to suggest the problems associated with the involuntary displacement of poor residents, and it has been applied primarily to developments since World War II, I will use it in this book as a neutral term indicating simply a change, a shift upward of any given neighborhood in socioeconomic status. Used in this way, the term can refer to a process that, like growth itself, is probably as old as cities.[7]

In Second Empire Paris, for example, as the boulevards sliced through congested old quarters, the poor were pushed out and the new apartment blocks were marketed to the expanding middle and upper-middle class. The displaced population, for its part, tended to move outward to industrial neighborhoods farther out in the city or to the inner suburbs. By the twentieth century, many of these inner suburbs, with their industrial facilities and cheaply built apartment buildings, had become a "red belt," a set of working-class neighborhoods that regularly voted for the Communist and other leftist political parties. Outside the Red Belt, especially during the 1920s, many suburbs saw an explosion of single-family houses for more prosperous working-class families and those of a burgeoning middle class, all happy to trade the noise and congestion of the city for the relative calm of the suburbs.[8]

In North American urban areas the movement outward in the 1920s was even more of a mass movement than in Europe. The expansion and intensification of retail and office uses in the old downtowns led to a sharp decrease in the number of people who lived at the center of cities. In this trend, American cities followed the process long visible in the city of London in which the down-towns came to be intensely crowded during the workday and relatively deserted at night and weekends. Around the downtowns were the poorest neighbor-hoods of most American cities and the places where new immigrants and most African-American citizens lived. Gentrification was also clearly underway at the heart of many American cities, perhaps most strikingly in neighborhoods like Greenwich Village in New York City or Beacon Hill in Boston or parts of Central City Philadelphia. However, it tended to be a later and less conspicuous trend than in many European cities. Because it paled in comparison with the outward push of affluent people to the suburbs, moreover, most people at the time and subsequently have tended to see it as a highly local phenomenon in one or another city and not as part of a significant and continuous trend in the twentieth century.[9]

Unprecedented levels of affluence, excellent public transportation, and ris-ing automobile ownership allowed a large portion of the American urban popu-lation, including even a substantial percentage of blue-collar families, to have the option of living in single-family detached houses in the suburbs.[10] Much of this housing was developed in small subdivisions by thousands of small-scale real estate developers. In the 1920s, hundreds of square miles of houses sprang up seemingly overnight in places like Floral Park in Nassau County outside New York or Berwyn outside Chicago. To look at block after block of sturdy brick bungalows in Berwyn, with their solid front porches, Prairie-style leaded glass windows and tidy front yards, is to be reminded of the enormous step upward that this housing represented for its owners. Although few middle-class American suburban parents today would consider a 1,000-square foot bungalow an ideal place to raise a large family, for many families at that time a small single-family house where they could live under their own roof and enjoy their own yard represented a real revolution in expectations. Moreover, even many workers who couldn't afford the least expensive house in a subdivision could have their own home if they were willing to locate it in a less than ideal setting and do much of the work of building it themselves. To have one's own house in the city was once within reach of only a tiny part of the population. By the end of the 1920s in North America, it became available far down the social and economic scale.[11]

The most spectacular examples of suburban growth could be found in the fastest growing cities of the American West. In the Los Angeles area, by the end of the 1920s the majority of families lived in single-family homes and had automobiles.[12] In fact it is probably accurate to say that many of the character-istics that we tend to associate with postwar America, including a high degree of home and automobile ownership and large mass-produced subdivisions, of single-family detached houses were already quite evident in fast-growing and affluent urban areas like Detroit or Los Angeles in the 1920s and 1930s.[13]

There was also a substantial amount of exurban growth in North America between the wars. Some of this involved country estates, weekend houses, gentle-man farms, and resort cottages of the affluent. But there was also working-class exurbanization, both for occasional use and for permanent residence. The great attraction for many families was the substantially lower price of land outside the regularly developed suburbs. Although these families could not expect the same municipal services as their suburban counterparts, for many of them, the combination of low land prices and taxes and low construction costs if they did some or all of the work on their own allowed them to become homeowners.[14]

Contrary to the way many observers have described the decentralization of the city as primarily the result of families fleeing the city, in fact it was often the case that the jobs, particularly industrial jobs, went first and the people fol-lowed. In the interwar years, many industrial concerns in older cities moved from loft buildings immediately adjacent to old downtowns into new one- and two-story buildings in industrial parks farther out in the city. These large indus-trial companies sometimes relocated to areas where there was already a plenti-ful supply of labor, but just as often they moved with the expectation that the residential population would follow.[15] In 1900 a third of all manufacturing jobs were located outside the central cities in the United States. By 1950, this figure was already close to 50 percent.[16]

Particularly during the latter part of the 1920s, retail activities also decentral-ized quickly. Large new commercial districts appeared within or just outside central cities at places like the Hub and Fordham Road in the Bronx, the Sixty-ninth Street area just west of Philadelphia, Uptown and Englewood in Chicago, or Hollywood and the Miracle Mile in Los Angeles. These shopping districts, which, by the end of the 1920s, had started to rival the retail sales of the tradi-tional downtowns, had their own department stores, offices, and theaters and operated like miniature versions of downtowns. Department stores also opened branches in the suburbs, and drive-in markets and strip centers made their appearance.[17] The result was a massive increase in retail sales outside the his-toric downtowns. In the Chicago area, for example, by 1935 fully three-quarters of all retail sales were outside the city core.[18]

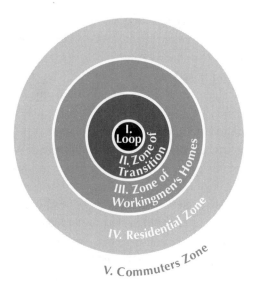

Figure 5. The city as seen in the 1920s. In the years between the two world wars, sociologists at the University of Chicago such as Robert Park and Ernest Burgess used Chicago as a case study in their attempt to understand urban structure and growth. In their "ecological" model, residents, as they became more affluent, would tend to move constantly outward in the urban area, replaced by newer, less affluent residents in a pattern analogous to the way various kinds of plant life would succeed one another on a newly formed sand dune. Although this model was not really very good at capturing the complex reality of the American city at the time Park and Burgess formulated it, and problems with it have become ever more apparent over time, still, diagrams like this one had such clarity that they still influence the way many people think of urban development. (Redrawn by Dennis McClendon from Robert Park, Ernest Burgess, and Roderick McKenzie, *The City* [Chicago: University of Chicago Press, 1925].)

One of the things that made all of this growth and movement possible was a notable expansion of infrastructure. During the interwar years American cities finally finished the process of paving streets and sidewalks, installing curbs, gutters, streetlights, and sewers, and generally completing the package of urban amenities we now take for granted. These decades also saw a remarkable expansion of the highway system in many cities, including the removal of dangerous railroad grade crossings, construction of a number of limited-access superhighways, and planning for a great national superhighway network. This highway network, revived after World War II and financed by federal dollars, became the interstate highway system.[19] By the end of the 1930s, the outlines of the multinucleated city, with its adjacent suburban and exurban zones that we usually associate with the postwar era, were already clearly visible.

The forces of decentralization appeared to many Americans to have tri-

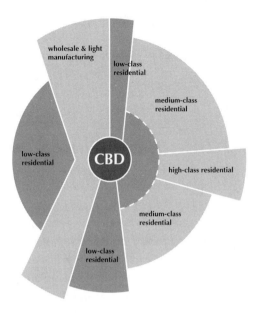

Figure 6. Homer Hoyt's sector diagram. It was clear from the beginning that the concentric rings of the Park and Burgess model of the city failed to account for many of the things that could be seen in Chicago or many other American cities at the time. Homer Hoyt observed that, in reality, development in cities didn't expand outward in tidy rings but instead various kinds of uses pushed outward in distinct sectors and at different rates. (Redrawn by Dennis McClendon from a diagram published in Chauncey Harris and Edward Ullman after Hoyt in "The Nature of Cities," *Annals of the American Academy of Political and Social Science* 242 [November 1942], 13.)

umphed definitively over the forces of centralization in the period between the wars. This explains one of the most important developments in urban thought during these years. In the 1920s a group of sociologists at the University of Chicago started doing significant work analyzing and mapping the modern city. Using Chicago as their prototype, Robert Park and Ernest Burgess tried to create a model that could explain the form and growth of the city. They concentrated on the movements of people and activities out from the downtown toward the periphery over time (fig. 5).[20]

Deploying an organic metaphor, they described this process as "ecological." According to them, successive waves of people and activities moved from more central locations into an adjacent neighborhood farther out and eventually dominated it, only to be replaced by the next wave in a process analogous to the way grasses, low bushes, and trees might establish themselves one after another on a sand dune. They illustrated this process by a famous diagram of the city as a series of concentric circles. In this drawing, the inner circle contained the central business district: the Loop and its environs. Beyond this a zone in transition, an area that housed many of the city's poorest residents in communities like Chinatown, Little Sicily, and the "Ghetto," was being invaded by business and light manufacture. Farther out still lay a third ring, consisting primarily of housing for the working class who had escaped the deterioration closer to the center. This was followed by a fourth ring of single-family residential areas, and finally, a "commuter zone" of suburbs and satellite cities located from thirty to sixty minutes from the central business district. The Park-Burgess model quickly became a standard way for many Americans, particularly planners and urban experts of all kinds, to conceptualize the city. Its popularity is not hard to understand. It seemed to simplify and abstract the dynamics of urban growth in such a fashion that most people could immediately grasp how it worked.[21]

It was obvious to many close observers from the beginning that there were major limitations to the Park-Burgess model. Industry did not concentrate in concentric bands. In Chicago, as in other American cities, industry followed lines of water and rail transportation in a radiating fashion with the largest industries clustering together in well-defined districts, often far from the center, for example, in the area around the great Western Electric works in Cicero. Already by the 1920s, when Park and Burgess were writing, moreover, large cities no longer had a single center. As we have seen, large new business districts, like Englewood in Chicago and Hollywood in Los Angeles, had already appeared.

Growth around Chicago was not uniform in all directions, and even within each ring of the Park-Burgess model, there were wide variations of income and social class. Areas near the Loop contained both the Gold Coast, with wealthy residents, and slums like Little Italy, with some of the poorest residents of the region. The same was true of the farthest ring, which Park and Burgess described as "high-class residential." This ring did house wealthy suburbanites, but it also housed a considerable number of poor people and factories.[22]

One attempt to correct the problems of the Park-Burgess model, to account for the diverse population within each zone and the asymmetrical way that the city developed, was a variation of the old diagram developed by Homer Hoyt in the 1930s (fig. 6). In his "sectoral" model, Hoyt retained the basic dynamic of ecological succession, with residents constantly moving farther out as they were able, but he chose to segment the urban area into different pie-shaped wedges that behaved quite differently, one from another.[23] This revised model corrected

some of the shortcomings of the original, but it did so only by increasing somewhat the complexity of the diagram, a process that led to a corresponding loss
of graphic clarity. Although it did succeed in taking into account several important features of urban life already visible in the years between the wars that
were not visible on the Park-Burgess diagram, it was still unable to incorporate
others. One of the most crucial was the growing evidence that urban development was not, as Park and Burgess or Hoyt had assumed, unidirectional, that
is, with affluent people always moving farther out. As we have seen, gentrification of the core of cities in both Europe and North America had already demonstrated that this was not necessarily the case. In fact, many neighborhoods
were constantly changing in ways that simple ecological succession could not
explain.[24] Nevertheless, for many people the Park-Burgess, or the variant by
Hoyt, remained the standard view of urban development in the United States,
buttressing the common but quite erroneous notion that the city is constantly
expanding outward with the most affluent residents in the vanguard.

4 Sprawl in the Postwar Boom Years

After World War II, the American experience and the European experience diverged for a brief period, with sprawl much more visible in the United States than in Europe. There were several reasons for this. One was that the desperate need for immediate rebuilding in European cities after World War II led to major public interventions in the development process. This, in turn, gave public planners the opportunity to exercise a great deal of new authority. In many countries, a planning elite could implement ideas about reshaping the city and its hinterlands that they had been advocating, largely in vain, for decades.

The other, and probably more important, reason for the divergence in urban development patterns between the United States and Europe was the simple fact of numbers of people and degree of affluence. Many of the European countries had been decimated by the war, and many of the largest cities grew slowly, if at all. While a few major metropolitan areas, for example, the Paris region, grew substantially from 1940 to 1970, many other cities such as Hamburg, Berlin, Vienna, Glasgow, and Birmingham saw their populations remain stable or even decline.[1] In the United States, on the other hand, basking in postwar prosperity and experiencing a prodigious baby boom, the population jumped from 150 million people to over 200 million people in the first two full decades after the war. The population gains of some individual cities were faster still. The figures for the Los Angeles urban area, for example, more than doubled in these two decades, jumping from under 4 million to over 8 million. The rate of growth was faster still in several smaller cities of the American South and West. The Miami urbanized area grew nearly threefold, the Phoenix area nearly fourfold, and the San Jose area more than fivefold. None of these figures convey the real impact of this population growth on the land, however, because it was accompanied by an even larger growth in the number of households. As the baby boomers started to mature, average household size fell, and unprecedented affluence meant that these smaller family units were able to secure for themselves more living space.[2] The result was a sharp reduction in densities at the core and a spectacular growth in suburban areas that were very low in density by any historic standards.

The Postwar Suburb

Although many books have been written on the subject of the postwar American suburb, they have tended to tell specific parts of the story, notably, the construction of the interstate highway system, the rise of the suburban shopping center, or the creation of mass-produced suburbs such Levittown on Long Island or Park Forest, Illinois. The majority of books and articles that have been published on the American postwar suburban experience, moreover, tend to perpetuate stereotypes that were popularized by upper-middle-class anti-suburban writers during the 1960s.[3] Many of them suggest that postwar suburbanization and sprawl were different in kind from what went before. As we have seen, this was far from true. Postwar suburbanization and sprawl were different in scale but not really different in kind from what had gone before. In fact the sprawl of the postwar years was really just an extrapolation of the process visible in London since the seventeenth century or in American cities for more than a century, particularly in the boom periods of the 1880s and 1920s.

Nor were the highly publicized techniques of William Levitt at Levittown, as many writers have suggested, a new departure in American development patterns. Levitt was merely the most successful builder of his day in pushing further the process of reducing costs through large-scale production and standardization that had been underway at least since the beginning of the nineteenth century. Levittown, although ingenious, was no different in kind from the work of large developers like Samuel Gross in late nineteenth-century Chicago or the new subdivisions created by defense contractors in

Los Angeles in the 1930s.[4] So successful were these early twentieth-century builders, along with many homeowners who did much of the contracting or the labor themselves, that already by the beginning of the war, well before the great wave of postwar building, the majority of urban American households lived in areas that were suburban in character, and almost half owned their own homes.[5] High homeownership and suburban living was not a new postwar American development; it was an accomplished fact at the outset of the war.

The everyday postwar suburban landscape, while more expansive than anything seen before the war, was actually remarkably similar to its predecessors. The typical minimal postwar house, for example, a small "raised ranch" or Cape Cod house, was not so different in plan and equipment from the interwar bungalow. True, the postwar house tended to sit parallel to the street on a larger lot, but this too was merely part of a longstanding trend. The average lot size at the turn of the century, in a typical residential neighborhood in a large northern city like Chicago, was 25 × 100 feet, meaning that a single-family residential neighborhood might have had sixteen housing units per acre. By the 1920s, lots in a typical middle-class suburb might have been twice that size, or 50 × 100 feet, meaning that an acre would accommodate eight houses. By the 1950s, a typical suburban lot reached 100 × 100 feet, which is to say about a quarter acre or four houses per acre. Given the simultaneous decrease in household size, the total population per square mile of a typical neighborhood at the edge of the metropolitan area would have declined from nearly 60,000 in the late nineteenth century to less than 25,000 in the 1920s to less than 10,000 in the 1950s, a remarkably long-term and steady progression.[6]

Also contrary to a great deal of what has been written about the "Ozzie and Harriet" suburbs of the 1950s, American suburbs were not a uniform mass of white, middle-class bedroom communities, and they were not distinctly different from central cities. Some suburbs were primarily residential, but many were commercial centers, accommodating office buildings and factories for the expanding number of companies relocating from locations closer in. Many of these companies had already, during the interwar years, left loft districts immediately adjacent to the old downtowns of the older American cities to settle in landscaped industrial parks at the periphery of the central city.[7] After the war, many of these companies spilled out into the suburbs of America's older cities. This was again only the continuation of a long process of decentralization, but it seemed to be novel to many observers because, unlike the earlier movements, the companies now crossed the boundary between central city and suburb and for this reason showed up prominently in statistical tables compiled from census figures.[8]

Many suburbs did house affluent white residents, but there were also suburbs catering to a working-class population and suburbs that had large minority populations.[9] The creation of a large number of suburban governmental units, far from fostering a homogenous suburban world, as is often argued, probably allowed for a greater differentiation among places as residents chose the kind of community and services they wanted.[10]

According to many historians, the postwar years saw the wholesale abandonment of public transportation, especially urban rail systems, in favor of the automobile. This does not really give a good idea of what actually happened. The automobile, for example, did not really replace the streetcar in any direct way. Instead, streetcar lines, whether in American cities or those elsewhere in the affluent world, were usually converted into less expensive and more flexible bus lines, many of which still operate. What the automobile more directly replaced, over the course of the twentieth century, was the private carriage. The shift from mass to individual and from public to private transportation happened because, given the management practices and available technologies, it allowed ordinary middle-class citizens the kind of privacy, mobility, and choice once only available to the wealthiest citizens.

Although European cities experienced substantial suburbanization in the postwar period, for various reasons it was far less conspicuous than in the United States. In the first place, because there was less growth in urban areas overall, there was less pressure to develop in the countryside. As we will explore in more detail in part 3, most of the expansion that did take place was highly regulated. In Paris, for example, a good deal of the suburban growth consisted of publicly funded high-density housing, most conspicuously the large housing projects called *grands ensembles*. There was also some development of single-family houses, of course, for example, some subdivisions created by American developer William Levitt.[11] Because the new suburbanites were much more likely to be lower-middle- and working-class inhabitants than in the United States, there was much less comment among elite observers (fig. 7).[12]

Figure 7. The postwar working-class suburb in Paris: Bobigny. For a brief period after World War II, urban development in the United States and Europe diverged sharply. In part because of war damage, in part because of a decimated economy, and in part because of a long tradition of top-down control of land use, European planners and other government officials were able to intervene in city development more actively than their American counterparts. Much of the new housing around Paris was either built directly by governmental bodies or heavily subsidized by them whereas in the United States, Canada, and Australia, the private-market single-family home was the norm. As Europe recovered from the war and grew in affluence, however, citizens increasingly spurned housing projects and demanded single-family dwellings. Polls have repeatedly shown that the vast majority of French urban dwellers, like urban dwellers almost everywhere that these polls have been conducted, would prefer to live in single-family detached houses. (Photograph by Robert Bruegmann, 1999.)

The Crisis of the Central Cities

While the population was exploding outward in American cities in the postwar decades, the older central cities struggled as never before. Large industrial cities of the Northeast lost staggering numbers of industrial jobs as manufacturing companies, confronting the problems of old facilities, high union wages, and mounting competition from abroad, either closed their doors, moved operations to the suburbs, or departed the metropolitan area altogether. In the case of retail, many observers had already realized during the interwar years that the old central business districts, many of which had aged without adequate reinvestment, were clearly at risk as newer districts developed further out in the city. These problems were compounded, starting in the 1950s, by competition in the form of large-scale suburban shopping malls. These regional shopping centers have been a convenient scapegoats for observers who lament the decline in vitality of the central city, but the malls only contributed to a process well underway before the large regional centers started to appear.[13]

By the end of the postwar boom years the inner cities of Newark, Detroit, Saint Louis and others reached crisis stage. As jobs and residents disappeared, many owners simply walked away from buildings. Some of the buildings were demolished; others were destroyed by deliberate arson. In many American cities additional areas were leveled through urban renewal projects that city officials hoped would remove some of the oldest and least economically viable physical fabric in the city and allow rebuilding to make the cities more competitive with the suburbs. It became common to compare American city centers with "Dresden after the war" and to marvel that a country rich enough to put a man on the moon could let such a thing happen to its city centers.

By the early 1970s, many observers feared that all or most American central cities might implode. Dozens of books appeared with alarming titles like *The Urban Crisis in America, Sick Cities,* and *Cities in a Race with Time.*[14] Most of these books blamed the decline of the central cities on the rise of the suburbs. As other writers of the era noted, however, a perceived decline is often just the symptom of a major reordering. In virtually every city throughout history, dismay and confusion have accompanied the decline of older economic activities or urban forms and the creation of new ones. Most writers who have discussed the abandonment of vast tracts of housing in central Newark, or Saint Louis, or Detroit have concluded that this was the result of malicious intent or bad public policies in specific cities. In fact, much of the housing that was destroyed after World War II was old and unsanitary, and the reason it could be abandoned was that so many of its inhabitants were able to move to much better housing farther out.[15] Cities that escaped most of the abandonment were not necessarily wiser, moreover. They were mostly in a different phase of their economic cycle or they benefited from waves of new immigrants who were grateful for the housing that the native population no longer wanted.

This episode provides good testimony to the fact that throughout the turbulent course of urban history, a setback for one group often provides an opportunity for another. A drop in house prices, perceived as decline for an existing population, offers affordable housing and a golden opportunity for potential new residents. In some cases, the "decline" of neighborhoods after World War II meant better housing for poor minorities. In other cases, it led to gentrification. It is for this reason that precisely during the worst years for many central cities, the process of gentrification sped up significantly. Entire districts like Boston's Back Bay and South End, Philadelphia's Society Hill and Rittenhouse Square, Washington's Georgetown and Old Town Alexandria, Chicago's Old Town and Lincoln Park, and San Francisco's North Beach and Western Addition were transformed with the arrival of new demographic groups, often young artists, gay people, and other bohemians in the vanguard, eventually followed by single professional people and childless couples. They stripped the woodwork in small houses in the little streets of Philadelphia and painted the frame houses of San Francisco in brilliant colors. This was the era that launched the phrase "back to the city" to describe a process of central city revitalization.[16] The phrase was misleading, though. Although there was a move of new residents into gentrifying areas, typically the population dropped as the gentrifiers occupied more space and densities declined.

During the postwar years, as scholars attempted to keep up with the changes that they saw around them, problems with the old Park-Burgess concentric circles became ever more apparent. The best known attempt to portray the dispersal and regrouping of activities appears in the "multinucleated" model created by geographers Chauncey D. Harris and Edward L. Ullman immediately after World War II (fig. 8).[17] Even the Harris-Ullman model, however, was soon seen to be inadequate because it assumed that each city, with all its peripheral development, was a discrete entity. The model did not account for the tight clustering of cities that formed a single urban region in places like the industrial belt that stretched between Cleveland, Ohio, and Pittsburgh Pennsylvania, the Pottery Belt around Stoke-on-Trent in England, or the coal-mining region of the Ruhr Valley in Germany. These places were all clearly part of a single urban system but without a single dominant center.[18] In like manner, the cities of New York, Newark, and New Brunswick were clearly all part of a single urban place. This meant that Newark could be simultaneously a satellite settlement of New York City and a city in its own right. Suburbs like the Oranges or Montclair were suburbs both of Newark, which was closer, but also of New York City, which was farther but which exerted a stronger gravitational pull. Nor did the

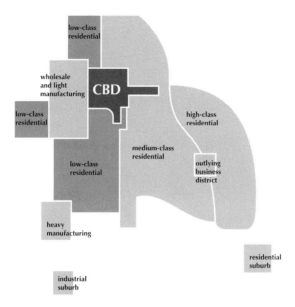

Figure 8. The Harris-Ullman model of city growth. Immediately after World War II, Chauncey Harris and Edward Ullman decided that the simple diagrams of Park and Burgess from the 1920s (fig. 5) and Homer Hoyt from the 1930s (fig. 6) failed to convey the complexity of American cities, which, well before the onset of World War II, had become enormous multinucleated regions. Harris and Ullman produced a diagram that, at the time, was widely believed to be the logical successor of the early attempts. What they may have gained in verisimilitude, however, was apparently lost in diagrammatic clarity because, for all its advantages, the diagram has not been much used in recent years. Nor has anyone been able to offer a satisfactory alternative. (Redrawn by Dennis McClendon from Chauncey Harris and Edward Ullman, "The Nature of Cities," *Annals of the American Academy of Political and Social Science* 242 [November 1945], 13.)

Harris-Ullman model adequately represent the large exurban areas extending dozens of miles out into the countryside with varying degrees of connection to the central city or, in some cases, to several cities. The resulting pattern of intersecting urban, suburban, and exurban rings was much more complex than anything any of the previous models had indicated.

This complicated and constantly shifting metropolitan pattern was best described in the postwar decades by the geographer Jean Gottmann, who coined the term "megalopolis" to describe the vast multicentered northeastern seaboard of the United States.[19] Gottmann's formulation worked quite well for many other places and still today is a useful description of many scattered, multicentered urban areas worldwide, from the settlements in the North Carolina Piedmont to the Pearl River delta in China. Perhaps because of the very complexity of the system, Gottmann did not offer any visual diagram of his ideas such as Park and Burgess had offered. Perhaps for this reason, the older models continued to have a life of their own.

5 Sprawl since the 1970s

During the last several decades of the twentieth century, cities across the world have had a prodigious growth both in population and land area. Where historically only a few cities anywhere reached a population of a million people, by the end of the twentieth century, China alone had more than thirty cities with a million people—many of them places that few people in the Western world have ever heard of. The largest metropolitan areas today, places like Tokyo-Yokohama, New York City, and Mexico City now number over 20 million people and sprawl across vast territories, incorporating in their urbanized area freeways, shopping centers, industrial parks, subdivisions, airports, and many previously separate urban entities. The most affluent of these, for example, the region from Tijuana in Mexico to Santa Barbara in Southern California, can extend for over one hundred miles, contain more inhabitants, and boast a larger economy than all but a few nations.[1]

In the affluent industrialized world since the economic upturn of the 1970s a great many cities have been turned inside out in certain respects as the traditional commercial and industrial functions of the central city have been decanted to the edges while the central city and close-in neighborhoods have come to be home to an increasingly affluent residential population and a high-end service economy. With the penetration of urban functions far into the countryside, the old distinctions between urban, suburban, and rural have collapsed. It is often difficult to explain or even characterize change when it is happening all around us all the time, and it appears that we have only begun to scratch the surface in understanding the urban transformations since the 1970s.[2] In what follows I will try to sketch in a picture of the course of sprawl over the past two or three decades by looking, in turn, at each of the large zones in the contemporary urban region and how sprawl has affected it.

The Central Business District

Although at first glance many city centers, particularly in Europe, appear to have changed relatively little over the past fifty years, the way these centers work has been transformed. These city centers once dominated the economic life of the urban region. Today, the core of most central cities contains only a small share of the population or the jobs in the metropolitan area, and the number is dropping constantly. In the Paris region during the 1990s, for example, the city of Paris proper lost 200,000 jobs and the inner ring of suburbs gained only 20,000 while the outer suburban ring added 160,000.[3] In the United States, the situation has advanced even further. By the year 2000, most traditional downtowns in American cities housed fewer than 10 percent of the jobs in their respective metropolitan areas.[4] In addition, many city centers that once functioned independently now find themselves competing with other centers in multicentered urban regions. This pattern is seen, for example, in the San Francisco Bay Area where San Francisco, Oakland, and San Jose serve as administrative centers in a single urban system or in the Dutch Randstad, where Amsterdam, Utrecht, Rotterdam, and the Hague together with their satellite communities today form an urbanized ring around a less-developed "Green Heart," resulting in a curious inversion of the London model of central core surrounded by greenbelt.[5]

Despite the move of offices and manufacturing out of the central cities and competition from suburban regional shopping centers, few of the direst predictions by American urban experts of the 1960s have come to pass. The historic core of most American cities has not disappeared. Many citizens who could have moved remained, and they helped define for their city centers a viable niche in the new urban system as a command post for government and high finance and a magnet for culture and tourism. The historical core of San Francisco, like that of London or Paris, has experienced a commercial gentrification, becoming a kind of "boutique" downtown, catering to international business, luxury retail, culture, and tourism and providing accommodations for an increasingly affluent and privileged residential population. Increasingly, the downtowns of cities like Chicago or Denver are following in the path of Paris or

San Francisco, and even places like downtown Detroit and Newark, considered hopeless by many people only a few years ago, are showing new signs of life.

In many ways, the gentrification of the core and sprawl at the edge, far from being competing tendencies, are flipsides of the same coin.[6] The first phase of this relationship was quite obvious. As many of the more space-intensive activities of the center—for example, manufacturing, warehousing, and back-office functions—moved to the urban periphery after World War II, it left many city centers with a large stock of underutilized buildings. Some of these were razed, leaving vacant parcels that were converted for use as parking lots. Although this process seemed merely destructive to many people, it provided space for new activities and functions.

It was at this exact moment, moreover, that nostalgia for the historical city and an interest in preserving what remained of it became a major popular movement. During the past few decades, in cities and towns all over the country, historical societies and preservation groups have burgeoned. Landmarks have been inventoried and protected. Historic districts have multiplied. Owners have restored and cleaned facades, and city officials have replaced postwar light fixtures, benches, and other street furniture with historic fixtures.

Eventually, the empty lots in many American downtowns were filled. The eroded urban fabric visible from the top of a tall building in Chicago or Los Angeles started to mend. New buildings took their place amid restored landmarks. What few people seemed to notice was the way the rising fortunes of the center, like their earlier decline, were directly connected to developments at the edge. As more and more businesses and people, including even some of the least affluent members of the urban community, arrived at the urban periphery, it lost much of its exclusivity and social cachet. The number of individuals at the very top of the social ladder who wished to buy large houses in the farthest subdivision declined dramatically in the last decades of the twentieth century. As this happened, the central city and older established suburbs began to regain some of the luster they had lost in the postwar decades. The stage was set for a remarkable revival of the center.

One of the ironies of this revival is that while central cities have traded on their "traditional" character, much of what is most attractive about them is the fact that so many of the things that once defined them have disappeared. The decanting outward of all kinds of manufacturing and warehousing functions led to a dramatic reduction in street congestion, truck traffic, and pollution. This allowed city centers to become increasingly attractive to those who have the choice to live anywhere they wish in the metropolitan area and who in previous decades might well have chosen to live in the suburbs or exurbs. The boom in affluent population at the core of American cities has been made possible in part by the rapid development of the condominium form of ownership since the 1960s.[7] The conversion of rental buildings, loft structures, and office towers into condominiums not only allowed for a rapid expansion of home ownership at the core of American cities, but the process made possible a large infusion of new money into old buildings. Behind the carefully preserved facades, many central cities have been thoroughly transformed as part of the same decentralization process that has been at work throughout metropolitan regions. They participate just as fully in sprawl as the farthest subdivisions.

The gentrification of the business core of many European cities has been underway longer, but in most cases has been even less immediately obvious than that in the United States. In part this has been due to the larger role of governmental bodies. Preserving the leading role of the historic city center, particularly the center of capitol cities, has long been a national priority in many European countries.[8] Affluent residents of Paris enjoy an enormous range of amenities paid for by the citizens of the country as a whole as well as by international tourists. This goes a long way toward explaining why the bustling streets and glossy shops around the Paris Opera look so different from those in the business districts of many American cities or even the centers of Marseille, Liverpool, Charleroi, Duisburg, or European industrial cities less favored by national governments.

The Inner or Central City

Many of the same forces operating on the central business district have also transformed large parts of the remainder of the old central cities. By the year 2000, the far left-hand side of the line recording the density gradient for virtually every American and European metropolitan area was much lower than it had been fifty or one hundred years before and very low indeed by any historic standards. The population of the central arrondissements of Paris, for example, which had reached over 200,000 people per square mile by the mid-nineteenth century, had dropped below 75,000 people per square mile by the year 2000. The city as a whole, which had hit its population peak in 1921 when it reached nearly 3 million people, had fallen to 2.1 million by 1999 giving it a density of just over 50,000 people per square mile.[9] Because, as in American cities, the center has lost population while the periphery has boomed, the city of Paris itself has housed a constantly smaller percentage of the population of the metropolitan area. Although the densities at the historic core remain higher than in American urban areas of comparable size, in Chicago, for example, the urban processes at work are no different. In fact the shift of population from the center of Paris to the suburbs has been greater than that in Chicago.

In the United States in the year 2000, only two central cities reached a density of even 10,000 people per square mile. The five boroughs of New York City contained just over 26,000 people per square mile, the average after the 70,000 inhabitants per square mile figure for Manhattan was balanced with the low densities of parts of Staten Island and the other boroughs. The next densest city, Chicago, had less than 13,000 people per square mile. It appears that 10,000 people per square mile is a threshold for the extensive use of public transportation systems, a fact that helps explain why these two cities together account for a large percentage of all public transportation in America, and even in these two urban areas, public transportation is a dominant force only for transportation into the central business districts. Many of the cities that have grown most quickly in recent years are among the least dense of all. The city of Phoenix, for example, in 2000 had a population of just over 1.3 million spread out over an area of 475 square miles or more than ten times the size of Paris, giving it an average density of 2,782 people per square mile.[10]

In both Europe and North America, the residential districts surrounding the business core of central cities are gentrifying. In Paris, for example, entire quarters that used to house working-class families are now filled with affluent citizens. Emblematic of this transformation has been the fate of the Communist Party headquarters in the northeastern part of Paris. Once firmly entrenched in a working-class district, today the party chiefs looking out their windows can see abundant signs of a rising tide of affluent bourgeoisie. This gentrification tends to produce lower densities, which helps explain the sharp decline in the population of Paris in the twentieth century. These figures would be lower yet had it not been for the fact that a large part of the industrial sector, in particular the factories, docks, and warehouses that used to fuel the city's economy and supported the working-class neighborhoods, has been replaced with other land uses, primarily upscale housing. Another conspicuous development in Paris, also visible in New York, London, and other major commercial and cultural centers, is the growth in the number of units owned by individuals with their primary residence elsewhere. In the most affluent districts in the western arrondissements of Paris, the number of second houses and professional pieds-à-terre account for as much as 10 percent of the total housing stock.[11]

In the residential quarters of many North American central cities the same combination of industrial conversion, historic preservation, and gentrification has produced similar results. Among North American cities, this process is perhaps most dramatic in San Francisco, where the gentrified area has expanded to virtually every part of the city.[12] This, in turn, has pushed a large percentage of the poorest families into other parts of the Bay Area. Incomes in San Francisco have risen to the point where they are now higher in the city than in most of the surrounding suburbs.[13] San Francisco is no aberration. Even in many of the poorest communities of urban America there has been a marked rebound.[14]

Another important source of rejuvenation in many European and American cities has been an influx of immigrants, many of them initially poor but willing and able to build bustling communities. This process is quite visible across the United States, from the Vietnamese neighborhoods of suburban Los Angeles to the African-Caribbean enclaves of New York City. When central-city populations have grown, it has been almost entirely the result of new immigrants who are willing to live at higher densities than most of the rest of the population. As the new residents become affluent, however, they have tended to disperse like all of the groups before them. Although the term "gentrification" has been used almost exclusively when the newcomers are affluent white residents, particularly when they displace minority residents, in reality, in neighborhoods all over North America, it is Asian-Americans, Latino-Americans, and African-Americans with rising incomes who are doing the gentrification.

As in the case of the central business district, gentrification in inner city residential neighborhoods is closely connected to sprawl at the edge. As the number of working-class families moving to the edge for cheaper land prices has mounted, affluent families have been increasingly less willing to move farther outward, particularly since many prestigious jobs in business, law, medicine, and the cultural and nonprofit worlds have either remained or have been newly created in the traditional city centers and close-in suburbs, and automobile commutes from the edge to the center have become longer and more unpleasant. This fact has played a major role in the rise of property values and the influx of affluent newcomers immediately adjacent to rail stations. In turn, this development, along with a rise in car ownership even among the very poor, has led to a seemingly paradoxical situation in many cities that an increasing share of the subsidy for public transportation, paid for by all taxpayers, benefits most directly individuals at the upper end of the social and economic ladder.

As the pace of gentrification has picked up, it has led to an outward march of population groups that displays many curious parallels with the old Park-Burgess ecological model of the city. As each neighborhood improves and property values climb, the initial gentrifiers, often gay people, artists, and other traditionally "bohemian" types, are pushed out by rising rents or lured by the attractions of less costly places farther out. Their places are taken by single or childless professionals or "yuppies" and, eventually, by families at the top of the income scale who can afford to send their children to private schools. Whether gentrification continues to intensify probably depends in great measure on the ability of central cities to improve their schools enough to compete with those of the suburbs. This pressure of rising expectations is one of the factors fueling the increasingly raucous national debate over school-funding formulas, vouchers, and the creation of new charter and magnet schools.

Some American cities, such as Philadelphia, Cleveland, or Saint Louis, are still decanting large numbers of people without much in the way of a new population to replace them. In other cities, Los Angeles, Chicago, or Denver, for example, the outward flow appears to have slowed and the newly revitalized urban cores are attracting an important influx of residents. In the early years of the twenty-first century, it appears that the forces of renewal and gentrification are becoming dominant in an increasing number of central cities. The old "crisis of the central city," in which jobs were departing and property values plunging, could well turn out to have been a short-lived phenomenon, perhaps triggered in the short run by the very programs—urban renewal, neighborhood revitalization, public housing—that were created to "cure" these urban woes. However, contrary to much accepted wisdom that has stressed the short-term negative effects of these programs, many of them seem to have been quite effective in the long run. The new crisis of the inner city may turn out to be a crisis in affordability caused by sharply rising prices.

Many smart growth activists believe that as people return to the city in greater numbers, this movement of people will create population gains and an increased density that will reduce the pressure for outward expansion. Increasingly, however, as affluent citizens have moved to the center, they are doing just what their counterparts have long done in the suburbs. They have found that they can use zoning ordinances, historic preservation measures, environmental regulations, and other means to resist continued change, to control the appearance and character of their neighborhoods, and to stop densities from rising. In city after city across the country, the old zoning codes have been downzoned time and again to reduce the ultimate possible population and prevent existing densities from rising.[15]

Suburbia

During the last several decades, as in the past, the creation of new suburban communities at the edge has set in motion a chain reaction as people throughout the metropolitan area move and adjust. In the process, some suburbs see their population get younger or older and housing prices rise or fall, depending on their location, the kind of housing stock, the strength of the local economy, and many other factors. By now many of the inner suburbs look and feel much like the adjacent communities within the central city. The differences between city and suburb have blurred as the suburbs have become more diverse and heterogeneous than ever.

Although at first glance it appears that new housing developments simply continue the trends of the postwar decades, there have been some significant shifts. For one thing, single-family houses have become much larger than they were in the postwar decades, as the average size of a new house has mushroomed from around 1,000 square feet at the end of the war to nearly 2,500 square feet by the end of the century. Many of the new subdivisions, moreover, have explored new forms of internal governance, particularly through the use of homeowner associations that have came to provide a kind of private local governmental structure. In addition, an increasing number of new residential communities have been gated. These recent shifts have been the source of new variations on the venerable theme of suburban criticism—the idea that suburbanites are selfish and self-absorbed in their increasingly privatized, exclusionary realms.[16]

A surprising amount of the new housing has not been conventionally produced single-family houses in traditional subdivisions. A substantial number of the units in many metropolitan areas are now mobile (or "manufactured") homes. Some of these, where it is not forbidden by municipal regulations, are parked in mobile home parks.[17] In other cases, several units are assembled, placed on foundations, and look like conventionally built housing. There is also a greatly expanded number of suburban row houses, garden apartments, retirement apartments, and other kinds of multifamily construction, some of it rental and some of it in condominium ownership. Along with these residential developments have appeared new shopping centers, business parks, office parks, and large suburban "edge cities," all connected with freeways.[18] Much of this new development is larger in scale than anything seen in the past.

One of the main ideas fueling fear of sprawl in the United States is the notion that sprawl is accelerating and that the suburbs are expanding at ever-lower densities. A closer examination of recent trends suggests that this is far from an accurate assessment. It is true that suburban growth has by no means stopped. Vast amounts of acreage around virtually every American city have been converted from farms and forests to housing subdivisions. However, given the large increase in population in American cities, some suburban growth is all but inevitable. The more important question is whether the rate of sprawl is accelerating—that is, whether suburbanites are using more and more land per capita. In fact, there is little evidence that suburban sprawl is accelerating and considerable evidence that the opposite is occurring.

We can use the Chicago area as a typical example. For years, sprawl opponents trumpeted the "fact" that between 1970 and 1990 the metropolitan area grew in population by only 4 percent but grew in land area by 46 percent.[19] This kind of statistic, juxtaposed with a photograph of a new subdivision under construction in a cornfield conjures up images of a juggernaut moving inexorably across the countryside, flattening farms and forests, replacing country roads with highways lined with wall-to-wall strip centers and an endless sprawl of large-lot subdivisions.

Even if the figures were accurate they would not necessarily represent a crisis. There is no shortage of land in Illinois, and the pace of decentralization has been less rapid than that seen in many other places at other times—around London between the wars, for example. But the statistics on Chicago sprawl were both inaccurate and misleading. To start with, subsequent and more accurate estimates of urbanized land soon led the Northeastern Illinois Planning Commission, the organization that initially popularized the figures, to quietly amend their original estimate of increased land use downward from 46 percent to 35 percent.[20] This was a minor adjustment, to be sure, but few anti-sprawl activists seem to have seen or used the revised figures.

More problematic was the basic assumption that land use should be compared to the growth of population. Since much of the increase in land was due to new houses, the more appropriate statistic would logically have been the increase in the number of households. Throughout America, during the years when the baby boom generation matured, household sizes declined rapidly. Nationwide the number of persons per household sank from 3.14 in 1970 to 2.63 in 1990. This would suggest a rapid expansion in the need for housing even without a growth in population. So, for example, in the Chicago area, where the population grew only 4 percent in this period, the number of households increased 20 percent. Then consider the fact that the workforce of the Chicago metropolitan area increased by 21 percent during this same period, in great part because of the entry of women into the workforce. Making the reasonable assumption that every additional worker requires some additional amount of space, both for the actual work and in the form of support spaces, and the presumably "disproportionate" growth in land use completely disappears.[21]

There is a more basic objection to the 4–46 percent formulation. The time period described is narrow. When the anti-sprawl advocates used these figures, it was usually in a context that suggested that this decentralization was part of a rising trend, that suburban decentralization in these twenty years was greater than what happened in the period 1950–70 and that decentralization since 1990 has been even faster. In fact, the opposite is true. The rate of suburban sprawl has actually decreased in each of these successive periods.

The most useful and consistent collection of information on densities in American metropolitan areas can be found in the statistics for "urbanized areas" compiled by the U.S. Census Bureau since the 1950s.[22] These figures are important because the other commonly used statistical categories, for example, the figures for municipalities or the various permutations on the "metropolitan area," are defined by essentially arbitrary political lines on a map. This makes them all but useless in determining densities. For example, once part of a county near a large city becomes sufficiently populous, the census bureau will count the entire county as part of the metropolitan area even if much of the county remains rural. This is not a problem in the total metropolitan population count, which is the information most people want, but it makes metropolitan density figures all but useless. The problem is particularly visible in the urban West. Riverside County and San Diego County are urban in their far western portions, so they are counted as part of metropolitan areas. However, these counties extend across many miles of nearly empty desert, all the way to the Nevada border. Obviously the inclusion of these counties in calculations of metropolitan density gives a distorted idea of actual urban densities.

For this reason, many of the statistics used in analyses of sprawl have been fundamentally misleading. If a metropolitan area continues to contain the same counties over a number of decades and population increases, it will often seem to rise in density even if the population is spreading out beyond these counties at exceedingly low density. Conversely, and much more commonly, when the urban population spreads outward, this will trigger the addition of a new county to the metropolitan area by the census bureau. In this case, the metropolitan density appears to plummet simply because of the addition of the new county no matter whether the density in the actual urbanized portion of the area was rising or falling.[23] The widespread use of this kind of misleading statistic has needlessly alarmed a great many people.

The "urbanized area," by contrast, was devised by the census bureau to provide a functional definition of the city. It includes all the land with a strong connection back to the central population centers and more than 1,000 people per square mile.[24] Although by no means a perfect measure for defining city and suburbs, the 1,000 people per square mile figure does approximately correspond to the threshold between the regularly developed suburban subdivisions and the exurban areas beyond because 1,000 people per square mile is today about the lower limit at which full city services like water supply and wastewater treatment can be provided in a way that most public and private agencies consider economical. For this reason, it is probably the most important tool available for measuring densities in the cities and suburbs (fig. 9). What the data on urbanized areas show is that although Chicago and many cities of the northern and eastern United States continued to decentralize in the late twentieth century, they decentralized more slowly than they had in the immediate postwar decades. In fact, they seem to be in the process of reversing this trend and actually becoming denser. Chicago seems to have reached this stage during the latter part of the 1990s.[25] Researchers at the Urban Transportation Center of the University of Illinois at Chicago, who have made the most careful study to date of decentralization in the region since World War II, have suggested that the rate of decentralization after World War II peaked in the 1960s and has been declining ever since then.[26]

The declining rate of suburban decentralization is quite evident on the ground. Lot sizes in new subdivisions at the suburban edge of Chicago and most other cities are, on average, quite a bit smaller than those of the 1950s, and there is a higher percentage of row houses and multifamily buildings

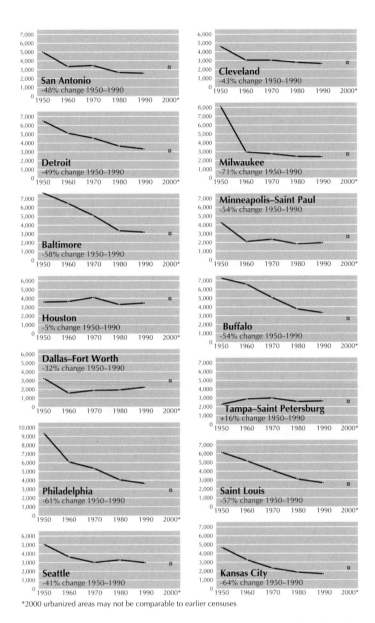

Figure 9. Densities of selected American urbanized areas. The Census Bureau's figures for "urbanized areas"—that is central cities and areas around them that have densities of at least 1,000 people per square mile and that are functionally related back to the central cities—provide a good way to track urban densities since World War II. These charts demonstrate graphically how most of the older, denser, and most heavily industrialized urbanized areas of the Northeast have declined sharply in density due to massive decentralization after World War II. A number of the newer cities of the American South and West, in contrast, although much less dense to begin with, have seen a pronounced rise in density. The

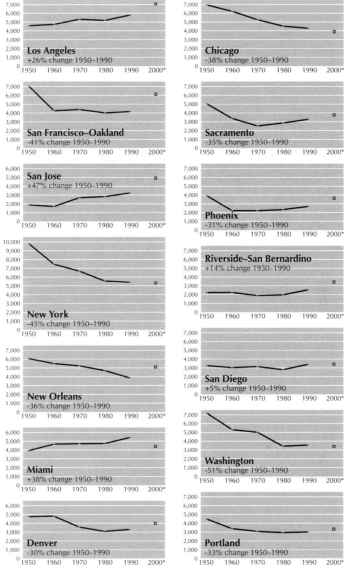

Los Angeles
+26% change 1950–1990

Chicago
-38% change 1950–1990

San Francisco–Oakland
-41% change 1950–1990

Sacramento
-35% change 1950–1990

San Jose
+47% change 1950–1990

Phoenix
-31% change 1950–1990

New York
-45% change 1950–1990

Riverside–San Bernardino
+14% change 1950–1990

New Orleans
-36% change 1950–1990

San Diego
+5% change 1950–1990

Miami
+38% change 1950–1990

Washington
-51% change 1950–1990

Denver
-30% change 1950–1990

Portland
-33% change 1950–1990

*2000 urbanized areas may not be comparable to earlier censuses

result has been a convergence between the older and the newer cities. In virtually every case the decline in density of the postwar years has either slowed or stopped since the late 1970s, with many American urban areas now becoming more, rather than less, dense. Chief among these is Los Angeles, which is today the densest urban area in America and at least as dense as many urban areas in Europe. (Charts by Dennis McClendon based on the compilation of urbanized area statistics from the U.S. Census Bureau by Wendell Cox and www.demographia.com. The figures for 2000 were calculated using a slightly different formula so that they cannot, in all cases, be directly compared with the figures from 1990 and before.)

Figure 10. The American suburb today. Despite a widespread perception that American cities and suburbs are constantly expanding outward at ever-lower densities, in fact, the peak of decentralization seems to have occurred between the 1920s and the end of the 1950s. Today, an increasing number of cities and suburbs in the United States, particularly those in the fastest-growing cities of the American South and West, are actually becoming denser as central cities rebound and suburbs cater to an ever-expanding number of working-class and minority families. Much of the new housing at the urban periphery, for example, as shown here, in Naperville, west of Chicago, is actually attached or multifamily. Exurban development, however, continues to expand in the older cities of the American North and East. (Photograph by Robert Bruegmann, 2000.)

(fig. 10). Row houses now make up as much as a quarter of all housing starts in the Chicago region, a statistic no one would have predicted even ten years ago and probably the largest number since the great fire of 1871.[27] In addition, many parcels skipped over in the earlier building eras are now being filled in. The standard wisdom about accelerating sprawl in American cities and suburbs is misleading. Within the city and suburbs, the national trend is toward a slowing, if not reversing, of the long decline in density that took place earlier in the twentieth century.

In this process, Chicago is among the many cities following in the wake of developments in the fastest growing cities of the American South and West. Census figures show that many of these urban areas have been getting denser for some time now. For example, the Los Angeles urbanized area saw its density rise a startling 26.4 percent in the years 1950 to 1990 and even more quickly

between 1990 and 2000. In other words, the overall density gradient for the Los Angeles area, while still flattening, is no longer falling; it is actually rising fairly quickly. The density of the Los Angeles urbanized area, as calculated in the 2000 census, was just over 7,000 people per square mile, nearly twice that of the Chicago urbanized area and significantly denser than the New York area. No one really knows exactly why this has happened. It is not clear how much is due to the imposition of governmental regulations and land-use controls of all kinds and how much is simply part of a natural cycle in cities as individual families constantly move to take advantage of more convenient commutes and better housing, schools, and social opportunities. Given the extremely high cost of land and increasing calls for tighter and tighter regulations in Los Angeles and elsewhere, however, there is no reason to believe that the process will reverse itself any time soon.

Although the idea of Los Angeles as America's most densely populated urbanized area might seem fantastic to those who have heard for years that Los Angeles is the quintessential example of American sprawl, it will be no surprise to anyone who has actually taken a close look at the city from a plane. It is true that central Los Angeles never had densities like those of Manhattan, but it is also true that there are few areas of really low density as there are in many parts of the New York region. From the air, virtually the entire Los Angeles basin appears as a dense carpet of buildings, with most houses packed together on lots that are considerably smaller than their counterparts in eastern cities. In addition, and in sharp contrast to many eastern cities, there are few vacant lots. There is also no appreciable exurban penumbra. Because of the problems of supplying water, in Los Angeles, as elsewhere in the American Southwest, where the relatively dense subdivisions stop, the desert begins (fig. 11).

The high average density explains the surprising fact that any chart show-ing America's most densely populated municipalities will contain a number of suburbs of Los Angeles. The city of West Hollywood, for example, with its many apartment buildings and intense pedestrian life, registers a density of over 19,000 people per square mile, near the top of the chart. In addition, many areas to the east of downtown that house large numbers of Mexican immigrants have very high densities even though they mostly consist largely of single-family houses. This happens because so many people are crowded into each house. Unincorporated East Los Angeles, for example, now registers nearly 17,000 people per square mile, and densities are also high in neighbor-ing El Monte and La Puente. Densities were so high in some parts of Orange

Figure 11. At the periphery of suburban Phoenix. Cities like Phoenix, Los Angeles, and Las Vegas are often described as the ultimate in sprawl. In fact they tend to be rather compact settlements with little abandoned housing or vacant land at the center and almost none of the exurban penumbra that surrounds almost all of the older cities of the American northeast. Where water has been available, Phoenix has developed outward in a surprisingly orderly way, with densities that hardly vary between the center and far periphery. This has given it one of the flattest density gradients in urban history. Where the water mains end, the desert begins. (Photograph by Robert Bruegmann, 1998.)

County's Santa Ana that the city tried to reduce them by prohibiting new apartment construction. As is often the case, this kind of simple planning solution backfired as the continuing flow of new residents crowded into existing houses, making the density problem even worse.[28]

From the air, the remarkable number of bright new tile roofs almost overflowing their small lots in the Los Angeles area is graphic proof of the ongoing process of urban infill. The new construction occupies parcels of redeveloped land and hold-out lots, pieces of property that for one reason or another were not developed earlier, usually because of negative environmental factors or because the land was unavailable or too expensive. As long as it was easier to develop elsewhere, particularly at the edge, these parcels were left fallow. Now, after major increases in the price of land throughout the region, these parcels are newly attractive as investments, particularly if they can be developed at high densities. This accounts for the remarkably high percentage of townhouses and garden apartment complexes. This is a good demonstration of why complaints about "scattered" or noncontinuous development as wasteful and land consuming are not necessarily convincing. Scattered development often results, in the end, in densities higher than those that would have been achieved with continuous development because it allows for infill at higher densities in the second and third waves of growth.

At the edge of the Los Angeles region the process of densification is even more apparent. Lot sizes in the region have always been smaller than those in eastern cities. There is virtually nothing in the Los Angeles region to compare with the large estates of the wealthiest residents of suburban Westchester County, New York, or Fairfield County, Connecticut, for example. It is rare to find a five-acre residential parcel, let alone a twenty-five-acre parcel. Since the 1950s, moreover, fewer of the most affluent residents of the Los Angeles area have chosen to live anywhere near the urban fringe than their counterparts in cities in the north and east of the United States. In fact, most of the fastest growing parts of Ventura, Riverside, and San Bernardino counties are being settled by families with unusually modest incomes. Even in more affluent Orange County the densities have risen sharply over the years. A driver headed southward through the county today sees detached houses developed in the north part of the county during the postwar years, built at densities of four or eight to the acre, gradually give way to higher density houses, finally reaching, in the southernmost part of the county and northern San Diego County,

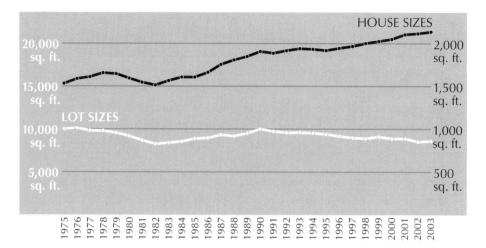

Figure 12. Changes in median house size and lot size, 1975–2003. Since World War II, as affluence has increased, the median size of American houses has risen dramatically. Median lot sizes in cities and suburbs, in contrast, after fluctuating in the 1970s and 1980s, started a significant decline in the 1990s. This change is immediately visible on the fringe in most metropolitan areas, where not only are lot sizes noticeably smaller but more of the dwellings are attached or multifamily units. This chart shows primarily the houses built by developers in urban and suburban subdivisions because developers were the chief source of information for this census category. This means that the chart excludes most very low-density exurban development. (Chart drawn by Dennis McClendon based on "Lot Size of New One-Family Houses Sold," 1976–2003, and "Median and Average Square Feet of Floor Area in New One-Family Houses Completed by Location," 1973–2003, U.S. Bureau of the Census, Construction Statistics.)

houses on exceptionally small lots, townhouse clusters, and garden apartments at twelve to twenty units per acre.[29]

The patterns visible in Chicago and Los Angeles are in evidence nationwide (fig. 12). Nationally, the lot size in American urban areas, which averaged about 10,000 square feet or about a quarter-acre in the mid-1970s, held steady or declined slightly during the 1980s and early 1990s. Since the mid-1990s, lot sizes have dropped sharply downward with median lot sizes falling from 10,000 square feet in 1990 to 8,750 square feet in 1999 even though, during this same period, the average size of the houses built on these lots increased from 1,500 to well over 2,000 square feet.[30]

Where virtually all large American cities grew much faster in urbanized land area than in population in the 1950s, by the end of the 1990s this process had slowed down or reversed itself. Today, densities are rising in at least half of the largest urbanized areas. A number of scholars, looking at other kinds of evidence, have confirmed that the peak years of decentralization apparently occurred in American cities and suburbs between the 1920s and the end of the 1950s and that decentralization has been moderating or reversing itself since then.[31] Although the sheer size of America's continuing population growth has meant that the outward push of American urban areas since the 1970s has been larger in scale than anything that came before, American city and suburban dwellers are using less land per capita. Thus we can conclude that the campaign against suburban sprawl, which became most strident in the last years of the twentieth century, was reacting to a trend that actually peaked some forty years earlier.

Another curious feature of the fight against sprawl is the fact that this campaign has been most conspicuous in the largest and fastest-growing cities, which are, virtually without exception, much denser than smaller cities and small towns. Anti-sprawl agitation is much more intense in the Los Angeles region, with over 7,000 people per square mile, than it is in Little Rock or Lubbock, with densities under 2,000 people per square mile. In many small towns where there is no agitation against sprawl at all, the highest densities may well be under 1,000 people per square mile. If the anti-sprawl crusade were really about using less land or using it more efficiently, the biggest metropolitan areas are illogical targets.

A final misconception about urban history that figures prominently in anti-sprawl literature is the idea that the major reason for the rapid growth of the suburbs has been that city dwellers, instead of fixing the problems where they live, simply flee to new places. They infer from this that the problems of the inner city will inevitably spread outward from the central city to the inner suburbs and then the current outer suburbs as urban residents continue their outward push. While it is true that some neighborhoods, as they age and face competition from outlying areas, do seem to sink in socioeconomic status, this is by no means inevitable. Even a cursory glance at the location of many of the most affluent suburbs will confirm that many of these communities today are the same ones that held this distinction in the 1920s or even the 1880s. Even when communities "decline," meaning that house prices fall or fail to keep up with others in the metropolitan area, this is not necessarily a bad thing for everyone. It is the most important supply of affordable housing in urban areas.

Rather than declining, many suburbs, usually those with natural amenities or particularly good access, have become increasingly gentrified. One of the most visible results of this has been the dramatic rise in the number of teardowns: the replacement of smaller houses with much larger ones. One might have thought that teardowns would be welcomed by anti-sprawl forces because they clearly represent a desire to reuse and revitalize older communities. But many of the same organizations that fight sprawl also want to discourage teardowns on the grounds that they destroy the character of communities. This suggests that the real target might be less sprawl than change itself.[32]

Suburban "Parks" and "Centers"

Although at first glance the story of urban development in the last half century might be seen as one of continuous decentralization, in reality it, like all urban development, has been a mix of forces tending toward centralization along with forces tending toward dispersal. Although there has been a net out-migration of population from the central city to the suburbs, for example, there has always been a countervailing process of in-migration, particularly of young adults and empty nesters. Within the suburbs themselves, both centrifugal and centripetal forces have been in evidence. One of the best places to see this is in the development of centers and parks, as in the shopping or business center and the industrial or office park. The frequent use of these terms suggests a simultaneous desire to enjoy the benefits of the intensity of interactions created by a compaction of functions in a "center" and the tranquility created by their dispersal in a "park."

One of the most remarkable developments of the last years of the twentieth century has been the rise of the industrial and office park. Although the first of the industrial parks were created at the turn of the century, and the earliest office parks in the 1950s, they have both become really common only in the past thirty or forty years.[33] The "park" idea has spread widely. From the air, enormous swaths of economically successful regions like the area stretching from Atlanta to Raleigh-Durham along the piedmont region of the Carolinas or the Lombardy region of northern Italy appear as a series of large boxes surrounded by parking lots and connected by highways.[34]

The shift of manufacturing from the central city to outlying locations has been responsible for the notion that today's urban areas are postindustrial. This is not a helpful concept. In many metropolitan areas, the amount of manufacturing has increased, not decreased. It is simply located farther from the center and requires fewer workers. This decentralization and mechanization has caused considerable social and economic dislocation, but it has provided great benefits as well. For several hundred years, most industrial production, usually housed in buildings tightly packed into a grim industrial landscape, was dirty and dangerous. In the new industrial parks, often quite low in density and heavily landscaped with clean and efficient new buildings, work can still be low paying, repetitive, and sometimes dangerous, but the differences in physical setting between white- and blue-collar workers has narrowed dramatically with sprawl.

As decentralizing forces are almost always offset to some extent by centralizing forces, so the rise of the suburban "park" as an ideal setting for business has been paired with the rise of the suburban "center." Although retail activities have continued to disperse throughout metropolitan areas in the past several decades, there has been some movement toward recentering as well. As suburban shopping centers increased markedly in size in the postwar decades, they started to incorporate activities other than retail activities within and around them. Where the earliest suburban shopping centers had professional buildings for doctors and dentists, newer malls started to incorporate office buildings, theaters, hotels, and restaurants, even, at the West Edmonton Mall in Canada or the Mall of America, outside Minneapolis, entire amusement parks (fig. 13).

In the 1970s and 1980s a number of these malls became the nuclei for giant suburban business centers like Tyson's Corner outside Washington, DC, or Schaumburg outside Chicago, or Costa Mesa–Irvine in the Los Angeles region. Sometimes called "edge cities," a term coined by journalist Joel Garreau, these places were mostly large regional shopping centers with office buildings around them.[35] Almost overnight, it seemed, from the late 1970s through the mid-1980s, the Woodfield area of Schaumburg, northwest of Chicago, became the second largest business district in Illinois, outpacing Rockford, Peoria, and Springfield. In the case of Houston's Post Oak Galleria district, the new center actually surpassed the old downtown in key indicators such as the dollar value of retail sales or number of hotel rooms.

The "edge cities" label is misleading. First of all, they are not cities. They are business centers with some, but not all, of the functions of the old downtowns. Nor is the "edge" part really accurate. Many were nowhere near the edge when they were built. Stamford, Connecticut, or White Plains, New York, or Bellevue, Washington, were old suburban satellite downtowns that were rebuilt as regional business centers. Few edge cities are anywhere near the edge today. In fact, after the 1980s few new ones have appeared. It seems that the sudden growth of these centers might have been only a brief transitional phase in a much longer process of decentralization. They were the successors to the outlying urban centers, like Hollywood or the Englewood district of Chicago in the

Figure 13. The mall as city. At the West Edmonton Mall outside Edmonton, Alberta, it is possible to take classes, go for a swim in the water park, stay for dinner, and then pub crawl into the wee hours, all within the climate-controlled spaces of the mall. Just as the residential homeowner association has transformed notions about the role of the public and the private in residential governance, so has the mall confounded many of the old assumptions about public and private space. (Photograph by Robert Bruegmann, 1994.)

1920s, and the suburban regional shopping centers in the 1950s and 1960s, but it seems that they, too, have been outflanked. Especially in the largest and fastest growing cities, businesses today are more likely to locate in linear strips along the freeways and large arterial roads than in concentrated centers.[36]

Many people have viewed all of these suburban parks and centers as antithetical to the old downtowns. In fact, it is probably more useful to think of all of them as siblings, always reacting to one other. It is, for example, conspicuous that many of the first suburban shopping centers were built by the same investors who owned and operated the downtown department stores. Many of the designs for these open-air suburban shopping centers were based directly on the old downtown shopping streets with many of the same stores and a similar relationship of store fronts to a central street.[37] In fact, the suburban centers were successful because they took the essential character of the old downtown and intensified it. The massive parking lots around these centers simultaneously enhanced accessibility for middle-class customers and at the same time allowed the central courts to be even more pedestrian-friendly than city streets.

Many downtown business groups responded by calling for the pedestrianization of their own major shopping street and the creation of new garages on the parallel streets immediately behind, thus bringing them more in line with the suburban centers. Likewise, the enclosed suburban shopping center was not an attempt to be anti-urban but owed a great deal to the old urban form of the galleria, for example, the great through-block galleries of Paris or Milan or Cleveland. No sooner had this idea of the enclosed multilevel center caught on in suburbia, however, than it was imported back into the city as the model for shopping destinations such as Water Tower Place in Chicago. At the same time the allure of centrality and an intensity of functions has always been present in the suburbs—witness the way many an old suburban shopping mall is being reconstructed and repositioned with the words "Town Centre" in the name.

The same process has marked the development of the office park. During the same years that these were sprouting in the suburbs, developers in the central city were creating large new office and hotel complexes with extensively landscaped grounds. In recent years, as many downtown business associations have tried to improve their competitive position by capitalizing on their historic heritage, restoring buildings, and installing traditional street furniture, developers of suburban places like the Reston Town Center in Virginia or the Easton Town Center in Columbus, Ohio, have countered by creating new suburban "downtowns" meant to look and function like historic city centers.

Suburbia outside the United States

While the suburbs of European cities or those of Australia or Canada have not developed exactly like those of the United States over the past several decades, in many ways the pattern has been similar. As we have seen, for example, during much of the mid-twentieth century, as Paris was losing population, the ring of suburbs immediately around it was gaining. However, since the early 1970s even these inner suburbs started to decline in population and density as the outer suburbs and exurbs have boomed. Between 1962 and 1990, as the city of Paris slipped steadily in population from 2.79 million to 2.15 million, the inner suburbs first gained in population, overtaking the population of the city and reaching just over 3 million by 1975, but then declined again, slipping back to 2.94 million by 1990. During the same period, the outer suburbs witnessed an accelerating growth rising from 1.66 million to 2.62 million. Beyond that an "exterior zone," including the rest of the large Parisian region, the Île-de-France, with its comprehensively planned new towns, exurban developments, and still-rural areas, grew from 1.2 million to 2.9 million.[38] By 1999 the Île-de-France had nearly 10 million people, meaning that the city of Paris accounted for fewer than a quarter of all Parisians. Despite efforts by the French central government to channel growth into specific axes of development and into planned New Towns with a carefully calculated balance of housing and jobs and adequate public transportation, the outer Parisian suburbs and exurbs, with their low-density subdivisions of single-family houses, shopping centers, industrial parks, and freeways, function and look increasingly like those in the United States.[39]

As in the United States, the Parisian suburbs have been the real economic engine of the region, the place where much of the actual production is accomplished and where the majority of the Parisian population now lives (fig. 14). Like the American suburbs, the French suburbs are extremely heterogeneous. They include elegant suburbs like Neuilly to the west of Paris, quite similar to the wealthiest quarters of the city itself, and poor suburbs like La Corneuve or Bobigny to the north and east with their bleak public housing complexes, concentrated minority population, and social unrest.[40] They also include the vast majority of the middle-class population of the Paris region, much of it living in the single-family housing that is the preferred living arrangement for the majority of people in the Paris area.[41]

Suburban development has been somewhat different in northern and southern Europe. In the more affluent countries of northern and western Europe the decentralization trend occurred much earlier than in the cities of southern and eastern Europe, but it has been highly regulated (fig. 15). Flying over Hamburg or Munich, for example, the traveler will see, extending in all directions outward from the central city, a pattern of relatively dense and self-contained suburban clusters carefully separated one from another by bands of green space.[42] This pattern, similar to the garden city idea advocated by Ebenezer Howard, has been enforced by government agencies that have channeled growth into relatively tight and self-contained islands in order to preserve open space and make it easier for public transit to function. Still, it is clear that, despite the efforts of public planners, the historic urban pattern has been supplanted by a new kind of low-density urban order as the scale of factories and suburban shopping cen-

Figure 14. A typical Parisian scene. The Paris known to most tourists and most academics is a very small piece of land that includes only the central neighborhoods within the city of Paris. Actually, at least four out of every five Parisians live in the suburbs that surround the city, for example, in this subdivision at Sénart. Beyond the outer suburbs, moreover, lies an enormous exurban belt. In much of the outer suburban and exurban territory, middle-class inhabitants live in single-family houses and use the automobile as their principal means of transportation much as they do in the United States, Canada, or Australia. (Photograph by Robert Bruegmann, 1999.)

ters has exploded the fine grain of the traditional city. In one of the best books to date on urban dispersal, German architect and planner Thomas Sieverts, looking primarily at German cities, has called this the *Zwischenstadt,* a term that means "intermediate" or "in-between" city.[43] According to Sieverts, the old image of the European city that many planners and individuals cling to so tenaciously has actually been largely superceded by a new pattern that occupies the land between the old core and the countryside and that he characterizes as the "urbanized landscape or the landscaped city."[44]

To a northern European primarily familiar with the patterns outside Hamburg or Munich, the view of the periphery of large cities in southern or eastern Europe can be unnerving (fig. 16). In Italy and Spain, for example, recent prosperity has brought with it decentralization that has been more rapid than in the north and with fewer controls. This explains why the low-density web of highways, residential subdivisions, and office and industrial parks at the periphery

Figure 15. The European suburb today. In this air view taken on the approach into the Franz Joseph Strauss Airport in Munich, the results of northern European urban planning are clearly visible. New development is channeled into compact nodes, usually surrounding preexisting villages, allowing for the preservation of agricultural and forest land. Although the appearance is quite different from that of American suburbs, the overall densities are similar, which has meant that, as in American suburbia, the private automobile has become the most common way for most residents to get around, and the landscape is increasingly marked by highways, big-box retail, vast industrial and warehouse facilities, and automobile-oriented commercial establishments. (Photograph by Robert Bruegmann, 2002.)

of Bologna or Barcelona looks a great deal more like the periphery of American cities than those in northern Europe.[45] In the case of Barcelona, for example, the city of Barcelona contains less than half of the population of the region and its share is declining as population densities fall in the historic core and rise in some of the more far-flung parts of the urban area, particularly along the B30 highway corridor in the western valley over the hills from the city of Barcelona.[46]

Given the low overall densities in European suburbs, it is not surprising that, particularly over the past decades, the private automobile has become the most common way for residents to get around (fig. 17). Even in the Paris region, which has one of the most extensive systems of public transportation in

Figure 16. Suburban sprawl in Palermo. Because the economies of cities in southern Europe tended to lag behind those of northern Europe and North America throughout the early twentieth century, the process of decentralization took place at a slower pace. Naples and Palermo, for example, remained several times denser than Hamburg or London through the post–World War II years. During the economic boom of the 1990s, however, many of the cities of southern Europe witnessed explosive decentralization as here in a view of an agricultural landscape near Monreale, outside Palermo, in the process of rapid suburbanization. As southern European cities like Palermo have sprawled outward, they typically have done so with fewer regulations than in northern Europe. (Photograph by Robert Bruegmann, 2003.)

Europe, public transit does not play much of a role through large parts of the territory. Although public transit is heavily used in the center, it accounts for only about 30 percent of vehicular travel in the region at large, and this figure declines further with each passing year.[47]

Use of the private automobile, in contrast, has been rising quickly throughout Europe. This is not surprising since, outside the central core, the automobile is almost always a quicker means of getting from one place to another. The average commute to work in the Parisian region, for example, is twenty-seven minutes by car, quite comparable to figures for the highest-density cities in the United States; the average commute by public transport comes in at fifty-three

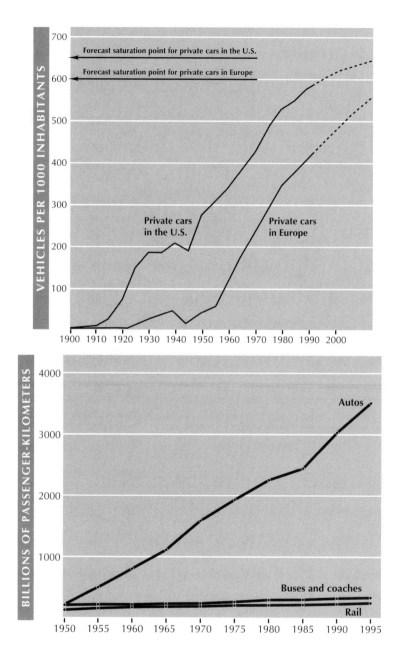

Figure 17. Automobile and transit use in Europe and the United States. The *upper chart* shows the rise in the number of private cars in the United States and Europe. The *lower chart* shows the way bus and rail ridership in Europe has been largely flat over the period since World War II, while the use of private automobiles has skyrocketed. The data suggest that Europe has been following very much in the same trajectory as the United States only with a time lag. (Redrawn by Dennis McClendon from Christian Gerondeau, *Transport in Europe* [Boston: Artec House, 1997].)

minutes.[48] For this reason it is no surprise that there has been such a massive switch from public transit to the automobile even though the French government, along with those of all of the other Western European nations, in an effort to discourage automobile use and to finance public transportation, has levied much higher taxes on automobiles and gasoline than in the United States.

Charts of growth in automobile ownership and use in Europe show a pattern strikingly similar to those in the United States, albeit with a delay of several decades.[49] In fact, as American automobile ownership is leveling off due to market saturation, automobile ownership and use are rising in Europe.[50] Even with the bias of funding toward public transportation, freeway construction in Paris and other European cities has continued so that today the superhighway system at the periphery of the Paris region or that outside many other cities in Europe is not significantly different in kind from that seen outside Boston or Dallas.[51]

Many of the suburban patterns in Europe are also are visible in the affluent English-speaking countries of Canada and Australia where the planning systems are more like those in Europe than in the United States. In the Vancouver or Sydney regions, there are many fewer miles of freeway, there is much heavier investments in public transportation, and the central cities are more likely to be more affluent and the suburbs less affluent than in the United States. Despite these differences, however, the overall configuration of Toronto or Sydney is surprisingly similar to the pattern in cities in the United States. This is even more the case in cities like Calgary or Perth, relatively new and wealthy and with land-use patterns not so different from those in Minneapolis or San Jose.[52]

In many developing countries outside the affluent Western world, there are even more compelling reasons to decentralize than in Europe or the United States since so many central cities never really had a good transportation infrastructure or service network to begin with.[53] Cell phones and other portable communication technologies have severed the connection between accessibility and centrality, allowing residential communities and businesses to bypass entire stages of infrastructure development. So, in São Paolo, many of the largest businesses and even—unlike the case in the United States—some of the biggest banks have moved from the old downtown, first to the Avenida Paulista, about a mile and a half to the south, then to places farther afield like the Avenida Faria Lima and the Marginal Pinheiros freeway, and finally to business parks like those around the airport at Congonhas. In fact, many of the cities that have proved most attractive to foreign investors, particularly those interested in setting up high-tech businesses, are those with the most benign climates and the lowest densities. For this reason, the view from the top of a hotel in Bangalore in India, over miles of low-rise stucco and tile-roofed structures, looks surprisingly like the view from the top of a building in San Diego or Montpellier on the French Mediterranean coast.

As I have already suggested, the consistent flattening of the density gradient since the 1970s that has characterized most mature, older cities does not apply to many cities in the developing world. Here, in many cases, the left-hand side of the density gradient continues to rise as enormous numbers of extremely poor rural people flood into central districts after crop failures or agricultural mechanization forces them off the land. This is particularly true in places like Lagos in Nigeria or Calcutta, India, where officials are unable to enforce even minimum housing standards. There is, however, almost always a considerable amount of building at low densities at the edge by a small, extremely affluent segment of the population (fig. 18).

Neither has a decentralization trend appeared to such a degree in places where there was no effective private market in land or that were subject to tight top-down centralized planning. During the Stalinist era in some Eastern European cities, there may have been times when the density gradient actually reversed itself, rising from left to right, as planning authorities worked to preserve the scale of the historic centers that housed party and government officials and to settle all of the increase in population in dense apartment complexes on the periphery.

Exurbia

Beyond the suburbs, at least in cities with an ample water supply, is the band I have called exurbia, the very low-density region beyond the regularly built suburbs that is still economically and socially tied back to the central cities (figs. 19, 20). This is the most dynamic part of many urban areas, particularly older urban regions in the eastern United States and Europe. By the late twentieth century, vast increases in wealth, together with widespread automobile ownership and new communications technologies, have put "country" living within the reach of millions of middle-class families.[54] Exurban regions are increasing much faster in land area than in population as lot sizes continue to rise.[55] By some estimates, over half of the new land used for residential purposes in the United States between 1970 and 2000 was in lots over ten acres, and over 90 percent was in lots of one acre and over. According to other experts,

Figure 18. Suburban development in developing countries. Next to the highway toll plaza outside Istanbul, first world–type high-rise apartment towers and warehouses abut third world informal settlements. Despite all of the efforts of governments throughout the developing world to stop self-built housing and move residents to rationally planned and sanitary rental housing developments, the self-built informal community has persisted as the most important means of housing for large parts of the population. In part, this has been the result of a lack of govern-mental resources. In part, however, it is due to the way these self-built houses, like suburban subdivisions in the affluent cities of North America and Europe, provide families some degree of ownership, control, and choice. (Photograph by Robert Bruegmann, 1996.)

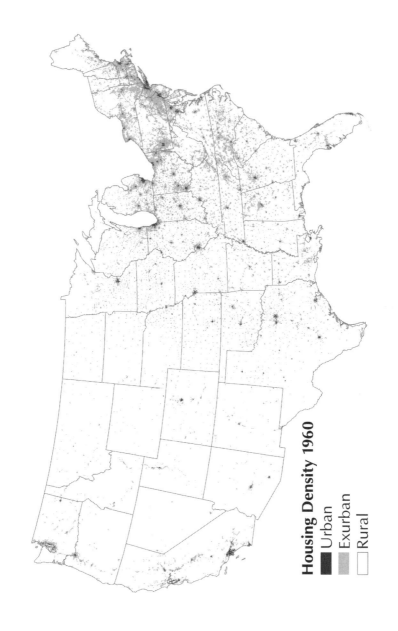

Housing Density 1960
Urban
Exurban
Rural

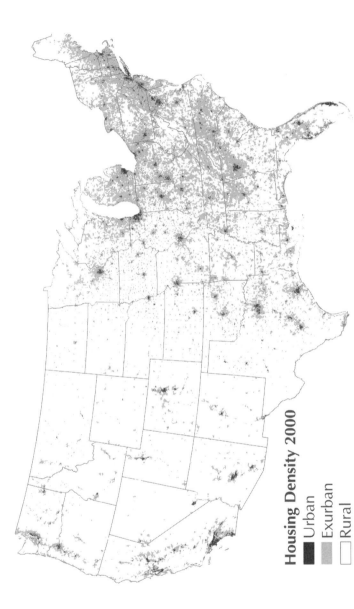

Housing Density 2000

- Urban
- Exurban
- Rural

Figure 19. Urban, exurban, and rural America, 1960–2000. Increasingly in the twentieth century, the old distinctions between cities, suburbs, and rural areas have blurred. The urbanized areas, including the city and its suburbs, are now surrounded by a low-density penumbra of exurban development that can extend for dozens, even hundreds, of miles from multiple urban centers. At the same time, new transportation and communications technologies have extended what is essentially an urban culture to almost every part of the country. In a striking set of maps, David Theobald has shown how new development radiating out of cities has created a complex and overlapping pattern that resembles the stars in a galaxy. The result, particularly visible in the great regional clusters of the northeastern seaboard, Great Lakes, southern Piedmont, and the California coast, is what geographer Peirce Lewis has described as the "galactic metropolis." (Maps by David Theobald published in "Use Dynamics beyond the American Urban Fringe," *Geographical Review* 91, no. 3 [July 2001]: 544–64.)

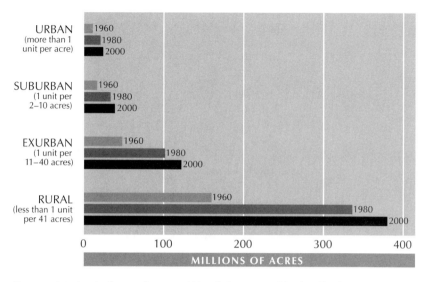

Figure 20. American land use, 1960–2000. Although the amount of developed land in American urban and suburban areas has increased since the 1960s, this increase has been due primarily to an expanding population and not to any increase in the amount of land used per person. By far the greatest increase in residential land use has been in exurban and rural areas on large lots—that is, over ten acres in size. Some of this land would clearly be considered sprawl by most observers, but a great deal of it looks entirely rural and is owned by individuals and families determined to protect it against what they consider sprawl. (Redrawn by Dennis McClendon from a chart published by David Theobald in "Use Dynamics beyond the American Urban Fringe," *Geographical Review* 91, no. 3 [July 2001]: 544–64.)

by the end of the 1990s exurbia accounted for more than 30 percent of the land in the contiguous forty-eight states and was home to 60 million Americans. There may soon be more exurbanites than suburbanites or inhabitants of central cities.[56] If sprawl is a problem and this is sprawl, this is where the greatest challenges lie. But is exurbia sprawl?

Unfortunately we know little about exurbia. When the term was coined in the 1950s it referred to a select group of wealthy, low-density bedroom communities at the outer edges of the suburban belt, particularly around New York City. What I am calling exurbia was not really studied until the late 1970s, when a number of social scientists started writing about a development they called variously "counterurbanization," or "rural renaissance," or "back to the land" because the census seemed to show the greatest growth in "nonmetropolitan" counties. In retrospect it seems apparent that there was no significant rural renaissance, and the phenomenon was more a statistical artifact than a good description of what was happening on the ground. Growth was simply going to more remote parts of the extended urban realm. In some cases, this growth consisted primarily of primary houses on lots larger than those in suburbia. In other cases, it involved weekend or summer places. In either case, much of the rural renaissance disappeared when significant parts of these counties reached suburban densities and the census bureau reclassified them from nonmetropolitan to metropolitan in the succeeding census. For this reason, starting in the 1990s serious observers started using the term "exurban" to describe these large areas that are neither suburban nor rural but are still connected back to central cities even when they extend dozens or even hundreds of miles out from them (figs. 21, 22).

Figure 21. In the Brandywine Valley. Although this scene looks entirely rural, it is actually part of a carefully tended urbanized landscape of gentrified villages and country houses along the Brandywine River between Wilmington, Delaware, and Chadd's Ford, Pennsylvania. The tone was set by members of the DuPont family and their associates and peers, who created elaborate estates with extensive gardens in the area. Comparable exurban areas—for example, Gates Mills outside of Cleveland, parts of the Hamptons at the eastern tip of Long Island, or the Napa and Sonoma valleys in Northern California—follow in the tradition of the aristocratic European exurban enclaves seen in figure 3. (Photograph by Robert Bruegmann, 2002.)

Figure 22. Upper-middle-class American exurbia: a golf course community near Luray, West Virginia. This far-flung exurban extension of the Washington, DC, metropolitan area has been growing rapidly because of its scenic amenities, notably the spectacular views of the Blue Ridge Mountains seen in the background in this photograph. This growth has been fueled by middle-class Americans who can now afford houses that rival in size those built earlier in the century by the country's wealthiest captains of industry. These houses are the most visible indication of a vast, if unequal, growth in wealth in the late twentieth century and the appearance of the world's first mass upper-middle class. (Photograph by Robert Bruegmann, 2004)

Around a large city like New York, huge regions of western Connecticut, western and southern New Jersey, or eastern Pennsylvania can be usefully be described as exurban. Even more dispersed is a vast swath of the Piedmont between Atlanta, Georgia, and Raleigh-Durham, North Carolina, where there are no really large cities but a cluster of smaller centers like Greenville and Spartanburg, South Carolina, and Charlotte, Greensboro, and Winston-Salem, North Carolina.[57] In this extended area, families can live in apparently rural surroundings but participate fully in an extended urban culture. The same is true for the "Gold Rush" country in the foothills of the Sierra Nevada Mountains of California.[58]

Along with the outward surge of population has gone an equally remarkable outward dispersal of jobs. Two or three counties away from the central city, clusters of brilliant glass office towers rise out of cornfields alongside the superhighway while enormous one-story distribution buildings hug the lushly landscaped ground in new industrial parks.[59] Today, on any given morning, a middle manager living on the outskirts of Bethlehem, Pennsylvania, may be getting dressed well before dawn in preparation for a long commute by car to a job at an AT&T facility in Parsippany in central New Jersey. An advertising executive who works primarily from her home in the tiny enclave of Washington Depot, Connecticut, will be driving to the train station in Pawling, New York, for a business meeting in Midtown Manhattan. In both these cases the trip still involves a "classic" commute inward toward the center. More often, these days, the commute will be in the other direction or laterally across suburban and exurban territory. It might include a professor of English at Wesleyan University taking a taxi from her Upper West Side apartment to catch a train to meet her 11 A.M. class at the campus in central Connecticut or a resident of Scarsdale in suburban Westchester County, New York, waiting at the airport in White Plains for a corporate jet to take him to the airport at Islip, Long Island, where a waiting car will take him to Melville to meet other business executives for a round of golf.

All of these affluent residents have clearly chosen a form of lifestyle that requires long commutes, and in many cases they have learned to make the commuting time unobjectionable if not pleasant. This is not the case with a great many less affluent residents, for example, the dishwasher at Newark Airport who spends an hour and a half each way getting from a mobile home park in central New Jersey to the airport on three different buses. However, even if her options are fewer and less attractive, the dishwasher still makes choices to create for herself the best living conditions she can obtain.

The net result of a vastly increased mobility has been a major reordering of travel patterns. The old edge-to-center commute that once loomed so large has been submerged in a new pattern where there are often more people commuting out from the historical center to jobs in the suburbs than from the suburbs into the center, and both are dwarfed by the number of commutes across the suburban and exurban periphery. One characteristic result is that in virtually all large American cities, traffic is worse at certain points near the edge than it is near the center, and the afternoon inbound or "reverse" commute is almost always more crowded in the direction of the most affluent suburbs than the "regular" or outbound commute. In addition, the commuting trip, which is relatively easy to chart, represents today only a small and constantly declining part of total travel, with a result that congestion is much more common during a much longer period and far less predictable than it once was, and it is increasingly difficult for anyone to foresee future travel patterns.

Extensive exurban development is a characteristic of only some American cities. In the cities of the American West and Southwest, where water is in short supply, there is little exurban settlement because it is almost impossible to build without a dependable public water supply, and government agencies and utility companies can't afford to overextend their systems. In many fast-growing cities, moreover, even where water is available, exurban development is often not a prominent feature in the landscape because it is constantly in the process of being redeveloped into higher density suburbia. Where exurbia is most conspicuous is around the older cities in the northeastern part of the United States with the slowest population growth.

Because many cities in northeast Ohio have been severely depressed economically and have grown in population only slowly if at all, the extensive exurban sprawl around them is at first glance rather surprising. Driving around the edge of Cleveland's suburban fringe, the line between suburbia and exurbia is usually fairly clear. On one side sit houses in suburban subdivisions, most often on lots no larger than an acre and increasingly much smaller than this. On the other side is a patchwork quilt of farmland still occupied by farmers, farmland occupied by urban residents who either farm as a hobby or contract the farming out, and a good deal of land that has been converted to urban uses. The nonfarm parcels include small lots owned by working-class families along the highways out of town as well as five- and ten-acre "ranchettes" and country "estates" of affluent city dwellers who use their properties for weekend use.[60] Densities are usually well under 1,000 people per square mile and most of the land is unincorporated. The fact that few houses have municipal sewer service reinforces this low density since most states and counties require fairly large minimum lot sizes for owners with private septic systems. In addition to the individual houses are small villages, some of them, like Chagrin Falls or Hudson, originally farm towns but today highly gentrified commuter communities.

This exurban zone covers an enormous area, not just around Cleveland but across much of northeastern Ohio, particularly around the older industrial cities like Akron, Canton, Youngstown, and even smaller places like Ravenna or Kent. On the country roads outside of Youngstown today it is possible to see a surprising number of large exurban houses, the kind often referred to as McMansions, with their quarter-mile driveways, acres of carefully tended lawn,

>eculiarly American. They have been pervasive characteristics of urban
around the world for at least a century whenever cities have become
fluent.

▸f the most remarkable things about the development of European and
▪n cities and suburbs since the 1970s has been the way in which they
◦ be converging. In part this is because an increasing number of Ameri-
tral cities are becoming denser while most European cities continue
ntralize. Moreover, the edges of cities everywhere, with their super-
's, supermarkets, and subdivisions, look increasingly similar, one to
In fact, the parts of suburban Phoenix that have developed in the past
venty years are actually quite comparable to the Parisian suburbs that
▸wn at the same time.[66]

striking result of this convergence is that the view out the airplane win-
◦ be similar whether the plane is landing in Minneapolis or Madrid,
k or Buenos Aires, Sidney or Stockholm (fig. 23). There is usually the
▪st territory of suburban development, low factories, warehouses, and

Airport city. In cities worldwide, the airport has become a major urban center in its own right,
eeways, office parks, industrial parks, and subdivisions that surround it are surprisingly similar
re. This is the view on the approach into Bangkok, but it could be Boston or Buenos Aires or
ywhere else. (Photograph by Robert Bruegmann, 1990.)

and an assortment of late-model cars and boats sitting in front of vast garages. This kind of phenomenon has baffled and upset many observers. Northeastern Ohio has not been a major economic growth area. Cleveland's metropolitan population is one of the few in the country that has actually declined over the past several decades. Youngstown finds itself in an even worse position. It was devastated by the departure of much of its steel industry, the town's industrial mainstay. Much of the central part of town, once filled with factories, is now a series of vacant fields. Its once-vibrant business district can appear deserted in the middle of a Saturday afternoon.[61] How can the vast expansion of exurban settlement around Youngstown be considered anything other than unnecessary and illogical?

Actually it is not necessarily either. That the land is not really needed for agriculture is evident from the way that, even with no residential expansion, farmers have been abandoning large tracts of cropland for decades now. Affluent residents of Youngstown who move to the exurban fringe are merely exploiting one of the most important assets available in the metropolitan area—a large supply of attractive land at low prices. Although at first glance it appears that the dispersal to the edges does little other than eviscerate the central cities and displace agriculture, in many cases, the possibility of building a house on a large tract of inexpensive land in the exurban fringe is the one thing that continues to attract middle-class residents who might otherwise flee to more dynamic regions. If, as is quite likely, Youngstown's downtown and central residential districts revive, it will not be despite sprawl but because sprawl has made it possible for the metropolitan area to retain residents during extremely difficult years. Moreover, as industry and working-class families leave the center, they relinquish space for other individuals and activities that might benefit from a location downtown. Although this possibility is probably difficult to imagine for most visitors to Youngstown today, it is likely that the process is already underway.

Is this exurbia really different from suburbia or just an extension of it? Is it sprawl? It is difficult to answer these questions or even characterize land-use patterns that run so counter to our traditional categories of land use. Most people would call a subdivision of two-acre ranchettes with mowed front lawns merely an extension of the suburban fringe and an example of sprawl. But would they say the same for the old farmhouse on twenty acres where the husband commutes to a job in a central city but the family farms the land themselves?

Would it matter if the land is worked by someone else under contract?[62] Would the term be usefully applied to a mobile home park with densities higher than almost any urban neighborhood?[63]

Certainly, most residents of exurban areas don't consider themselves as living in or contributing to sprawl. In fact, affluent exurban residents are among the most zealous guardians of environmental quality and the rural feel of the landscape. They are often the ones most adamant about preserving much of it exactly as it was when they arrived, if not in actually turning the clock backward. In large parts of New England the exurban trend has brought things back full circle. After a century of declining rural populations, as farmers abandoned their farms for the cities, these rural areas are now being repeopled, often at nineteenth-century densities, by urban families who want to go "back to the land." They want the look of nineteenth-century rural New England but with all of today's urban conveniences. In some ways, these back-to-the-land enthusiasts are motivated by desires similar to those involved in the back-to-the-city movement. Both want the aesthetic experience of a "traditional" kind of settlement without all of the inconveniences of life usually associated with that kind of landscape. In fact, these are often the same people in different circumstances or at different times in their lives.

The development of exurban Europe has proceeded in a way that is fundamentally similar to the pattern seen in North America. As we have already seen, exurban development was quite pronounced around Paris as early as the eighteenth century. Over time, these areas of exurban weekend or summer houses tended to become denser and the houses often came to be used as primary residences. With the gradual introduction of municipal services, they became suburbs. At the same time, exurban development moved farther out.

Today, residents in the region of Paris, tightly bunched in the city and inner suburbs, more loosely scattered in the outer suburbs, sprawl across the entire Île-de-France basin and beyond in a vast patchwork quilt of country houses, farm properties, and gentrified villages. The creation of this exurban region, in a process the French have called *rurbanisation* or *periurbanisation,* appears to have increased considerably since the 1970s, due in part to vastly increased affluence of Parisians but also fueled by fears of unrest in the wake of the riots of the late 1960s in the city of Paris and the disturbances in Parisian suburbs in more recent years.[64] In 1990 there were nearly 400,000 second houses owned by Parisians in a huge swath of land around Paris and its suburbs extending

---

far into the interior of the country on the sou
Normandy Coast to the north. In this vast i
for 10 percent of the total number of housing
although a Parisian family living in an apartm
in the city than their counterpart in an Ame
land they use is taken into account, it is by no
the most land.

Converging Cities

Much of the literature comparing American a
these are fundamentally different kinds of u
the center of Phoenix and Paris would suggest
common. However, comparing the center of a
to that of an old European city like Paris is a li
boy with a twenty-five-year-old man. It's true t
less and have a smaller vocabulary, but the wa
likely be quite similar. Of course, because urb;
a residue that persists into subsequent eras, th
is largely confined to the parts of the city that
be quite different from that of Phoenix, which
development after World War II.

A more telling comparison would be to loo
same time and the larger trajectory of change
core density and its subsequent decline would
ies. The major differences would be primarily
and when it experienced its most important gr
est spurt of growth at the end of the nineteenth
Manchester, or Berlin—typically reached max
than did cities that grew fast earlier in history.
empty out, however, they did so more quickly,
flattening and lowering of the density gradien
ies. This means that the gradient for a relative
could look similar to one for an older Europear
the behavior of these graphs is a good indicatio
many historians and sprawl reformers, suburb

---

are not
growth
more a
One
Ameri
seem t
can ce
to dec
highw
anothe
ten or
have g
One
dow c
Bangk
same

Figure
and th
everyw
almos

Figure 24. Strip mall. The strip mall, because it is a logical building type in areas where many people drive, has become a new worldwide vernacular building type. This one is in Bangalore, India, a city that, by Indian standards, is extremely low in density and one that has become a magnet for high-tech industry. (Photograph by Robert Bruegmann, 1997.)

shopping centers. Wherever there has been both rising affluence and some kind of land market, the trajectory of settlement patterns has been similar. This is not surprising since in all of these places residents and business owners display the same desire to inhabit an easily accessible, uncongested, well-landscaped environment (fig. 24).

Unfortunately we don't understand our new urban areas very well. One of the reasons we don't is that many of the individuals who are best equipped to describe them—historians, social scientists, planners, urban theorists—have been so quick to condemn that they have never looked carefully. The famous architectural and social critic Lewis Mumford, spoke of the Eastern Seaboard of the United States as a vast "undifferentiated urban tissue without any relation either to an internally coherent nucleus or an external boundary."[67] This statement testifies more to his lack of curiosity than it does to the territory he was describing. This kind of view has been common among many urban intellectuals. However, even a little time spent studying the map and then driving around an urban area will disprove this notion. The location of subdivisions, industrial parks, and office clusters is just as much a function of resources and accessibility as any settlement pattern at any time in urban history. Observers with some basic knowledge of real estate practices can orient themselves quite readily in almost any new city that they visit.

That many individuals have trouble seeing this order is in great part because of aesthetic prejudices and because our analysis and descriptive efforts haven't kept up with the pace of change on the ground. Certainly neither the concentric circles of Park and Burgess nor the multinucleated city of Harris and Ullman provide anything like a good picture of the complexity and constant changes visible in the landscape. Although Jean Gottmann's concept of the megalopolis has proven more satisfactory, a more recent metaphor, the "galactic metropolis," as used by geographer Peirce Lewis, perhaps provides an even better way of thinking about these areas.[68] Using this metaphor, we can set aside the traditional distinctions between urban, suburban, and rural and think instead of settlements across a vast landscape as if they were stars, planets, and other celestial bodies, each exerting a force field, stronger or weaker according to their size and density, and changing in intensity across time.[69]

This metaphor provides a good description for the patterns seen on the enhanced satellite images of cities, which may be currently our best way of visualizing urban areas as a whole.[70] It is particularly apt in explaining the way in which suburbia clings tightly around old urban cores while exurban settlement at a greater distance is much more diffuse. It seems to account for the way settlements of decreasing density coalesce in bursts outside cities. It provides a way of understanding the striking manner in which many cities located close to each other, for example, Chicago and Milwaukee or Dallas and Fort Worth, have grown together and have each exerted a pull, more or less strong, on all of the land in between them. Better than any factors related to soil quality, it explains the remarkable difference between the $8,000-per-acre value of agricultural land in New Jersey and the paltry $383-per-acre in South Dakota, where there are no large or fast-growing cities for hundreds of miles.[71]

Finally, it suggests the ways in which every change in the urban system affects everything else in the system. It is possible that when even a small, remote star explodes, this event can reorder the entire gravitational system of a galaxy. A slight wobble in the axis of a planet can mean drastic warming in one place and cooling in another. So it is with urban systems, the main difference being that the most basic element in the urban system is the individual human being who can think and make decisions. Any change made by any member of any neighborhood affects, to some degree, everyone else in the metropolitan area. When a great many individuals make changes in a certain direction, it can lead to major shifts in the pattern of development. To understand sprawl, it is necessary to look constantly back and forth from edge to the center, from the most specific to the most general, and from the individual to the neighborhood to the urban system as a whole.

6   The Causes of Sprawl

Before leaving this short survey of the history of sprawl, we might ask what seems at first like a simple question: What causes sprawl? The answers to this question have been remarkably varied and contradictory. Let's consider briefly several of these, starting first with those that assume that sprawl is peculiarly American and attempt to explain why the United States is different from other places and then moving to more general explanations.

Anti-urban Attitudes and Racism as a Cause

A number of observers, usually highbrow Europeans or Americans who live and work in the central city, account for the massive amount of sprawl in the United States by claiming that it is the result of national character traits. American cities are so different from European cities, they say, because Americans are at heart anti-urban, attached to unfettered individualism, low-density living, and automobile usage.[1] But, as I hope I have shown, the history of urban decentralization seems to suggest that many of the supposed differences in American and European cities and suburbs are less the result of inherent differences in these societies than a matter of timing. Cities on both continents are, if anything, converging when it comes to space used per capita, automobile ownership, or other similar measures. All of this casts considerable doubt on theory that Americans are uniquely anti-urban.

In fact, it is probably only possible to call Americans anti-urban if one accepts a specific set of assumptions about urbanity made by members of a small cultural elite. This group likes to think of urbanity as the kind of life lived by people in apartments in dense city centers that contain major high-brow cultural institutions. In these dense centers, they believe, citizens are more tolerant and cosmopolitan because of their constant interaction with other citizens unlike themselves.[2] It is this definition of urbanity—in many cases based on an idealized vision of the European city of the late eighteenth and nineteenth centuries—that many Americans and, increasingly, citizens throughout the world reject or, more often, simply ignore. If they thought about it at all, they wouldn't agree that highbrow culture is necessarily better than their own middle-class culture, and they would probably have little patience with the argument that they would be more tolerant if they lived in apartment buildings on densely built city streets or were forced to interact with people they would rather avoid. Most Americans do not like the dirt and disorder that characterized historic nineteenth-century industrial cities, and they may be indifferent if not hostile to the clubby culture of the downtown elite cultural groups, but there is little evidence that suburbanites are opposed to urbanity. They only want to rearrange the physical elements to make life more convenient and pleasant for themselves and to avoid the things that made nineteenth-century industrial cities so unpleasant for people who did not have a great deal of money.

It is true that some suburbanites see their environment as the opposite of the old central city, peripheral to their everyday lives and just another exit on the freeway. However, it is likely that the majority considers these two places as good for different things. For them, suburbia is a good place to live, work, and raise children, while downtown is a place to see ballgames, go to a nightclub, visit a museum, or do some special Christmas shopping. As the old downtowns remake themselves as tourist destinations and places of entertainment, it appears that they have, if anything, become a more valued part of the larger urban world.

Another common explanation of the growth of American suburbs and the rise of sprawl is that it was caused by white flight fueled by racism. Although no one would deny that race has played a key role in many aspects of American life, it is significant that urban areas with small minority populations like Minneapolis have sprawled in much the same way as urban areas with large minority populations like Chicago. It is also the case that when they have become affluent enough to do so, African-Americans have been just as willing as their white counterparts to move out to the suburbs. The suburbs they choose are often ones with largely African-American population. This suggests that there is no simple relationship between race and sprawl.

Nor is it plausible to suggest that the segregating out by income level, race, and ethnicity is peculiarly American. These kinds of segregation have been visible not just in American suburbs but in cities and suburbs all over the world, particularly when large disparities in income is a major factor. It was certainly the case in all nineteenth-century industrial cities and today, whether in the old public housing of suburban Stockholm or Paris or the favelas and shantytowns of São Paolo or Istanbul, segregation of immigrants and poorer residents by skin color, religion, and income level is a pervasive feature of contemporary urban life.

Economic Factors and the Capitalist System as a Cause

Probably the single most common explanation of sprawl is that it has been a direct by-product of an insufficiently regulated capitalist system. This argument rests in great part on two dubious propositions. The first is that economic forces are the prime factor in human interactions, the driving force in most aspects of life, and everything else is secondary. In fact, although economic conditions have always had a strong relationship to urban forms, the history we have reviewed suggests that this influence is much less direct and obvious than many people believe. Similar urban forms can evolve in very different economic circumstances; different urban forms can accompany similar economic circumstances. Further, the history we have reviewed suggests that urban form is not just an effect but also a cause of economic conditions. Every decision by every individual about where he or she lives or works or plays will have repercussions throughout the system.

The second dubious notion is that there are many circumstances in which the capitalist system inherently doesn't work well, leading to "market failure" and unhappy results on the ground. Many individuals have claimed that sprawl is a logical result of capitalism because this kind of economic system induces buyers and sellers to act in ways to further their own good even at the expense of their neighbors or the common good.[3] So, for example, many families, each acting to secure for themselves a location at the very edge of the urban area so they can enjoy proximity to nature, could produce a situation where only a handful will be able to enjoy the view, and even they will soon be outflanked. Or, it has often been claimed, developers, left to themselves, will maximize their profits by building at low densities no matter what their customers might actually want because building detached single-family houses is more profitable than building apartment buildings. Some observers claim that this fixation with the bottom line will inexorably produce settlement patterns that are inefficient, socially and environmentally harmful, ugly, or all of these. Therefore, government must intervene to produce better results.[4]

The kind of behavior that puts personal advantage over common good is hardly limited to matters economic, however. The same homebuyers who might try to maximize their personal advantage in buying a suburban house are the voters who elect government officials and who push for land-use regulations that will benefit them, often at the price of other parts of the population. Is it logical to think that landowners would suddenly act in a completely different fashion when they engage in political rather than economic transactions? Nor is the kind of behavior that puts personal interest above community welfare peculiar to low-density settlements. The resident of a central city who tries to block the badly needed expansion of a hospital next door to his apartment building because it would block his view is acting in a similar fashion. So it seems illogical to make any close link between the capitalist system and sprawl.

The notion that sprawl is the inevitable unhappy result of laissez-faire capitalism, moreover, turns on its head the analysis of reformers in the nineteenth and early twentieth centuries who were convinced that unregulated private forces would lead inexorably to excessively high densities. Housing advocate Benjamin Marsh, for example, bitterly attacked developers in 1910 for crowding as many people as possible into a single acre in order to maximize their profits. He was particularly indignant over the claim of some developers who argued that high density helped create community. He considered this to be no more than a cynical justification for greed and stated that the best solution for people of modest incomes was to move out of dense cities into detached houses surrounded by their own gardens.[5]

Another problem with the private-market-as-cause-of-sprawl argument is that places like London were already sprawling in the seventeenth century, long before there was a fully developed consumer market for land. Or, looked at from a different vantage point, there is the fact that the development patterns in many cities and villages at the end of the nineteenth century, all widely admired by anti-sprawl activists today, were achieved primarily by private builders with relatively little governmental intervention while during the last several decades, during a period when the amount of intervention by government agencies in the land development process has increased dramatically, there has been a rising chorus of complaint.[6] This might suggest that although there may indeed be market failures they are not necessarily more harmful than the "government failures" that have been caused by attempts to regulate the market.[7]

Despite some basic problems with the argument, the theme of capitalism causing sprawl has led to the creation of a major edifice of historical argument. One recurrent theme of anti-sprawl reformers in the United States is that Americans never really chose to live in the suburbs. In the extreme form of this argument, Americans were forced to settle there by some powerful cabal of big business with the complicity of government. A remarkable case of the willingness of anti-sprawl critics to believe this despite all evidence to the contrary can be found in the persistence of the urban myth of the General Motors conspiracy. This theory, popularized by a man named Bradford Snell in the 1970s, was an attempt to prove that American cities lost their streetcar systems because General Motors deliberately bought up the lines in order to close them down. As many authors have demonstrated, this theory was never plausible. General Motors may indeed have bought streetcar lines in a few cities, and some individuals at General Motors may conceivably have wanted to destroy a given streetcar system, but in the larger picture, the role of the automobile company was almost certainly insignificant. The streetcar has yielded to the less expensive and more flexible bus in virtually every city in the developed world, and most affluent cities, European and American, abandoned their streetcar systems with or without any intervention by General Motors.[8]

The persistence of this story as the explanation of the demise of public transportation, as reinterpreted, for example, in the movie "Who Framed Roger Rabbit," is explained by how conveniently it seems to encapsulate an entire worldview. From this point of view, the needs of ordinary city dwellers have been systematically denied in favor of the interests of greedy private entrepreneurs in league with corrupt public officials. Now greedy entrepreneurs and corrupt public officials there certainly are, and at times they undoubtedly have run roughshod over the needs of ordinary citizens. However, blaming greedy entrepreneurs, particularly real estate developers, for sprawl is highly problematic. Developers, if they possess anything like the guile attributed to them by the anti-sprawl crusaders, would be perfectly able to make money in the city as well as in the suburbs. They would certainly be able to make money building at high density, as Benjamin Marsh believed, and as the condominium-conversion boom of the 1970s seems

to prove. In fact, developers have often been the group most vocally opposed to large-lot zoning; they know that raising densities on a given piece of land can result in more units and higher profits.[9]

A recent version of the attempt to explain urban form by the inherent nature of the capitalist system is the widespread idea that sprawl has some relation to the increasing globalization of markets. Of course it is true that changes in market conditions will have repercussions on the land, but attempts to describe the built environment of a particular city or part of a city as the result of globalization have, to date, rarely been very useful. In the end, whether a bank is owned locally or by a multinational corporation headquartered in a distant country, the dynamics of local real estate markets seem to play out in similar ways.

Government as a Cause

Another group of observers, particularly in the United States, has tended to look at the other side of the equation and blame government failure, meaning bad policies at the local, state, and national level, for fostering sprawl.[10] The federal government, they say, fueled sprawl through homeowner subsidies, highway programs, infrastructure subsidies, and federal income tax deductions. Some anti-sprawl reformers go so far as to say that it was federal policies, not the private market, that all but forced tens of millions of Americans to live in the suburbs in single-family houses. According to this line of reasoning, if the federal government had not built superhighways, subsidized suburban infrastructure, fostered long-term self-amortized mortgages, initiated federal mortgage insurance, allowed "redlining" of neighborhoods, and provided massive tax breaks for suburban homeowners, many city dwellers would have preferred to remain in large multistory apartment buildings in the dense central city rather than move to a single-family house in the suburbs.[11]

None of these arguments is very convincing. First of all, the notion that the federal government, through the Interstate Highway Act, was responsible for advocating and planning these roads is misleading. Most cities and urban areas had extensive plans for superhighways in place already in the 1930s; many of them had allocated large sums of country and state money to begin construction of these roads long before the federal interstate highway program of the mid-1950s. These roads were heavily supported by central city interests because they were considered an important way to rejuvenate the city. Given the strong rebound of many of these cities in recent years, it is altogether possible that, at some point in the near future, most people will conclude that they were actually largely beneficial for central cities.

Another common assertion is that federal agencies starting in the 1930s specifically discriminated against city neighborhoods by introducing new low-interest self-amortizing mortgages that were made available to suburbanites but denied to many city dwellers. In fact, while agencies of the federal government helped to bolster the popularity of the long-term self-amortizing mortgage, this was not a new government invention of the 1930s or one that was specifically aimed at suburbanites. The self-amortizing mortgage had been used by private savings and loan associations in the early twentieth century and was common by the end of the 1920s. It is a policy that could have benefited any homeowner, whether in the central city or the suburbs. Nor was governmental "redlining" as important as anti-sprawl historians have claimed. The term "redlining" refers to a practice a line was drawn around certain neighborhoods, particularly poor and racially changing neighborhoods, that were considered too risky to lend in. The reason banks started this kind of policy was quite logical: to prevent financial losses in places where houses were likely to lose value. Federal agencies undoubtedly played a role in continuing and systematizing redlining. But neither the government nor the banks were doing anything either new or necessarily prejudicial to urban neighborhoods. Most banks, like most businesses, were perfectly happy to invest money in any part of the city or suburbs where they could make a profit. Their conclusion that older and racially changing neighborhoods, whether in the city or the suburbs, would inevitably see a drop in real estate values may have been too sweeping, and there probably was prejudice involved in rating the neighborhoods, but there was, in fact, a great deal of evidence over many years indicating that property values did tend to drop as neighborhoods got older and experienced ethnic or racial turnover. No amount of regulatory control would have altered this fact of life or made this kind of loan less risky.[12]

In fact, for a great many relatively poor buyers—white or black—throughout urban America, redlining wasn't an issue at all because the option of a bank loan for them was never a serious possibility. Instead buyers, whether Polish immigrant workers in the Back of the Yards neighborhood of Chicago or the African-Americans living in central Saint Louis, were forced to rely on help from their extended families or from institutions like churches or they turned to "contract buying," a practice where the seller provides the financing. The terms imposed on contract buyers were often onerous and unfair to the pur-

chasers, but for many buyers, in neighborhoods with or without formal redlining, it was often the only way they could own property. It did allow many poor
families to buy their own houses and apparently was an important mechanism
in achieving an unprecedented rate of nearly 50 percent homeownership in the
United States before World War II.

The final, and most important, federal policy blamed for sprawl has been
homeowner deductions in the federal income tax.[13] These deductions have
undoubtedly had a major impact on all aspects of American life. However, the
United States is far from the only country with such provisions. Many other
nations have instituted similar incentives.[14] Furthermore, these tax incentives
were clearly not part of any plot to entice city dwellers to the suburbs. They
were part of the federal tax code from its earliest days. The intention of the
deduction for mortgage interest and for local property taxes, for example, was
to avoid the taxing of money that was arguably not part of income because it
either was already going for taxes or would go to other parties who would pay
tax on it. Other observers have argued that homeowners reap another windfall
in the tax code because they don't have to pay taxes on the "rent" that they would
have to pay to a landlord if they didn't own the property. According to this line of
thought, for tax purposes homeowners should be treated both as investors and
occupants. For their investment in the property to be treated the same as any
other investment, they would have to pay taxes on their investment income, in
this case the net income that would remain after they deduct all expenses from
income, which would be primarily the rent they pay themselves.[15]

There is little doubt that homeowner tax deductions have fueled a great deal
of suburban residential construction, but this does not mean that it inherently
favors the suburbs or larger lots in the suburbs. That the American tax code
favors wealthy homeowners over poorer homeowners and all homeowners over
renters is quite true, and perhaps should be amended or repealed on those
grounds, but the advantages of the deduction are not tied to any geographical location.[16] The deduction could have been used for any house, whether in
city or suburbs. It is conspicuous, for example, that these tax deductions only
became important for many people when incomes and tax rates increased dramatically after World War II. By the 1960s, when these deductions had became
a really significant feature for many Americans, legislation was already in place
to allow the deductions on any kind of single-family unit, whether a house in
the suburbs or a condominium in a high-rise downtown. Most large American
cities in the 1960s had a considerable supply of vacant land or land with rela-

tively inexpensive buildings that could have been redeveloped at higher densities. In just these years, moreover, there was a boom in conversions of rental housing to condominiums.[17]

Thus, if the demand had existed, construction in American cities could have outpaced construction in the suburbs, and mortgage interest deductions taken by city dwellers could have dwarfed those taken by residents of suburban areas. The reason that they did not is probably because most middle-class Americans in the late twentieth century had little interest in staying in the city if they could buy a larger and less expensive home in the suburbs. It is quite likely that the homeowner deductions have fueled some of the growth in house sizes since World War II by making them relatively more affordable. It might be logical to assume that the deductions would also have led to similar, automatic increases in lot sizes, but the fact that the total value of the deductions has risen dramatically while the average size of suburban lots has declined over the last fifty years suggests that the link between homeowner deductions and sprawl is weak.

In short, none of these governmental policies connected with home ownership explain sprawl. For this reason, it is not surprising that already by the end of the twenties, well before any of the federal policies that supposedly favored homeowners in the suburbs took hold, the move to the suburbs was in full swing, and close to half of all American families were able to own their own home. Even more striking is that, even with the mushrooming value of these incentives for homeowners, the rate of homeownership increased only from 50 to 67 percent during the second half of the twentieth century despite two of the most important boom periods in American history and the massive growth of low-density suburbs.

Another favorite explanation of the federal influence on sprawl is that it was caused by the government spending more federal dollars in the suburbs than in the central cities. In fact, it might be true that more money in recent decades has been spent on infrastructure projects in suburban areas than ones that are located in the central city. This is not surprising, however, since this is where the vast majority of metropolitan residents now live and where the vast majority of growth is taking place. To prove that this is inequitable would require a much more elaborate accounting than the typical studies to date in which a piece of freeway that was constructed in a suburban area gets entered into the one column and any road built in the city shows up in the other. For one thing, most transportation networks still converge on the central city and serve it. For another, this accounting would fail to consider the value of total federal expenditures over history. In any such accounting, the spending by the federal government since the eighteenth century for ports and railroads, bridges and highways, universities and hospitals located primarily in the central cities would have to be factored in.[18] Looking beyond infrastructure, if all spending by the federal government is taken into account, federal spending today goes more heavily per capita to central cities than to suburbs, primarily because of the enormous price tag of social security payments, which go primarily to an older population that remains disproportionately in the central cities.[19]

Other observers lay the blame for sprawl more with the states and local governments. The states, they say, have mostly refused to invoke the authority over land use reserved to them by the Constitution to compel local governments to plan rationally. In the case of local governments, it has been argued, building codes, zoning regulations, subdivision ordinances, and municipal rivalries fuel sprawl. In the most cynical interpretation of the evidence, some observers suggest that sprawl is all but inevitable in the current system because developers merely buy local politicians who will vote for sprawl.[20] However, even if one believed that developers were this powerful, this conclusion would only be plausible if sprawl were inherently more profitable than building at higher densities, which is far from self-evident.

More moderate critics point especially to the use of zoning provisions that segregate land uses, restrict mixed-use developments, and impose minimum lot-size requirements.[21] It is true that if all land-use restrictions were abolished, American cities might redevelop at somewhat higher densities and with more mixed use. Knowing exactly how this would play out, however, is virtually impossible because the cause-and-effect factors here are so difficult to disentangle. For example, it is clear that zoning itself cannot be blamed for most of the sprawl that has occurred because sprawl was well underway long before zoning became common in American cities, which only started to happen in the 1920s.

Most early zoning ordinances, moreover, did not try to foster any new pattern of development. Instead, they extrapolated from historical patterns. This included the kind of sorting out of land uses in neighborhoods that had been underway for at least a century, as those who could afford to do so increasingly left crowded neighborhoods with incompatible land uses at the center to settle in neighborhoods at the edge where residential land was better protected by deed restrictions and other private covenants against industrial pollution and noxious land uses. What most zoning did was to take these private tools, make them public, rationalize them, and extend them across the entire city.

For this reason, most parts of Houston, which has historically been hostile to zoning, look and function very much like corresponding parts of other cities developed at the same time. In Houston, rather than zoning, it has been subdivision regulations and building codes that have mandated many of the features commonly found in suburban developments. But, like zoning, these provisions were mostly an extension and regularization of earlier private practices. Were these regulations the cause of urban form or were they the result of many years of experimentation with the kind of building patterns that city dwellers wanted? An important piece of testimony on this subject can be found in the history of private mechanisms to control the communities. In Houston, as elsewhere, the most important of these was the deed covenant, which could regulate everything from the size and shape of the building to the kind of people who could buy the property. Even when there was no zoning at all, wealthy individuals could and did protect their single-family neighborhoods by going to the courts at the first sign of what they considered an undesirable land use. One of the chief functions of zoning was to give a much larger part of the population the same kinds of control over their environment that the wealthy had always enjoyed.[22]

A final reason that zoning has not had the effect that many people have claimed for it is that, so often when there has been a conflict between market demand and the zoning code, it has been the zoning codes that have given way. Because these changes have happened incrementally, typically a few parcels at a time and over many years, it has been difficult to document the overall effect of these changes. Still, it is quite possible to make some educated guesses. For example, given the current situation of rising density and declining lot sizes at the suburban edge of many American cities, it is clear either that zoning was not what caused such large lot sizes in earlier decades or that zoning has changed as necessary to accommodate market realities. Ironically, one place where many people now agree that zoning has genuinely had an effect in increasing sprawl is precisely in those suburban and exurban jurisdictions where anti-sprawl advocates were successful in introducing large-lot zoning in an effort to try to stop sprawl by making subdivision more difficult.[23] Large-lot zoning, particularly favored since the 1960s, almost certainly forced many homeowners to buy more land than they otherwise would have wanted, leading to lower densities than would have been the case without the regulations. In short, the role of zoning in sprawl is much more ambiguous than the existing anti-sprawl literature would imply.

Another charge has been that the fragmentation of governments in metropolitan areas into many municipal jurisdictions has led to a situation where these governments compete with each other for new development rather than working together to plan for a less sprawling future.[24] However, the idea that a fragmentation of local governments causes sprawl is not at all clear in actual practice. It is true that Saint Louis, which has a relatively small central city and a large number of suburban districts, has become one of the most decentralized cities in the United States and has experienced widespread abandonment in the central city and massive sprawl. By way of contrast, Melbourne or Sydney, Australia, places with even smaller central cities, have been held up as models of anti-sprawl. At the opposite end of the spectrum, central cities that occupy most of their urban region are not necessarily more compact. Tucson, Indianapolis, and Jacksonville, for example, occupy large parts of their metropolitan area, but they are all very low in density and are dispersed.

Technology as a Cause

Another favored explanation for sprawl is that it was caused by new communications and transportation technologies. One of the most common explanations of the changes in city form in the past two centuries is the notion that the railroad tended to concentrate growth then the automobile dispersed it. This is, we are told, the primary reason the dense city of the early twentieth century yielded to the highly dispersed postwar city in the same period as mass transportation yielded to the automobile.[25] This argument, plausible as it sounds at first glance, actually leaves a great deal unexplained. In the first place, as we have seen, the automobile did not directly replace any sort of mass transportation; what it more directly replaced was the private carriage. In fact, it would be more accurate to say that private transportation and mass transportation have coexisted and developed together through the nineteenth and twentieth centuries as the automobile replaced the private carriage and as the bus replaced the streetcar, which in turn replaced the cable car and horse-drawn street railway.

It is true that the use of private means of transportation has soared while the use of mass transportation has remained steady or declined in the same period of time that the population dispersed in virtually every major metropolitan area in the twentieth century. But this does not prove any simple cause-and-effect relationship. There is no more reason to think that the automobile causes decentralization than to believe that rail transportation can only work to centralize cities. As we have seen, the outward dispersal of urban population started centuries before the advent of the automobile. Certainly by the early twentieth century, suburbanization was in full swing using rail transportation as a principal means of dispersal. The Los Angeles region had become one of the most decentralized, dispersed, multicentered urban places the world had seen already by the time of the First World War, well before the impact of the private automobile was felt in any really significant way. It was the steam railroad, the cable car, the streetcar, and the interurban rail system that had made this possible. Even more important, the Los Angeles region has become dramatically denser since the 1950s in an era when the vast majority of people have relied on the private automobile. The fast-increasing rate of automobile ownership at the very heart of some of the densest urban regions in the affluent world today offers proof that high automobile ownership does not automatically lead to low densities.

In a similar way, it is not really logical to blame postwar urban freeways for sprawl. These roads were heavily supported by central-city interests because these individuals believed that these roads, like the railroads before them, would reinforce the centrality of the downtown and make it easier for people from throughout the region to get to it. In fact, they did make getting downtown much quicker. Also like the railroads, they made leaving town simpler, but there is no particular reason to think that the decentralization caused by roads has been any different in kind than that caused by the railroads. In fact, both caused some dispersal and both caused some centralization.[26] The amount of each depended on a great many other factors and millions of individual choices.

If one were willing to believe in simple cause-and-effect relationships in urban development, one could turn the entire transportation argument on its head. From this perspective, the individual desires of large numbers of families wishing to live at lower densities could be seen as the primary cause of the growth in the successive development of the carriage industry, the railroad, public transportation, and finally the automobile industry. Each of these means of transportation did, in fact, give families increased mobility. It is this enormous increase in mobility, and not any specific means of transport, that has been a key factor in the large population dispersal that we have chronicled. What we can conclude is that although this increase in mobility certainly made sprawl possible it did not necessarily cause it.

Affluence and Democratic Institutions as a Cause

Perhaps a better way of looking at the causes of sprawl is to leave aside for the moment the question of why cities sprawled and instead to ask what were the forces that worked against sprawl and kept cities from dispersing even more than they did before the mid-nineteenth century. After all, in many ways it is puzzling that so many people would have chosen to live uncomfortably on top of one another in walled cities for such a long time when there was attractive land all around the city. According to Thomas Sieverts, this would seem to be a very unnatural condition, quite opposed to the "natural" habitat for man that appears to be neither the completely open field nor the enclosed forest but the areas that lie at the border between the two. In like fashion, he suggests, humans seem to favor neither a high degree of compaction nor a high degree of diffusion but a moderate clustering. If so, the compact historical city, such as seen in Europe before the nineteenth century, may turn out to have been an aberration, a short "interlude" in urban history. What sustained the compact city even beyond the period when it was necessary for defense, Sieverts suggests, was the concerted effort of a small elite of individuals and institutions who erected a system of "priest kings and religious associations, temples and churches, walls and markets, feudalism and the guilds." It was perhaps the wane of these forces in the seventeenth and eighteenth centuries even more than the advent of the railroad, telecommunications, and other innovations of the nineteenth century that really made sprawl possible.[27]

Although sprawl has developed differently at different times and in different places, the history of sprawl suggests that the two factors that seem to track most closely with sprawl have been increasing affluence and political democratization (fig. 25). In places where citizens have become more affluent and have enjoyed basic economic and political rights, more people have been able to gain for themselves the benefits once reserved for wealthier citizens. I believe that the most important of these can be defined as privacy, mobility, and choice.

By privacy, I mean the ability to control one's own surroundings. This might take the form of a co-op apartment on Fifth Avenue in New York with a door-

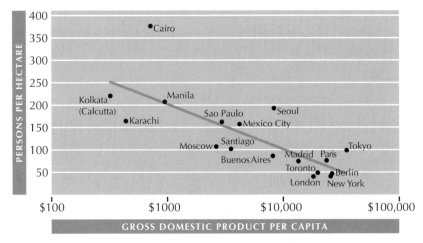

Figure 25. Affluence and sprawl. The relationship between affluence, as measured by gross domestic product, and sprawl, as measured by density figures or space used per capita, is a close one. The more affluent urban dwellers become, the more space they are likely to demand and to be able to afford. (Redrawn by Dennis McClendon based on the charts prepared by Marcial Echenique for his article "Mobility and Space in Metropolitan Areas," in *Cities for the New Millennium*, ed. Marcial Echenique and Andrew Saint [London: Spon Press, 2001], using data from H. Beyer, "Plan regulador metropolitano de Santiago: El peso del Subdesarrollo," *Estudios Públicos*, no. 67 [1997], 147–65 and World Bank, World Development Report [Oxford: Oxford University Press, 1997].)

man at the sidewalk and a chauffeured car at the ready, or it could take the form of a modest house on a small plot of ground in the suburb (fig. 26). One of the major reasons the suburban house has been so successful is that it has been a way to obtain many of the advantages of privacy enjoyed by the millionaire on Fifth Avenue at much less cost.

By mobility I mean both personal and social mobility. Where, in the nineteenth century, only the richest and most powerful urban dwellers could maintain their own carriages and get around urban areas on their own power at will, by the end of the 1920s private transportation was in reach of tens of millions of middle-class suburbanites particularly in the United States. The option of using an automobile has given city dwellers around the world an enormously increased mobility. City dwellers everywhere travel on average vastly more than they did at the beginning of twentieth century. This physical mobility has allowed a dramatic expansion of educational and employment opportunities. In turn, this has led to increased social and economic mobility.[28]

Figure 26. The single-family house as universal ideal? Despite the enormous variety in the location, climate, and culture of cities in today's world, it appears that most urban dwellers, when they become affluent enough to have real choices in housing, prefer single-family detached houses. Polls show this to be just as true in France, Germany, or Russia as in the United States, Canada, or Australia. Shown here is a model house near the freeway in Bannewitz, outside Dresden. (Photograph by Robert Bruegmann, 2000.)

Finally there is choice, perhaps the most important element of all and the most hotly disputed. Many members of cultural elites are not interested in hearing about the benefits of increased choice for the population at large because they believe that ordinary citizens, given a choice, will usually make the wrong one. Sprawl has certainly increased choices for ordinary citizens. At the turn of the century, it was primarily wealthy families who had multiple options in their living, working, and recreational settings. An affluent New York banker and his family could live in many different communities in the city or its suburbs. They could summer in the Adirondacks or at Newport, winter in Florida or on the French Riviera. They had the luxury of ignoring their neighbors and choosing their friends elsewhere. Today, even the most humble American middle-class family enjoys many of these choices. And even if the alternatives aren't thrilling, the very fact of having choices at all makes virtually any situation more tolerable. The most convincing answer to the question of why sprawl has persisted over so many centuries seems to be that a growing number of people have believed it to be the surest way to obtain some of the privacy, mobility, and choice that once were available only to the wealthiest and most powerful members of society.

It would not be wise to conclude from this, however, that affluence causes sprawl. The fact that some of the wealthiest individuals in every large city continue to live at very high densities at the center suggests that affluence is compatible with many different settlement patterns. If everyone became wealthy enough, it is quite possible that a large number might want to live in places like Park Avenue in New York or an apartment in the sixteenth arrondissement in Paris and that new urban districts would be built to accommodate this demand. In the case of urban areas and sprawl, as in the case of virtually any vast and complicated human or natural system, there is very little simple cause and effect. Rather, there are innumerable forces, always acting on each other in complex and unpredictable ways.

PART 2

the diagnosis: three campaigns against sprawl

7   Early Anti-sprawl Arguments

As I noted at the beginning of this book, the term "sprawl" has never had a coherent or precise definition. This has been one of the reasons it has been such a powerful polemical tool. Thinking of it as a blank screen on which a great many people project their own feelings of discontent with contemporary urban conditions is a good way to approach the history of the anti-sprawl movement. Because of the lack of a precise agreement about what sprawl is, individuals have been free to rally around certain broad but quite abstract concepts as a way to explain what is wrong with developments they see around them without necessarily agreeing on any specific diagnosis of the problems or any concrete set of prescriptions. It has allowed people with radically different assumptions to find common cause. A review of the history of the anti-sprawl movement and its diagnoses provides compelling evidence for the complexity and changing character of these assumptions over time.

Although the current use of the word "sprawl" originated only in the twentieth century, the arguments that cluster around low-density unplanned settlements have had a much longer history. As we have seen in part 1, cities have sprawled from time immemorial and for a wide variety of reasons. As long as only a small number of the wealthiest and most powerful families occupied the most land in the most attractive locations, there was very little sustained or organized protest. Whenever a newly affluent or empowered part of the population started to enjoy this privilege, there was a backlash.

By the eighteenth century, the suburban and exurban exodus had grown enough in scale to inspire an impressive literature of complaint from the period's self-appointed arbiters of good taste. Wrote one observer:

The Town has tinged the country; and the stain
Appears a spot upon a Vestal's robe
The worse for what it spoils.[1]

As these lines suggest, by this time the British countryside was not just a place to produce food but a nearly sacred idea. The poet obviously assumed that there was a proper "natural" state of the countryside that was violated by inappropriate human use. Of course, the British countryside had long since ceased to be natural. Already, centuries earlier, it had been reworked into a thoroughly manmade landscape of agricultural lands, villages, and great country estates. To critics of the newly evolving urban middle-class landscape, however, this older landscape was the natural order of things, and anything else on the land was a moral offense, a violation of all that was good and beautiful.

As far as the critics were concerned, matters only got worse in the nineteenth century. London, already very low in density compared to cities on the Continent, spread across an enormous territory. Hundreds of miles of modest row houses lined the streets in neighborhoods punctuated by factories and gasholder houses, crisscrossed by rail lines elevated above the landscape on great brick viaducts, the whole blanketed in the nearly perpetual soup of industrial smog so graphically described by Sir Arthur Conan Doyle in his tales of Sherlock Holmes. It was common to describe the outer areas of London as dreary, chaotic, monotonous, congested, and polluted, the inevitable result of greedy unthinking developers and railroad builders out to make a quick profit. In fact, virtually every argument leveled against sprawl today can be found in these descriptions of London and other European industrial cities in the nineteenth century.

From that day to this, wherever and whenever a new class of people has been able to gain some of the privileges once exclusively enjoyed by an entrenched group, the chorus of complaints has suddenly swelled. Not surprisingly, this has happened during every period of major prosperity because during these times a greater number of families have enjoyed a greater choice of living arrangements. Predictably, every time this has occurred, in the judgment of certain already well-established groups, the newcomers have made the "wrong" choices. Also predictably, criticism of sprawl has virtually always been aimed at people outside the speaker's or writer's own circle.

8   The First Anti-sprawl Campaign: *Britain in the 1920s*

As I noted in chapter 3, rising prosperity in London and other British cities in the 1920s allowed an unprecedented number of families to move outward into areas of greatly reduced density. The incredible growth of the suburbs with their miles of semidetached houses led to a violent reaction among members of Britain's literary and artistic elite.[1] "We are making a screaming mess of England," a typical jeremiad started. The author continued with this arresting metaphor: "A gimcrack civilization crawls like a gigantic slug over the country, leaving a foul trail of slime behind it."[2] The book in which this essay appeared was edited by the most tenacious and vociferous of the opponents of suburban growth in this period and almost certainly the era's most interesting anti-sprawl prose stylist, the architect Clough Williams-Ellis. Williams-Ellis in an earlier publication, his scathing 1928 volume *England and the Octopus* spared no adjectives in his war on developers: "There was no attempt at an intelligent general lay-out plan; all was cut-throat grab, exploitation and waste—a mad game of beggar-my-neighbor between a host of greedy little sneak-builders and speculators—supplying the demand for homes meanly and usuriously."[3] But, a few pages later his target was the inhabitants themselves: "As the Joneses fly from the town, so does the country fly from the pink bungalow that they have perched so hopefully on its eligible site. The true countryman will know that the area is infected—the Jones have brought the blight of their town or suburb with them—and in all probability they and their home will be followed by an incursion of like-minded people similarly housed, and the country will be found to have further withdrawn itself beyond the skyline in its losing retreat towards the sea."[4] This passage is drenched in class resentment. It seems clear that for Williams-Ellis the "true countrymen" were members of the great landed aristocracy of Britain who had controlled the bulk of the country's land since the medieval period. The true countrymen apparently also included a small cultural elite, namely, people like himself. A group of these individuals had formed the Council for the Preservation of Rural England in 1926 in order to stop middle-class encroachments into a landscape that had been largely shaped by feudal rights.[5] It is also clear who Williams-Ellis believed could resolve the crisis. It would be skilled professionals, particularly architects like himself, operating, as he believed, outside the realm of the marketplace and the political process.

Many of these themes are even more explicit in the slightly less exuberant but equally passionate writings of the prominent British planner Thomas Sharp. In his book *Town and Countryside* of 1932, Sharp wrote: "The new houses and town extensions sprawl out in a sloppy diffuseness all over the countryside. London begins to roll over the Home Counties; Birmingham, Manchester, Glasgow, and all the big and little towns in the kingdom spread and sprawl proportionately."[6] One can almost hear Sharp reading this passage, drawing out the word "sprawl," here used as it had been for a great many years as a verb meaning to spread out in straggling fashion. Sharp, like Williams-Ellis, offered a clear diagnosis, unapologetically founded on class-based assumptions. The cause of suburban blight was a breakdown in social and moral order as the middle class gained economic and social power from the old aristocracy. The degradation of the English landscape was the direct result of the advent of "dull democracy" and the lessening influence of "enlightened autocratic control."[7] Sharp certainly did not believe that his ideas were merely his opinion. He argued that they were instead based on eternal, even biological verities:

> Tradition has broken down. Taste is utterly debased. There is no enlightened guidance or correction from authority. The town, long since degraded, is now being annihilated by a flabby, shoddy, romantic nature-worship. That romantic nature-worship is destroying also the object of its adoration, the countryside. Both are being destroyed. The one age-long certainty, the antithesis of town and country, is already breaking down. Two diametrically opposed, dramatically contrasting, inevitable types of beauty are being displaced by one drab revolting neutrality. . . . The strong, masculine virility of the town; the softer beauty, the richness, the fruitfulness of that mother of men, the countryside, will be debased into one sterile, hermaphroditic beastliness.[8]

This is the language of evangelism, of a man intent on turning back the clock to return to God-given ordering principles. And, of course, the very landscape he was describing, which for him was already hopelessly degraded, has, in subsequent generations, been taken as the natural state of things, the wonderful British landscape that more recent development is constantly on the verge of destroying, forever.

In the nineteenth century, the word "sprawl" had sometimes been used as a noun, as in a "sprawl of people," but it was apparently not until the early twentieth century that it was commonly used in this way to refer to the built environment. It was used this way frequently in Britian in the 1920s and 1930s.[9] By 1938, the American social critic Lewis Mumford could use the term without definition or explanation in several places in his monumental survey of urban history, *The Culture of Cities*. Mumford's criticisms mirror those of Sharp and other British writers, not surprisingly since Mumford drew heavily on British planning ideas.

> Circle over London, Berlin, New York, or Chicago in an airplane, or view the cities schematically by means of an urban map and block plan. What is the shape of the city and how does it define itself? As the eye stretches toward the hazy periphery one can pick out no definite shape, except that formed by nature: a banked river or a lakefront: one beholds, rather, a shapeless mass, here bulging or ridged with buildings, there broken by a patch of green or the separate geometric shapes of a gas tank or a series of freight sheds. The growth of a great city is amoeboid: failing to divide its social chromosomes and split up into new cells, the big city continues to grow by breaking through the edges and accepting its sprawl and shapelessness as an inevitable by-product of its physical immensity.[10]

The heart of Mumford's criticism, like that of most of his peers, was aesthetic. Because he could not discern the order underlying contemporary urban regions, he rejected them as amorphous and shapeless.

Although aesthetic and symbolic aspects dominated the anti-sprawl rhetoric of the interwar years, there were also more practical concerns. Particularly around London, some observers charged, suburban development was eating up some of the most productive agricultural land in England. There was also a continuous problem with traffic congestion. It was widely assumed that the continuous move of families out from the central cities was leading to greater congestion. Building new roads did not appear to help. Every time a bypass road was built around a village, it seemed, new "ribbon" or what Americans today call "strip" development would appear along the bypass, and traffic would quickly fill the road. In other words, the argument of postwar anti-sprawl reformers that new highways "induce" traffic was already in use at least as early as the 1920s in Britain.

9 The Second Anti-sprawl Campaign: *The United States in the Postwar Years*

With Europe's population and economy decimated, the United States became the most important battlefield in the war against sprawl in the first decades after World War II. What triggered this new campaign was the prosperity of the 1950s and 1960s and the resulting building boom. As in the booms of the 1880s and the 1920s, the majority of the new growth took place at the periphery and at lower densities than ever before. It appears that lot sizes in subdivisions in the United States, which had been expanding since the late nineteenth century, reached their apogee in the 1950s when a large number of American families were able to purchase suburban lots of a quarter acre or even larger. Even if the settlement had been much more compact, however, increases in population and affluence of the magnitude seen in the United States in the postwar years would have necessitated a vast amount of building, and all of this new construction would have led to severe strains on the existing urban systems. By the middle of the 1950s, a strong reaction against decentralization and suburbanization was underway among urban professionals.[1]

Fortune Magazine Conference

In the late 1950s the topic of sprawl caught the eye of journalist William H. Whyte, a young and precocious staff member at *Fortune* magazine who was already well known for a pioneering study of the postwar suburban community of Park Forest, outside Chicago. Whyte convened what was probably the first conference specifically devoted to sprawl. In attendance were some of the most important names in American city planning and architecture.[2] After the conference, Whyte gathered essays by some of the participants into a book called *The Exploding Metropolis*.[3] This book was a hymn of praise to the dense traditional city and a bitter attack on postwar suburban development. Whyte's own introduction and his essay entitled "Urban Sprawl" brought the term to a wide reading public. On the first page of his essay he informed readers that "huge patches of once green countryside have been turned into vast, smog-filled deserts that are neither city, suburb, nor country and each day—at a rate of some 3,000 acres a day—more countryside is being bulldozed under."[4] While the assumptions and language of this passage were obviously inspired by British critics of the interwar years, Whyte then introduced a new, more specifically American target as his prime example of all that was wrong with contemporary urban development: Los Angeles. He described the flight in an airplane from Los Angeles to San Bernardino as "an unnerving example of man's infinite capacity to mess up his environment." In the decades that followed, the suburban subdivisions of Los Angeles replaced the slums of Manchester as the ultimate urban horror, at least for intellectuals and academics living in the dense old industrial cities of the American Northeast.[5]

The various authors of the essays in the *Fortune* magazine book announced most of the themes that would dominate the second campaign against sprawl. In what follows I will consider these under six principal subheads proceeding from the most specific and practical to the most subjective and general.

Costs of Sprawl

Starting in the 1960s, a burgeoning new empirical literature started to accumulate on the supposed detrimental economic effects of suburbanization and sprawl. The centerpiece of this literature was the monumental three-volume *Costs of Sprawl* report of 1974, which finally appeared at the very end of the second campaign against sprawl and provided a kind of summary statement for it.[6] Unlike most previous attacks, which were journalistic broadsides, long on opinion but short on research, this study was funded by the federal government and carried out by the Real Estate Research Corporation, a respected private organization doing real estate consulting work in Chicago. The authors of the *Costs of Sprawl* did not really spend much time looking at actual landscapes. Instead they used two different techniques, the first an extensive review of the literature to see what other researchers had already found and the second a statistical analysis to determine how much sprawl actually cost.

The literature review was published in volume 2. In it, the authors performed a great service by assembling almost all of the available literature and summarizing it. Predictably, a preponderance of published work supported the assumption that sprawl was a problem and more costly than compact development. It would have been remarkable if this had not been the case, however, given the anti-suburban orientation of many academics in the social sciences and the understandable bias of most writers on planning toward the notion that the answer to most land-use problems is more public planning. Moreover, as in the sciences, "publication bias," the tendency to publish results the author would consider "positive" or tending to support a preconceived thesis, was clearly a factor. On any issue, an individual who feels that conditions need to be changed is more likely to spend more time and energy arguing the point than those who don't feel that basic changes are needed. Taking two bodies of literature—a large body that supported the idea that sprawl is a problem and more costly than "unplanned" development and a smaller one that suggested that neither was necessarily the case—the authors of *Costs of Sprawl* felt justified in simply asserting that the weight of evidence was on the side of the former. In reality, these were simply different points of view based on different starting assumptions about urban life.

The statistical analysis, based on an elaborate computer model of the projected costs involved in building various kinds of new communities at the edge of existing suburban areas, was described in volume 1 (fig. 27). These communities ranged from high-density "planned" development to low-density "unplanned" development. The authors concluded that planned communities were less expensive than unplanned communities and that higher densities, more mixed use, and more compact development would be less expensive than low-density sprawl.

Critics of this report quickly came forward to produce a series of devastating attacks on all of the fundamental assumptions of the study. They noted that the authors of the report had failed to control for things like the difference in the size of apartments and houses. One of the main reasons high-density settlements appeared to be less expensive than low-density counterparts was simply because the units were much smaller and so cost less to build. This obviously did not prove that low density was inherently more expensive. Others demonstrated that what worked in the model was not necessarily what happened on

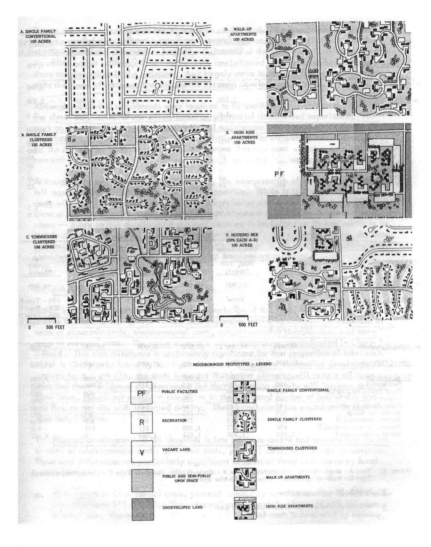

Figure 27. Costs of sprawl, 1974. In this landmark study, the Real Estate Research Corporation used computer modeling to compare the costs of various kinds of settlement patterns. They concluded that sprawl (*upper left*) was more expensive than higher-density "planned" development (*lower right*). However, critics charged that most of the reported difference was simply due to the difference in the size of the housing units. In addition, they noted, in actual practice, the heavier upfront costs and reduced flexibility of planned developments make them more vulnerable to changes in the market. Many individuals have attempted to correct the problems of the previous studies and to provide conclusive evidence that sprawl is indeed more costly than more compact, highly planned development, but none has been entirely convincing. (Real Estate Research Corporation, *The Costs of Sprawl* [Washington: U.S. Government Printing Office, 1974], 1:5.)

the ground. Master-planned communities, for example, although theoretically able to achieve a greater economy of scale, were not as flexible as communities without master planning and were therefore more vulnerable to changes in the market. Still others showed that "scattered settlement," which the report criticized for causing an inefficient pattern of low-density development, could, over time, turn out to be a highly efficient way to produce high densities as intervening lots were filled in at higher densities than the original development.[7]

More basically, the report clearly demonstrated a chronic problem with social science studies: the belief that clear, objective methods can lead to clear, objective policy conclusions. Unfortunately, in anything as complex as human settlement patterns, because the data are almost always incomplete, many of the basic assumptions in dispute, and many of the most important factors not easily quantified, the conclusions are inevitably highly dependent on the point of view of the observer. None of this deterred the growing band of anti-sprawl true believers. For decades, the conclusions of this report, no matter how shaky, have served as a statistical rock on which the anti-sprawl lobby has erected the ever-growing edifice of an argument that sprawl is inherently inefficient and therefore must be curbed.

Social Problems

Parallel to the efficiency arguments against suburbia were those of an entire generation of academic sociologists and other "high-minded" social critics. Particularly troubling, according to these writers, were the high levels of dissatisfaction and alienation they discerned in the suburbs. In addition to William Whyte's description of the residents of Park Forest as compulsive joiners and organization men came a flood of literature describing the social, intellectual, and artistic poverty of life in America's middle-class suburbs.[8] Popular books soon followed with titles like *Crack in the Picture Window* and *The Split-Level Trap*.[9] Curiously, this alienation was exactly what a previous generation of intellectuals had associated with life in high-density central cities.

Not everyone went along with the sweeping condemnations of middle-class suburbia. Perhaps the most famous rebuttal came from the sociologist Herbert Gans, who actually went to live in Levittown, Pennsylvania, in order to describe the life in a typical working-class suburb. After some observation, he concluded that this was a society as rich and complex as that in any central city neighborhood. Yet, Gans suggested, many people, including a great percentage of the national opinion makers, were unable to understand a place like Levittown because of their "upper-middle-class ethnocentrism." According to Gans in his influential 1967 book *The Levittowners,* an upper-middle-class citizen was likely to see "the lower middle and working class with whom I lived in Levittown as an uneducated, gullible, petty 'mass' which rejects the culture that would make it fully human, the 'good government' that would create the better community, and the proper planning that would do away with the landscape despoiling little 'boxes' in which they live." [10]

Several years later, Gans ringingly endorsed people's right to choose environments like that of Levittown if they wished. He also challenged the upper-middle-class condemnation of sprawl: "I have never seen any persuasive evidence that sprawl has significant bad effects, or high-density development significant virtues. Indeed, I doubt that density itself has much impact on people, except at levels at which it produces overcrowding or isolation. I therefore believe that people should be able to choose the density levels they prefer. Since most Americans who are able to choose have long preferred low-density housing, I favor urban policies that respect their preference, while not ignoring the minority preferring high-rise housing." [11]

Much of the academic establishment ignored Gans's eminently reasonable conclusions and, in the wake of massive unrest in American cities in the 1960s went even further in castigating the suburbs. In books like *Cities in a Race with Time, Metropolis in Crisis, Sick Cities, The Urban Crisis in America,* and *The International Urban Crisis,* the authors usually ignored the massive problems in the central city that had been visible for decades and instead explained the problems of the central cities as primarily the result of the rise of the suburbs and the flight of the white middle class. [12]

Environmental Objections

Another major force during the second campaign against sprawl was the rapid rise of the environmental movement. This movement, like the campaign against sprawl itself, represented a powerful fusion of diverse and often incompatible elements. [13] It grew, in part, out of a prewar interest in conservation, which had traditionally been about trying to preserve resources needed for economic growth. In a fashion that might at first seem paradoxical, it was precisely the enormous increase in affluence in the postwar years that allowed so many citizens to worry less about conservation as a way to sustain the economic boom and more about conservation as a way to prevent the damage that growth causes.

At first, the concern was related primarily to what people could see and what obviously did physical harm. The most obvious target was pollution. Of course, there had been some recognition of the deadly effects of air and water pollution as early as the nineteenth century and also some attempts to deal with them, but it was not until after World War II that these efforts really blossomed. In Pittsburgh, for example, the smoke that had once been seen as an inescapable, if unfortunate, corollary to economic vitality, was now seen as a problem that had to be solved in order to create a healthier, more efficient, and more competitive city. Civic and business leaders banded together and wiped out the pall of heavy smoke that once blanketed the city.[14]

The cause was bolstered by immensely popular books like Rachel Carson's *Silent Spring* of 1962 and Barry Commoner's *The Closing Circle* of 1971, both of which focused attention on pollution and the destruction of natural systems.[15] One of the major reasons that these books appealed so readily to postwar Americans was that so many Americans had moved to the suburbs precisely to have a more direct contact with the land than they could experience in an apartment in the city. These "backyard environmentalists" swelled the ranks of the Sierra Club and other environmental groups.[16] By the early 1970s, public opinion had clearly swung to the view that important corrective measures were necessary. This led to a flood of new legislation at all levels of government, most notably the series of federal environmental bills, which were primarily enacted during the Nixon presidency, including the National Environmental Protection Act and Clean Air Act of 1969, the Clean Water Act of 1972, and the Endangered Species Act of 1973.[17]

A number of anti-sprawl polemicists tried to link pollution with sprawl. This connection was problematic, however. Although an increased automobile usage had accompanied decentralization, the cause of the pollution was not sprawl. Automobile usage had increased everywhere, both in the city and the suburbs. Moreover, as many observers remarked, the higher density of automobile usage in the city meant that pollution was almost invariably worse in dense areas than in dispersed ones. The cause of the pollution was neither sprawl nor the automobile itself but, rather, the inefficient fuel source it used. For many of those in the anti-suburban camp, however, developing new and cleaner fuel sources was the last thing they wanted. It would only lead to more driving and more sprawl.

In like manner, although critics of sprawl charged, quite correctly, that paving over more landscape with roads and driveways made it harder for water to percolate down into the soil, created more run-off, aggravated flooding, and increased water pollution, the remedy for this was not necessarily to require everyone to live in dense urban areas where almost all the land is covered by impervious surfaces and where the only solution to the urban environment's impermeability was an enormous centralized sewer system. At low enough densities, it would be possible to trap and treat almost all of the water onsite or nearby and do without centralized wastewater facilities altogether. This ultimately could prove a more ecologically sound system than the "big pipe" engineering solutions of nineteenth-century industrial cities that continued to be used after World War II.

Limits to Growth

A related environmental attack on sprawl was made through a broader and more abstract set of arguments clustered around the concept of "limits to growth." This kind of thinking had had a long history by the end of the Second World War. Alarmists had been warning that mankind was in imminent danger of running out of resources since at least the late eighteenth century when Thomas Malthus famously predicted that population growth would inexorably outstrip food supplies. Virtually without exception, the frightful predictions of Malthus and his successors had turned out to be wrong. Nevertheless, predictions of this kind were extremely useful to zealous reformers because they implied the possibility of dangers potentially so great that immediate action had to be taken even if not everyone agreed on the diagnosis or the prescription.

A particularly important restatement of the Malthusian idea in the postwar decades was launched in the late 1960s with the publication of Paul Ehrlich's *The Population Bomb* (1968) and a 1972 volume called *The Limits to Growth*, which publicized the results of a large-scale computer simulation at the Massachusetts Institute of Technology by a group calling itself the Club of Rome. The predictions were dire. Ehrlich painted a scenario of 90,000 people dying in a killer smog in Los Angeles and a massive food famine in the United States by the year 2000.[18] With all of the growth in new technology and prosperity, this line of reasoning went, mankind was upsetting the balance between man and nature.[19] The only way to save mankind was to conserve and preserve, to limit and restrict, to turn the clock backward rather than pushing confidently forward into the future.

Not everyone was convinced either by the empirical research or by the philosophical assumptions. Critics at the time pointed out that the basic assumptions—that the technology and affluence are the major causes of environmental degradation and that the world is on the verge of running out of resources—were not well supported by the actual evidence. In fact, they argued, environmental degradation is typically much worse in poor societies than in rich ones and that although affluence can certainly cause environmental problems, particularly in the early stages of economic development, it is precisely affluence that, in the end, seems to create both the demand for environmental quality and the means for achieving it.[20]

Ehrlich's critics also rejected the idea that there was any immediate danger of running out of resources. Although theoretically there is a limit to the amount of energy available, they argued, in fact, given that the entire universe is energy, it is really more a matter of how this energy can be extracted, at what cost, and with what by-products. The real limits, for these observers, were those imposed by ignorance and social disorganization.[21] In societies not plagued by internal strife and repressive leadership, citizens would band together to increase the supply of available resources. For the critics of "limits to growth," it was highly likely that mankind would learn to harvest vastly larger and cleaner energy supplies when it became necessary and thus economically advantageous to do so. They further argued that any policy aimed at dramatically decreasing the use of resources could have a devastating effect on the poorest citizens of the world who needed more, rather than fewer, resources to pull themselves out of a cycle of destructive poverty and environmental degradation. Despite the considerable controversy stirred up by the limits to growth theories and a poor record in specific predictions, the notions underlying limits to growth have remained a foundation of the anti-sprawl edifice.

The Attack on the Automobile

Building on both the concerns about pollution and the limits to growth was an attack on the private automobile. Like the steam railroad, horse-drawn street railway, cable car, electric streetcar, subway, and elevated train before it, the automobile had clearly allowed for greatly increased mobility. This in turn made it possible to develop outlying areas not easily accessible heretofore. In affluent and fast-growing cities like Detroit or Los Angeles, the automobile had become the most common form of transportation for most families by the end of the 1920s. In the two decades after World War II, much of the rest of urban America reached this stage, and the majority of American households were finally able to own a car.

Not incidentally, it was exactly at this point, when the automobile ceased to be a luxury item for the affluent and came into the hands of a large middle class, that the anti-automobile sentiment grew really strident. As with criticisms of the suburbs, complaints against the automobile surged in the 1950s. Led by upper-middle-class residents of central cities in the Northeast of the United States, this group took a passionate dislike not just to the automobile but to an entire world-view that they believed supported it. For them the automobile was symptomatic of an individualistic, consumerist society run amuck. The years between the late 1950s and the early 1970s produced a large collection of vitriolic broadsides with titles like *The Insolent Charioteers, Superhighway-Superhoax, Autokind vs. Mankind,* and *Dead-End: The Automobile in Mass Transportation.*[22]

One conspicuous part of this attack was an assault on urban freeways. These roads were planned in part to alleviate the severe traffic congestion problems faced by many American cities starting in the 1920s. Although the freeways clearly did help enormously with traffic congestion, as anyone driving the free-ways of Los Angeles in the 1960s or 1970s could testify, they also had some undeniably bad side effects. Urban freeways displaced vast numbers of fami-lies, wiped out communities, and created barriers within once vital neighbor-hoods.[23] In many downtowns, the need to provide access roads and parking led to the demolition of many blocks of urban fabric.

The anti-highway activists weren't content to rehearse these problems, which hardly anyone disputed. They argued that the freeways had actually caused congestion rather than alleviating it. They convinced many people that all that highways did was to "induce" new driving. This, in turn, led to the widely used maxim "We can't build our way out of congestion." This observation seemed quite convincing to many people who saw with their own eyes that a given freeway, as soon as it was built, soon filled up with traffic. However, this may have only proved that engineers had sited the road correctly to handle growing demand. Certainly while roads in fast-growing cities leading to the areas most likely to be developed were soon filled, other roads, particularly those on the least favored sides of urban areas with stagnant economies, remained lightly used for decades, despite the fervent desire of public officials that they would induce traffic and new development. Moreover, although a given new freeway may indeed have soon become choked with cars, a careful observation of all of the alternative means of transportation in the area would almost certainly have shown that much of this traffic was caused by people switching from one route or means of transportation to a faster and more direct one. Yes, highways could induce traffic, but this was hardly a disaster. It was often just the result of many people using new roads to expand their choices in living, working, and recreational environments.[24]

One of the reasons the anti-road arguments were successful was a fateful decision made by an earlier generation of highway engineers and public officials. To gain public support for new roads, they pitched them as a way to relieve congestion. They were clearly successful in doing this, at least for a time in many American cities.[25] However, the vast increase in affluence of Americans at mid-century and the resulting demand for increased mobility virtually guaranteed that the engineers would rarely be able to completely satisfy demand and that most new urban roads would soon be filled. To make matters worse, the problem always seemed most acute in those places where the engineers expended their greatest effort. Despite the construction of new roads, the parts of cities that were growing quickly seemed to be the very ones that were perpetually on the verge of gridlock. In fact, of course, the disruption caused by the building of the roads itself contributed greatly to the congestion at least in the short run. This led many people to conclude that congestion in fast-growing places proved the failure of highway building. It would probably have been more useful to consider congestion in these regions more a testimony to an economy so vibrant and quality of life so high that people continued to move in and to drive despite the obvious problems.[26] Moreover, although it would not have been immediately obvious to many people, because urban dwellers constantly change their behavior in response to conditions, moving their place of residence or changing their jobs, gridlock never quite arrives. After booms subside, there is usually a significant easing of problems. By this time, though, the new highways have become part of the existing landscape and few people remember how bad traffic had been before they were constructed.

If highway officials had focused less on congestion and more on mobility, there might have been a more rational debate about induced traffic and about automobiles versus public transportation. It would then perhaps have been obvious that if the induced traffic proposition were true it would also invalidate the claims of the reformers that building transit can reduce congestion and discourage sprawl. To the extent that any transit system can, indeed, take cars off the freeways, by the logic of "induced traffic" the freeways would just fill up once again with other cars. Any increased capacity in public transportation would not only itself allow people to live even farther from their work and other activities, but the space freed up on the road would also allow for greater decentralization.

At base, none of these objections to their arguments really mattered to the most passionate anti-road crusaders. Theirs was merely an update of the hoary tradition of wanting to reform the lives of other people, particularly people who couldn't be trusted to make the right decisions on their own. These arguments provide a twentieth-century counterpart to the arguments against the construction of railroads made by the Duke of Wellington in the nineteenth century. Railroads, in the mind of the duke, "only encourage the common people to move about needlessly." [27]

Aesthetic and Symbolic Objections

In the prosperous postwar years, as increasing numbers of middle-class citizens were able to meet most utilitarian needs, they often turned their attention to less tangible, more subjective factors in urban life. In issues ranging from concerns about the ugliness of billboards to the growing perception of a need to preserve historic monuments, the public became more engaged in aesthetic and symbolic issues that had once been mostly of interest to a wealthy and cultured elite.

One matter of considerable concern was the preservation of landscape and open space. The interest in landscape was undoubtedly accelerated by the fact that, more than ever before, Americans were able to interact with the land either in their own backyards or farther afield as the automobile and the airplane allowed them to reach more remote parts of the country to fish, camp, and hike. Both experiences made them sensitive to the need to protect scenic land and recreational resources close to home as they watched the old, the familiar landscapes of farms and forests, disappear before the onslaught of the developers' bulldozers. As Joni Mitchell summarized it: "They paved paradise and put up a parking lot." [28]

Even though suburban growth was by no means new, and suburban development of the postwar decades actually occupied very little of the total land mass of America, this larger perspective was hard to grasp from the perspective of someone living in the booming growth corridors of Nassau County, Long Island, or the San Fernando Valley of Los Angeles. Especially for those stuck in traffic on the way to their weekend houses, it could easily have appeared, as Edward Higbee claimed in his 1960 book *The Squeeze,* that the country was running out of land. His book followed hard on the heels of a 1959 report by the Twentieth Century Fund, which offered this diagnosis: "The highways are packed, recreation places are saturated, the open landscape is increasingly devoured."[29]

The environmental movement would almost certainly not have become such a mass movement without a rising appreciation of the aesthetics of landscape. Although there had always been admirers of majestic mountain scenery and the seashore, after World War II many Americans were ready to appreciate prairies, cornfields, and wetlands as aesthetic landscapes, particularly since more Americans made their home at a comfortable distance from landscapes used for farming or mining or logging and weren't obliged to perform back-breaking labor to wrest a living from them. This process was greatly accelerated by writers like Aldo Leopold, whose evocations of the winds rippling across a great marsh in central Wisconsin in the 1949 volume *Sand County Almanac* resonated with thousands of readers.[30] In fact, once Americans learned to appreciate the vast prairies of the central part of the country and the scrub landscape and deserts of the West, there was very little left in the natural landscape that was considered uninteresting and unworthy of preservation. Land conservation and open space preservation became mass movements.

Anti-sprawl groups capitalized on both the rising appreciation of landscape and the perceived open space crisis as well as the graphic techniques of the environmentalists. They particularly favored the before-and-after photo spread: on one page, a photo of tranquil farms and hillsides, on the other a view of the same area after it had been bulldozed in preparation for development. The implication was that nature was being destroyed at an unprecedented rate. Of course, looked at from another perspective, it is clear that the landscape of the farm was no more the product of unaided nature than the subdivision, and the logged-over forest land would soon be covered with new growth. By the end of the postwar decades, moreover, many really egregious offenses against the environment—for example, the nearly total destruction of the tree cover of the upper Midwest by logging or the most destructive pollution caused by strip mining in Pennsylvania and West Virginia—were already a thing of the past.

The new appreciation of the natural landscape was coupled with a mounting distaste for the manmade landscape. Americans were barraged by a series of books that argued that much of what humans did to the landscape was deleterious. Stewart Udall's book, *The Quiet Crisis*, published in 1963, juxtaposed glorious color images of the coastal marshes of Virginia and the towering Rocky Mountains with black-and-white photos of dust storms in the Great Plains, logged-over timberlands, and streams whose topsoil and gravel had been washed away by miners. Later in the decade, landscape architect Ian McHarg, in *Design with Nature*, concentrated more directly on urban development and delivered a stinging critique of contemporary settlement patterns and a call for a greater sensitivity toward natural systems.[31]

From the pens of architectural critics came a barrage of invective. The new American landscape was the ultimate aesthetic wasteland, according to architect Peter Blake writing in *God's Own Junkyard*.[32] Lewis Mumford put it this way:

> Whilst the suburb served only a favored minority it neither spoiled the countryside nor threatened the city. But now that the drift to the outer ring has become a mass movement, it tends to destroy the value of both environments without producing anything but a dreary substitute, devoid of form and even more devoid of the original suburban values. . . . A new kind of community was produced which caricatured both the historic city and the archetypal suburban refuge: a multitude of uniform unidentifiable houses, lined up inflexibly, at uniform distances, on uniform roads, in a treeless communal waste, inhabited by people of the same class, the same income, the same age group, witnessing the same television performances, eating the same tasteless prefabricated foods, from the same freezers, conforming in every respect to a common mold.[33]

Mumford's attack was based on a typical highbrow disdain of middle-class culture. It echoes many of the hoary themes in anti-suburban writing, particularly the idea that their residents were unable to recognize the futility of the entire enterprise. According to Mumford, newcomers would inevitably outflank any new settlement and destroy the very environment that the initial residents were seeking. Of course, Mumford could have made similar observations about many other parts of the landscape. Exactly the same thing could happen to an individual who chooses to live in a high-rise apartment building because of the spectacular views of the city only to find these views blocked as newer and higher buildings rise around him. In fact, there was probably little evidence that Mumford could have found to show that suburbanites were any less successful than residents of any other part of the urban area in finding ways to preserve the amenities that were valuable to them.

Similar criticism of working-class and middle-class culture reached a new generation of American youth through popular culture and the radio where they could hear Pete Seeger singing:

> Little boxes on the hill side, little boxes made of ticky tacky.
> Little boxes, little boxes, little boxes all the same.[34]

The boxes that inspired the song were actually the houses in the relatively high-density suburb of Daly City, California, just south of San Francisco. Photographs of these houses were repeatedly reproduced in publications as an object lesson in the horrors of suburban conformity and the despoiling of the landscape. Of course, today, after time has passed and their landscapes have matured, they are being reappraised by hip, young urbanites who see them as charming period pieces and an important part of the Bay Area's architectural heritage.[35]

The *Use of Land* Report and the End of the Second Campaign

The year 1973, at the very end of the second campaign against sprawl, saw the appearance of a book entitled the *Use of Land: A Citizen's Policy Guide to Urban Growth*. This volume was the report of a blue-ribbon committee, the Task Force on Land Use and Urban Growth, which had been appointed by a federal committee and funded by the Rockefeller Brothers Fund. Like the group assembled by *Fortune* magazine at the beginning of the second campaign, this was a collection of prominent business and government leaders, most of them living and working in large cities in the American Northeast. The report was a comprehensive summary of what "right-minded" citizens of the day thought about the growth of the suburbs and sprawl.[36] The growth of the suburbs was producing inefficient settlement patterns, harming the central city, depleting open space, and contributing to pollution. Once again Los Angeles, "the symbol to many of how urbanization should not take place," represented all that was wrong with contemporary development.[37]

The conference had been effective because it managed to bring together, if only for a short time, academics antagonistic to what they called "mass culture," a central-city business elite interested in limiting suburban competition, and some established suburbanites who were themselves concerned about further development in the outlying suburbs. They shared a common platform of stopping "business as usual," which they characterized as unregulated growth and sprawl at the periphery. They also agreed, in principle at least, that this kind of growth could be replaced with a much more rational, carefully coordinated, and in many cases, much slower, process. Like most reform groups, the anti-sprawl coalition attempted to claim the moral high ground by portraying their activities as a disinterested attempt to make life better for everyone.

Skeptical observers at the time noticed that many of these individuals and groups, while claiming to be working altruistically for the population as a whole, were actually proposing measures that would provide great benefits to people like themselves. They also noted that the reformers, while claiming to uphold democratic principles, were attempting to impose their own aesthetic norms on the rest of the population.[38]

As with so many other attempts to stop or channel growth, the anti-sprawl movement faded with the next economic downturn, in this case the recession triggered by the fuel crisis of the 1970s. The gas crisis actually delighted many slow-growth and anti-growth activists because they saw it as the fulfillment of their predictions about the limits to growth and the force that would finally halt the insanity of sprawl. They were convinced that, as the costs of driving rose, Americans would abandon their infatuation with automobiles and suburbia and come back to live in central cities. Of course, nothing of the kind occurred. The gasoline shortages did not stop Americans from driving; the economy recovered; sprawl continued and came to be the target of another generation of reformers.

10 The Third Anti-sprawl Campaign: *Since the 1970s*

In many reform movements, by the time opinion coalesces around a given set of diagnoses and prescriptions, the conditions that caused the discontent in the first place may well have been transformed beyond recognition. So it is with the campaign against sprawl. Although the sheer volume of new construction since the 1970s at the periphery of American urban areas has exceeded in size anything that has gone before, this has been due primarily to the fact that the population of urban America has become so much larger. The same could have been said of urban dispersal in the 1950s or the 1920s or the 1890s. In fact, as we have seen, the actual rate of urban and suburban sprawl in the United States already reached its peak in the years between World War I and the end of the 1950s and since then has been declining, as an increasing number of urbanized areas have become denser rather than less dense. Nevertheless, the anti-sprawl campaign has, if anything intensified. In fact, in this campaign, the older anti-sprawl groups have been joined by a new set of reform activists. The anti-sprawl movement has achieved a great deal more public attention than any of the efforts in the past, not just in the United States and Europe but also in many other places worldwide.

The anti-sprawl reformers have undoubtedly been successful in getting their message across. Whenever the word "sprawl" is mentioned today, it triggers in the mind of most listeners an entire litany of alleged woes, ranging from objective ones, such as the loss of cropland, to highly subjective ones like the supposed ugliness of suburban subdivisions. The complaints against sprawl, no matter how unlikely, have been repeated so often, and in so many forms, that they form a kind of mantra. One objection to sprawl seems to follow the next in a seamless web.

For anyone taking the time to investigate any of the claims in detail, to check the footnotes of the impressive-looking reports, it is remarkable how often the assertions are based on simple and surprisingly obvious statistical errors or the source of information turns out to be simply another anti-sprawl tract or a sketchy opinion piece by a journalist. Nevertheless, when hundreds of these reports are collected, they create an edifice that can look quite solid, in part because it is so big that no single individual can ever examine very much of it in detail. I am not trying to suggest that all of the charges against sprawl are false. Some of the complaints about sprawl are justified, and some may turn out to be so important that they will eventually force everyone to conclude that sprawl must be stopped. However, for the time being, there is at very least a great deal of reason to be dubious.

In fact, by the time the most recent anti-sprawl campaign reached the zenith of its influence in the late 1990s it also stimulated, for the first time, an increasingly vigorous skepticism and even outright opposition. Some individuals object to specific parts of the analysis. Others feel that it is necessary to look at the benefits as well as the problems with urban decentralization. Still others are unwilling to see suburban or exurban living as an inherently inferior to living in the central city. Finally, there are those who won't accept the conclusion that low-density cities like Atlanta or Phoenix, which attract thousands of enthusiastic new residents every month, are bad places to live or unhappy aberrations from eternal urban norms. In what follows I will once again start with the more objective and quantifiable problems supposedly caused by sprawl—the costs of sewers or the loss of farmland, for example—and move toward the more subjective, difficult to quantify, but, in the end, most powerful arguments: those that deal with symbolic concerns, aesthetics, and culture.

The Costs of Sprawl Revisited

One of the most commonly heard arguments made in the current campaign against sprawl is a reprise of the old "costs of sprawl" argument. For example, as common sense might suggest, it must be less expensive to build houses close together because this would require less roadway and fewer feet of sewer. It must also be wasteful for an inner-city school district to close a school in a neighborhood where population is decreasing while a school district in a fast-growing community at the urban periphery is forced to build temporary class-rooms to handle the influx of children. The same ought to be true of most urban infrastructure. However, this argument is a little like saying that it ought to be cheaper to renovate an old building than to construct a new one. Some-times it is, but often it is not. In the case of cities, a little closer examination reveals that much existing infrastructure, schools, for example, or the facili-ties devoted to freshwater delivery, wastewater treatment, and transportation in the central city, were never really adequate to begin with and today would require extensive improvements to bring them up to current expectations. The cost of doing so, particularly in densely built-up cities, is often considerably higher than it would be to start afresh in an outlying area. As a result, it might make perfect sense to build relatively inexpensive and up-to-date new schools or roads for new residents at the suburban edge, allowing the existing roads or schools in the central city to better serve a reduced population until gentrifica-tion and rising land values make possible the very expensive renovation of the old infrastructure.

The complexity of this issue starts to suggest why the old costs of sprawl debate has ballooned into a cottage industry among social scientists. By far the most careful and comprehensive statement on this subject to date has been a pair of massive studies produced by a team under the direction of Rutgers pro-fessor Robert Burchell entitled *Costs of Sprawl Revisited* and *Costs of Sprawl—2000*.[1] The authors of these publications admit that the dire consequences predicted in the original *Costs of Sprawl* report of the 1970s were unjustified. However, these more recent reports suggest that the fault didn't lie with the method but with incomplete data. So the authors returned to the old questions and tried to generate even more comprehensive data.

As in the 1970s, the task they set themselves was probably an impossible one. It required, first of all, a precise and objective definition of "sprawl," a term, I have argued, whose very usefulness to reformers has depended on its highly subjective quality and ability to adapt itself to changes in circumstances and taste. In the case of *Costs of Sprawl—2000*, the authors defined "sprawl" as low-density, leapfrog development in rural and undeveloped counties.[2] They then created a highly complex system of statistical analysis based on county boundaries. As we have already noted, however, the use of anything as large and as arbitrary as a county as a unit of measure is almost sure to be highly unsatisfactory in measuring sprawl and is an extremely blunt instrument in any statistical analysis. The authors then proceeded to make the same assumption made in the original *Costs of Sprawl* report in 1974, namely, that they could usefully compare real "uncontrolled growth" with a hypothetical "controlled growth" that they could model on computers.

Even assuming, for a moment, that the basic analytical tools were adequate, the conclusions reached in the report were hardly gripping. The savings to government bodies in the costs of highways, streets, and sewers, although apparently large in terms of the total number of dollars, turned out to be surprisingly modest compared to the total cost of government personnel or the gross national product. Also, the authors presented no evidence that, even if sprawl were irrefutably more expensive than compact development, citizens wouldn't be willing to pay the necessary premium in order to have the lifestyle they wanted.[3] The issue in any public policy study of this kind, after all, should be about balancing what everyone pays with what everyone gets in return.

From the point of view of Soviet planners and budget officials, it was probably highly efficient to stack workers up in vast concrete dormitories at the edge of older cities, but from the point of view of many residents this efficiency may have been quite misguided. It might well be a good thing from the perspective of American state treasury officials for the state to spend less on new highways, but this would be a false savings if it meant that time lost by citizens of the state sitting in traffic caused by the lack of the new roads outweighed the savings in road construction. It is likely, in fact, that the relatively small savings to public agencies that might result from more compact development would be dwarfed by the increased costs to individuals caused by heavy land-use regulations. To be fair, the authors of *Costs of Sprawl—2000* admitted to many of the difficulties with their study in the text itself, which is probably why the conclusions seem so oddly muted.[4]

Automobile Dependence

One of the most important arguments against sprawl has been the notion that it leads to automobile dependence and that this in turn leads to congestion, longer commutes, more pollution, and the depletion of energy sources. Perhaps the most conspicuous campaign against sprawl on these grounds has been mounted by two Australian urbanists, Peter Newman and Jeffrey Kenworthy.[5] Their 1989 book *Cities and Automobile Dependence* almost immediately became one of the foundations for the third campaign against sprawl. However, their attempt to link low-density sprawl directly to pollution, increased energy use, congestion, or longer commutes proved to be highly problematic.[6]

As transportation experts like Peter Gordon and Harry Richardson have argued in a long series of publications, the notion that sprawl causes congestion or longer commuting trips is difficult to sustain in the face of data that show that commuting times in the United States did not increase very much during the entire period from the sixties through the eighties, even as cities declined dramatically in density. The reason was that the decentralization of residences was accompanied by a decentralization of jobs and other activities and the creation of additional and less congested roadway capacity at the periphery.[7]

In general, and quite logically, congestion and commuting times tend to rise, not fall, with density. Certainly all the evidence suggests that residents of very low-density Kansas City, Missouri, or Oklahoma City can get around their metropolitan area much more easily and quickly than those of relatively high-density New York or Los Angeles or Tokyo.[8] It is not surprising that the Tokyo area, despite the city's very high densities and one of the best public transportation systems in the world, has some of the world's longest commuting times.[9] Even if the travel times were longer by automobile than by public transportation, which is rarely the case, the comfort and convenience of the automobile would probably make it the transportation mode of choice for many middle-class urban dwellers. It is not surprising that, by the end of the twentieth century, the automobile has become the dominant mode of travel in all affluent nations, even in a country like the Netherlands, which has one of the highest densities of any country in the world.[10]

Clearly there are enormous hurdles ahead in accommodating the vast numbers of automobiles and trucks in urban areas. It is likely that there will need to be massive spending to upgrade transportation infrastructure, to allow the switch to less polluting fuels, to make both the roads and vehicles more intelligent with sensors and guideways so they can accommodate a much greater flow of traffic safely, and to create entirely new modes of public and private transportation systems, some of which may not use roads at all. None of this is aided by the single-minded fight against the automobile and sprawl.

The Destruction of Farmland and Open Space

Anxieties about the loss of farmland, while already a major factor in the second campaign against sprawl, have become even more acute in recent years.[11] In some ways this is curious. Although the actual rate of farmland loss and the role of urban development in this loss are hotly debated, no one seems to dispute that agricultural yields are going up and agricultural prices going down worldwide despite a reduction in the amount of land devoted to agriculture. In the United States, agricultural production has clearly outstripped demand. Even where there has been no conversion of farmland for urban uses, farmers have taken a considerable amount of land out of production because it was simply not needed. Across great stretches of the northeast of the United States, for example, agricultural landscapes have yielded to forest producing an "explosion of green."[12]

Even many anti-sprawl reformers now admit that there appears to be little evidence that urban sprawl poses any foreseeable threat to the world food supply.[13] In fact, within a few decades we have gone from Paul Ehrlich's dire predictions of widespread famine in America to the notion that sprawl is a major cause of obesity.[14] What clearly drives the current campaign to protect farms are aesthetic and symbolic concerns. In both the United States and Europe, as the number of people actually working the soil has declined, the symbolic role of the farm and farmer has risen correspondingly, and landscapes that were mostly about food production are increasingly seen as aesthetic amenities for urban dwellers.

It is in part this desire to protect the agricultural landscape that has given rise to massive government subsidies in most affluent countries in the world. They now amount to as much as half of all farm income in the United States, for example. There is, of course, nothing wrong with trying to protect farmland. It is difficult to imagine Europe without its magnificent agricultural landscape, for example. But efforts to protect farmland have many unintended consequences. It can, first of all, drive up the cost of urban land by limiting the supply of land that can be developed. A spectacular example of this can be found in Hong Kong, where there is actually a substantial amount of land now in agricultural production that could be developed without any fear of causing hunger or starvation if it were not for governmental policies protecting agricultural production. The result has been some of the highest land prices in the world.

Farmland protection can also come into direct conflict with the goals of environmentalists, who are increasingly worried about the pollution caused by agricultural production, particularly the erosion of soil and the run-off of chemicals from the field. Even more damaging has been the impact on the developing world of the massive subsidies given to American, European, and

Japanese farmers and the resulting food supply that is then sold overseas at cut-rate prices. Because agriculture is the primary component of the economies of many of the poorest countries, when farmers can't make a living because they can't compete with cheap, heavily subsidized food products from the developed world, the result on national economies can be devastating. The preservation of farmland is clearly important to many people for a variety of reasons, but the good these policies do must be weighed against their negative impact.

Agriculture aside, some observers, particularly those in the largest and fastest growing cities, believe that sprawl is consuming an excessive amount of land and is well on the way to paving over the entire American countryside. The use of the prejudicial term "consuming," even in supposedly dispassionate analyses, is symptomatic. It suggests that farmers or agricultural companies do not "consume" land but that any developer or suburban homeowner does even though the farmland is just as much a product of human action as the subdivision. In any event, by even the most generous estimates, the total amount of developed land today is probably no more than about 5 percent of the total of nearly 2 billion acres in the continental United States (fig. 28).[15] Looked at another way, it would be possible to accommodate the entire population of the United States, nearly 300 million people, at suburban densities within the slightly over 65,000 square miles of the state of Wisconsin. It is also important to note that the amount of land added to the country's supply of permanent open space, including public parks, national forests, and other areas set aside from development, has been increasing faster than the amount of urbanized land.[16]

Social Concerns and Equity Problems

Even though the population of the suburbs has always been diverse and in recent years has become even more varied, many writers have continued to claim that the outlying regions of urban areas lack the social and economic diversity of the center. However, both city centers and suburbs have been subject to the same forces, leading sometimes to a mixing of people by race, ethnicity, and income level and sometimes to a sorting out process. In fact, there is arguably more real economic and racial integration in most suburban malls today than on the streets of the central cities.[17] In any event, the current enthusiasm among an academic and social elite for "diversity" rests on a notion, far from obvious or proven, that different kinds of people living in close proximity

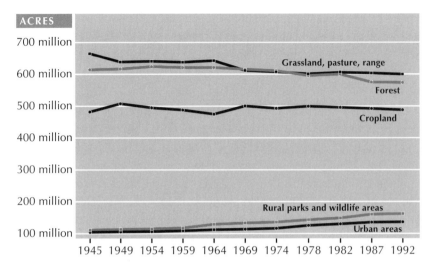

Figure 28. Land use in the United States, 1945–92. Although many people in fast-growing urban areas have the impression that the entire country is fast being paved over, in fact, urban areas, meaning cities and suburbs, occupy only a small percentage of the land in the country. For example, the entire urban population of the United States could fit comfortably into Wisconsin at suburban densities. As this chart shows, moreover, the amount of land set aside permanently for parks and wildlife areas has grown faster than urban land. What these government statistics don't show clearly is the amount of exceptionally low-density exurban development that now takes up enormous amounts of land around many American cities. (Redrawn by Dennis McClendon from a chart published by Samuel Staley in *The Sprawling of America: In Defense of the Dynamic City*, Policy Study no. 251 [Los Angeles: Reason Public Policy Institute, 1999], based on data from the National Agricultural Statistics Service.)

to one another will be more tolerant of each other than people who live in more homogenous groups.[18]

Another recurring theme in much recent writing has been a claim that the suburbanization of America has led to a sense of alienation or decline in "civic engagement."[19] Of course, just fifty years ago sociologists were describing how the central cities caused alienation and how residents of suburban areas were such compulsive joiners and volunteers. It is probably more useful to observe that the way community works has shifted. Extremely affluent people have always had the ability to choose their own kind of community, which might have nothing to do with the people who happen to be neighbors. Poorer citizens, for example, the residents of New York tenement buildings, were forced to interact with their neighbors. Today most citizens have a greater measure of choice in determining their own community.[20]

Another continuing complaint about sprawl is how it has hurt central cities and minorities. According to this line of argument, when affluent citizens leave the city and move to the periphery, they abandon the problems of the central city, instead transferring their civic concern and tax dollars to outlying municipalities. The poorest residents of the city are then trapped in cities without the resources to deal with its problems. Eloquent recent analyses of this sort have come from former Albuquerque Mayor David Rusk and Minnesota State Senator Myron Orfield, both of whom argue that the remedy is "regionalism," by which they mean governmental structures that encompass an entire region.[21]

There is no doubt that the concentration of very poor citizens in any part of the metropolitan area brings with it a great many social problems. However, many observers from both the political right and left reject the diagnosis that the cause of the segregation has been urban dispersal or that the remedy is regional government. They note that, in fact, many American metropolitan areas have long had area-wide governmental structures for things that everyone agreed on, such as water delivery or waste treatment. The reason that more robust regional governments have not been popular, they further argue, is that there is little consensus about more far-reaching policies, for example, schemes for major income redistribution. A proliferation of small governments, moreover, has made it possible for citizens not only to choose the kind of community and the kind of services they wish but also to have a larger voice in planning for the future than they would in a very large regional government.[22]

Other observers have argued that Rusk's statistical demonstration that "elastic" central cities—ones that are able to annex suburbs—are healthier than "inelastic" cities is more a statistical artifact than a description of urban reality. If any city were able to annex all of its suburbs overnight, that city might appear to be "healthier" economically on statistical charts but, of course, the annexation would do nothing in itself to improve the lot of any given individual living in the region. Others argue that the record of American experimentation with regional government has not been very encouraging. Although this kind of government might satisfy many residents in Minneapolis–Saint Paul, for example, the experience of Miami-Dade County and elsewhere gives little reason for optimism that pushing powers to a regional government will necessarily produce more efficiency or fairness than leaving them in the hands of many small municipalities.[23] Perhaps the best critique of the push by elite groups toward regionalism was penned by the famous social critic Jane Jacobs, certainly no fan of sprawl but even more suspicious of large-scale government and planning, when she wrote, "A region is an area safely larger than the last one to whose problems we found no solution." [24]

In fact, many of the most pressing social and economic problems in American urban areas today are not in the central city, which often has a relatively healthy tax base, but in the suburbs, often the far suburbs. In the Chicago region, for example, maps prepared by Myron Orfield demonstrate graphically that the city of Chicago is far from the poorest community in the area in terms of tax revenues per capita and that many of the poorest communities with the smallest tax revenues per capita are places like Ford Heights or North Chicago, located in the outer ring of suburban communities. [25] Channeling government dollars toward central cities and inner suburbs, as many proponents of regional planning are now advocating, would only hurt Ford Heights. Finally, there is the irrefutable fact that some of the cities with the greatest amount of sprawl at the periphery, for example, San Francisco, have thriving downtowns and central cities. Even some of the writers most critical of sprawl now acknowledge that blaming sprawl for the decline of downtown is unfair. [26]

Another common complaint about sprawl is that it depends on massive governmental subsidies that favor suburbanites and car owners. Of course, it is true that there has been more public funding for roads than for public transit in the United States. This is neither surprising nor inequitable, given the fact that private automobiles are used for the overwhelming majority of all travel in the United States. The calculations used by critics of the automobile to prove that transportation spending is unfair are highly problematic. They usually involve a balance sheet on which everything related to automobiles and roads is put into one column and then everything related to public transportation into another. This produces a highly misleading picture. For example, even if there were no suburbs and not a single private automobile, governments would still have to pay large amounts of money for roads because they are used for police cars, fire engines and other public vehicles, delivery trucks, taxis, and buses, which carry the vast majority of public transportation riders.

Most governmental funding for highways in the United States could reasonably be called a "user's fee" since it is largely funded by gasoline taxes paid by the users themselves. The same cannot be said for public transportation, where governmental subsidies per passenger miles traveled are much higher and they are paid for by a large number of citizens to benefit a relatively small group of users. [27] For these reasons, anti-sprawl advocates often resort to arguments involving a wide variety of indirect costs of automobile use, or "externalities," to prove their contention that the automobile is "subsidized." Air pollution would be an externality of automobile use, as would time lost by everyone in traffic jams. Having governments take externalities fully into account is, in itself, a perfectly reasonable demand. A very good argument can be made that automobile owners should pay more to compensate for the costs to society associated with their driving. However, every mode of transportation produces important externalities. The calculations made by anti-auto activists—which put all the pollution produced by roadway vehicles of all kinds and all of the money spent for American military action in the Middle East in the column of automobile externalities—do nothing to sort this out.

In fact, tilting the funding balance more dramatically toward public transportation might not in itself actually reduce externalities. Time lost in traffic obviously would drop if everyone was obliged to take public transportation. However, given almost any imaginable transit system we might produce, the total time spent in making these trips would almost certainly increase by an even greater factor since the automobile has proven itself so much more efficient in getting from any given point A to point B in our dispersed urban regions today. Moreover, automobile makers have been so successful in boosting fuel efficiency and reducing emissions, and public transportation in the United States today carries such light loads, that even with only 1.5 occupants per vehicle in cars, most new automobiles generate little or no more pollution per person per passenger vehicle mile than the average bus.[28] It would require a massive increase in the use of public transportation and improvements in transit vehicles for it to bring much reduction in energy use or pollution generated per passenger mile.

There are probably good reasons to provide more subsidies to some forms of public transportation in the United States today, but building traditional mass transportation systems is not likely to solve the problems associated with sprawl. Urban dwellers are already too dispersed and cities' residents already too accustomed to the comfort and convenience of individual transportation to go back to the cumbersome mode of buses and trains. There are a great many possible options for future public transportation, but the most promising for most situations in most urban areas today are those that involve something that acts and feels more like the private automobile or taxi on the ground or in the air than a passenger train. Certainly one of the biggest obstacles to finding these new solutions has been the notion that we can or should attempt to remake cities to fit traditional transportation modes rather than finding modes of transportation that can work in our dispersed urban environments. More competition rather than the near governmental monopoly on transit would probably also help.

Environmental Problems, Sustainability, and Global Warming

If there is a single factor that has galvanized the anti-sprawl movement during the last decades it has been a newly cemented alliance between anti-sprawl reformers and an invigorated environmental movement. In addition to all of the problems cited by the earlier anti-sprawl reformers, several powerful new arguments have come into play during the most recent campaign.[29]

One has been the idea of sustainability. Perhaps because it has been so difficult for environmental reformers to make a fully convincing case that concentrating people in dense cities is more environmentally friendly than dispersing them in lush, green suburbs, many environmentalists have tended to make the arguments more general and more abstract. A key phrase in the latest round of anti-sprawl has been "sustainability." According to the memorable definition in the so-called Brundtland Report, a document issued by the World Commission on Environment and Development in 1987, "sustainability" means "meeting the needs of the present without compromising the ability of future generations to meet their own needs."[30]

In many ways "sustainability" is the perfect foil for "sprawl." Where sprawl exudes a negative aura, sustainability is warm and fuzzy.[31] In place of the strip mall it conjures up an image of a child playing in a garden under the watchful gaze of a young mother. In reality, however, many of the advocates of sustainability base their assumptions on a very pessimistic view of the world and of mankind. They assume that the resources of today will be the resources of tomorrow and that humans will be unable to discover new ones or harvest the existing ones more efficiently. In other words, sustainability rests heavily on the dubious assumptions of limits to growth.

It is particularly difficult to reconcile the idea of sustainability with the reality of cities, which, by definition, draw in prodigious amounts of energy and materials from far beyond their borders in a process of constant destruction and rebuilding. It is quite possible, moreover, that today's low-density sprawl is actually more sustainable than the old nineteenth-century industrial cities that are usually described as its antithesis. At low enough densities, most citizens would probably be able to generate, using wind, water, solar, and geothermal power sources, a great deal of the energy they need on their own land, much like the New England farmer did in the nineteenth century.

A more specific charge against sprawl is that it has caused a major loss of habitat and, in the worst cases, species extinction.[32] This is clearly a significant problem. However, as many writers have observed, species extinction is still not well understood. Even the estimates of the magnitude of species loss due to urban development have varied wildly. The debates over species extinction, moreover, tend to veer back and forth between practical arguments—how much economic loss might be involved in species extinction—and moral arguments about the relationship between man and nature. It is clear that a vast amount of work needs to be done to reconcile human settlement patterns with the needs of other kinds of animals, but until more is known about the science involved in species extinction, stringent restraints on urban growth could easily do more to harm human habitat than help those of endangered species.[33]

An even more potent argument is that sprawl contributes to the production of greenhouse gases and therefore to global warming. If true this would perhaps be the strongest argument in favor of curbing sprawl. Despite the difficulty sorting out the exact extent of human impact on a pattern of global weather that has fluctuated very widely over the millennia with or without human intervention, the weight of scientific evidence today suggests that human activity has played a significant role in the current warming trend, and it is quite possible that this could have dire consequences.[34] Some important corrective action is almost certainly desirable. However, exactly what can or should be done by whom and at what cost is still very much in dispute.[35]

For our present purposes, the first and most important question is whether global warming is necessarily linked to sprawl. Although low-density living has undoubtedly been accompanied by more miles of driving and more energy use per capita and this in turn has led to the production of more greenhouse gases, it is certainly not clear that sprawl itself is the culprit. Even if everyone in the world came to live in the same way as the inhabitants of European central cities, this would certainly not, in itself, solve the global warming problem. It seems likely that the most effective remedy in this case—as with many environmental problems supposedly caused by sprawl—might be less in restricting or limiting low-density development, energy use, or automobile travel (although some of this might be advisable) but, instead, in exploring new ways to solve specific problems, most of which are the result of using inefficient and old-fashioned energy sources.

The greatest need, in the case of global warming, is a more intelligent debate about what we know about the problem and how we might most efficiently and equitably deal with it. Unfortunately, much of the debate about global warming, and about sprawl and environment more generally, often has very little to do with rational discourse about quantifiable conditions. If the issue were really about eliminating environmental horrors, the affluent citizens of the West would surely be less worried about the long-term and still very uncertain effects of global warming and more concerned about the absolutely clear and present problem of water delivery and wastewater treatment in the favelas and slums of the developing world, where millions of people become sick and die every year. Fixing these problems, moreover, would probably cost a fraction of what might be required to reduce even slightly the level of greenhouse emissions.

The underlying assumptions of many environmentalists worried about species extinction or global warming, as for many anti-sprawl reformers, are highly subjective and inextricably linked to moral judgments. One is the notion that nature is a purposeful and benign system that man has interrupted and that, therefore, man has an obligation to restore.[36] Another is the idea that environmental concerns are so urgent that they must be exempted from any cost-benefit analysis and trump every other consideration. But these assumptions are at best debatable. What very few people will deny is that sprawl, like compact cities, certainly causes environmental problems. However, environmental history seems to suggest that as societies become more affluent, citizens are likely to be less and less willing to tolerate these problems. The automatic equation of sprawl with environmental degradation has obscured the issues surrounding both the very real threats to our environment and the potential means of dealing with them.

Aesthetic and Symbolic Concerns

As we have seen, the most conspicuous early objections to sprawl were aesthetic, and these considerations have been the most important motivating force for many individuals ever since. In fact, it seems that as society becomes richer and the amount of time and energy devoted to securing things like food and shelter diminish, aesthetic issues inevitably loom larger. Certainly both the number of people complaining about the aesthetic impact of sprawl and the vehemence of the rhetoric have mounted during each successive campaign against it. In the most recent round, this literature culminated in a new round of tirades against the middle-class landscape and its inhabitants, such as James Howard Kunstler's *Geography of Nowhere* or John Miller's *Egotopia*.[37] These works are very much in the tradition of the outraged British observers of the interwar years, like Clough Williams-Ellis or Thomas Sharp, but less discriminating in their accusations and less skillful in their prose style.

As in previous campaigns against sprawl, there is an obvious class bias in these judgments. In very few cases have these indictments against sprawl targeted architecture or landscapes acceptable to upper-middle-class taste, no matter how scattered or low in density. Very few individuals link sprawl with the spectacular British villas and gardens of the French Riviera created in the 1920s or the great country houses built by American industrialists at the turn of the century on northern Long Island or in the Brandywine Valley in Delaware. Sprawl is subdivisions and strip malls intended for middle- and lower-middle-class families. Today it is notoriously "McMansions," which could be defined as houses judged by any given observer to be excessive in size and stylistic pretension.

New Urbanism

Perhaps the most potent attack on the alleged aesthetic deficiencies of sprawl has been the product of individuals gathered under the banner of the New Urbanism. This movement had its intellectual roots in the campaign against modernist architecture and urban renewal in the 1960s and 1970s and found important spokesmen in individuals like the London-based architect Leon Krier. The movement coalesced in the United States in the early 1980s with the creation of Seaside, Florida, designed by Andres Duany and Elizabeth Plater-Zyberk, who quickly became the most important voices for this cause (fig. 29). Along with other architects, such as Peter Calthorpe in California, they helped create the Congress for the New Urbanism in 1993. In lectures and articles and then in their influential book *Suburban Nation,* published in 2000, Duany and Plater-Zyberk have argued that most recent American development, particularly suburban development, lacks the kind of coherent fabric of traditional urban settlements. Their call for denser neighborhoods, more mixed in use, less dependent on the automobile, and more conducive to neighborly interaction, as well as their preference for regional historical architectural styles, has struck a chord with many people, both within the fields of architecture and planning and among the population at large. New Urbanist ideas are very com-

Figure 29. The New Urbanism. Andres Duany and other members of the New Urbanist group have mounted a sustained attack on the design of the typical American suburb and on sprawl. They believe that the design of American suburbs requires an excessive amount of automobile travel and is not conducive to any kind of real community feeling. In their own designs they try to incorporate lessons learned from traditional small towns across the country. The Florida resort community of Seaside, designed by the firm of Duany Plater-Zyberk & Company in the early 1980s, created a sensation when it opened because it seemed to some people to provide an alternative to normal suburban development and sprawl. However, most New Urbanist communities have been fairly low in density and located at the urban periphery. The question remains whether the New Urbanism is really an alternative to sprawl or just a tastefully designed variant on it. (Photograph by Robert Bruegmann, 2000.)

mon in professional and popular magazines today, and New Urbanist communities have proved to be very popular.[38]

One important reason for the success of the New Urbanists' critique of contemporary development is the way it picked up so many strands of thought from the earlier anti-sprawl campaigns and seemed to be so compatible with smart growth. However, it is not clear whether the New Urbanist prescriptions have any necessary relationship to sprawl. The vast majority of New Urbanist projects that have actually been built have consisted of relatively low-density residential subdivisions at the very edge of metropolitan areas. Although there may be a few shops, particularly if the area is frequented by tourists, these communities have been functionally very similar to standard suburban subdivisions, and there is little evidence that the actual behavior of residents has been different in kind from that of people living in more conventional suburbs.[39] This has led some observers to claim it is really just a kind of more attractive sprawl or, as one prominent observer suggested, the "New Suburbanism."[40] Nevertheless, the New Urbanists' critique of existing development has been undeniably influential and a major force in the anti-sprawl crusade. It is changing the look, if not the underlying character, of sprawl.

The Avant-Garde Discovers Sprawl

If history is any guide, the current revolt of the "sensitive minority" against sprawl, the landscape created by the "vulgar mass," will soon seem a quaint product of a bygone era.[41] After all, the very same row houses at the periphery of London that the aesthetic elite of the late nineteenth century considered a vulgar imposition on the land by greedy speculators are now being lovingly restored by members of the aesthetic elite of the current generation. A mounting respect, if not yet outright admiration, is now evident for the semidetached houses built around London in the interwar years that were so loudly castigated by English highbrow critics of that era. So it is with cookie-cutter houses in postwar American suburbia such as Daly City, California, now that their landscapes have matured and their original plastic-shaded pole lamps have become collectible. In like manner, as hard as it is to imagine today, by the time the landscape around the now-treeless subdivisions of look-alike stucco boxes at the edge of suburban Las Vegas fully matures, these subdivisions will be likely candidates for historic landmark designation. Most urban change, no matter how wrenching for one generation, tends to be the accepted norm of the next and the cherished heritage of the one after that.[42]

In fact, this process of revision seems to be well underway in the case of sprawl. When Los Angeles, for decades a byword for sprawl and all that was formless and chaotic in contemporary urban form, was reexamined by more sympathetic viewers, it became apparent that it had a structure as clear as that of any older city. The very things that made it anathema to the older critics—its large scale, pace of change, and lack of traditional monumentality—opened up a great many new aesthetic possibilities. This was the message of British architectural historian and critic Reyner Banham in his book *Los Angeles: The Architecture of the Four Ecologies,* published in 1971.[43] In his book Banham suggested that the Southern California gas stations of Ed Ruscha and the backyard swimming pools of David Hockney were different from but no less exciting aesthetically than the Paris streets and parks recorded by the Impressionists.

During the same years, the architects Robert Venturi and Denise Scott Brown looked at the images of sprawling cityscapes published in 1964 by Peter Blake in his *God's Own Junkyard* and saw, rather than the simple ugliness described by Blake, great urban vitality. They took a Yale architecture studio class to Las Vegas to study what they called the prototypical roadside strip. In *Learning from Las Vegas,* the highly influential book that grew out of that work, they suggested that "Sprawl City" wasn't necessarily so bad after all and that much could be learned from it. They then went on to do a studio on Levittown and found a good deal to admire there as well.[44] By the end of the twentieth century not just Los Angeles and Las Vegas but also Houston and quite a few other places that have been held up as the worst examples of urban sprawl had found their poets.[45]

Although the books of Banham, Venturi, and Scott Brown were very widely read, their assault on traditional aesthetic standards as inadequate to deal with the contemporary landscapes was largely ignored for many years. Only recently does there seem to have been a major upsurge of interest among highbrow architects and critics in trying to describe and understand the aesthetics of sprawl. Probably the most ambitious attempt has come from Dutch architect Rem Koolhaas, whose voluminous musings on the contemporary built landscape seem to alternate between careful analysis, condemnation, and celebration.[46]

In a similar fashion, in a recent book, architectural curator, critic, and trend-spotter Aaron Betsky juxtaposed images of sprawl with those of many current avant-garde architectural forms—sleek metal skins, landscapes that look like graphic designs, and interior spaces that are based on the intersection of blobs on a computer screen—suggesting that new forms of all kinds are often difficult to understand but that it is the duty of the avant-garde artist or critic to start this process. Sprawl, according to Betsky, "appears not to make sense, but perhaps that is because we have not figured out how to find what is beautiful in sprawl or because we do not yet know how to evaluate its forms."[47] Likewise the German architect and planner Thomas Sieverts writes about the tours he has led to the periphery of Cologne to give visitors a feel for the beauty of this discontinuous area of factories, warehouses, and freeways. For him the perception that peripheral areas are chaotic and fragmented is often due to a lack of imagination, an inability to appreciate their spatial and ecological richness.[48]

Forging the Anti-sprawl Coalition

The third campaign against sprawl really ignited in the mid-1990s when a number of major national groups began to coordinate their efforts. Several large organizations were already in the field. One was the American Farmland Trust, founded in 1980, which had become increasingly concerned with the way farmland near cities was being converted to urban uses.[49] Another was the Sierra Club, which had transformed itself over the previous decades from a small and elite group primarily interested in wilderness into a mass movement devoted to a wide range of issues including pollution, animal habitat, and land use.[50] The club's 1998 report "The Dark Side of the American Dream: Costs and Consequences of Suburban Sprawl" and other materials on its Web site have played a major role in the anti-sprawl coalition.[51] The most complete statements of the environmentalist objections to sprawl to date, though, have come from another environmental group, the Natural Resources Defense Council, in a 1999 volume written by F. Kaid Benfield entitled *Once There Were Greenfields.*[52]

In 1994, two other organizations, the Brookings Institution, a policy think tank in Washington, DC, and the Lincoln Institute for Land Policy of Cambridge, Massachusetts, jointly published a book by Anthony Downs entitled *New Visions for Metropolitan America.* Downs, a formidable figure in any discussion of land use and planning, had been an employee of the Real Estate Research Corporation when it did the original *Costs of Sprawl* report and in 1994 was the senior economist at Brookings. Downs had long recognized the problems caused by sprawl, but he had also been keenly aware of the problems that arise with any attempt to stop it.[53] His book was the most carefully argued and persuasive treatment of sprawl to that date.[54] In 1995 Brookings and the Lincoln Land Institute, along with the National Trust for Historic Preservation, sponsored a conference entitled "Alternatives to Sprawl," the most important gathering on the subject since the Task Force on Land Use and Urban Growth in the 1970s. Although the majority of participants were clearly anti-sprawl, the sponsors also invited several individuals not in sympathy with the dominant viewpoint.

The appearance of the National Trust for Historic Preservation at the 1994 conference may have surprised some observers, but it could be seen as an understandable, if perhaps risky, bid on the part of the trust to gain a new constituency.[55] In a manner parallel to the environmental movement, the preservation movement had grown over the decades since its founding in 1949 as traditional tasks, for example, the saving of single buildings, often for patriotic reasons, expanded to include the challenge of saving districts and entire regions. In this process, some preservationists turned their attention to sprawl, which, they believed, not only endangered the historic countryside but also threatened old downtowns and Main Streets by drawing businesses out to the suburbs and strips.[56] What really seems to have galvanized the anti-sprawl forces within the preservation movement was the appearance of Wal-Mart outside gentrified towns in New England. When Wal-Mart announced that it wanted to build several stores in Vermont in 1993 the National Trust put the entire state on their list "America's Most Endangered Places" and pulled out all the stops in a campaign against Wal-Marts and sprawl.[57]

The appearance of the environmental and preservation movements was extremely important to the anti-sprawl campaign because the laws passed in response to the efforts of these organizations claimed to have a basis in something more objective than mere personal opinion. This, in turn, allowed governmental agencies dealing with preservation and environment to wade into aesthetic and symbolic matters that they had traditionally avoided because they were so subjective and controversial. Anti-sprawl groups soon learned that they could use preservation laws or environmental impact reviews to stop demolitions or block new construction even when preservation or environmental concerns were never really the main goal.

The last years of the twentieth century also saw the creation of several broad-based coalitions of anti-sprawl groups, for example, the Sprawl Watch Clearinghouse, founded in 1998 and Smart Growth America. The Web sites of these organizations gave the various anti-sprawl groups a wide exposure.

The Counterattack: Anti-anti-sprawl

By the middle of the 1990s the anti-sprawl forces had become quite powerful. Even airline magazines, understandably loath to antagonize, considered anti-sprawl broadsides uncontroversial enough to occupy space on their pages. However, as often seems to be the case with reform movements, by the time the movement has reached the stage of wide acceptance, forces within and without have already severely undermined the foundations. In the case of the anti-sprawl movement, isolated opposition had already been in evidence during the second campaign. As we have seen, well-known sociologist Herbert Gans, who considered himself a liberal, was willing to speak out in defense of suburbia and sprawl for ordinary citizens. Further to the left were individuals, more often in England and the other English-speaking countries than in the United States, who saw most anti-sprawl regulation of the second campaign against sprawl as a misguided mainstream liberal movement aimed at protecting privilege and stopping social change. This coincided with the views of planner Bernard Frieden who argued in his 1979 book *The Environmental Hustle* that the environmental movement, which he says had started with quite reasonable attempts to control growth, had become an elitist juggernaut that was increasingly able to impose its own views on the land at the expense of housing affordability and the average American homebuyer.[58] To the political right were figures like Edward Banfield who, in his widely read *The Unheavenly City: The Nature and the Future of Our Urban Crisis* of 1968, was highly skeptical that the disadvantages of sprawl outweighed its advantages or that planners could produce a better system.[59]

Despite these voices of doubt and opposition, there was little organized opposition to the anti-sprawl movement in the United States until the mid-1990s when the movement really started to reach a broad audience. At least initially, opposition to the anti-sprawl movement came primarily from individuals and institutions identified either with the real estate industry or with Libertarian organizations. The first major salvo was a reaction to a 1995 publication called *Beyond Sprawl: New Patterns of Growth to Fit the New California.* The report itself was in many ways unremarkable. It contained a compilation of accepted anti-sprawl wisdom, and it was aimed at citizens in a single state. However, California had long been in the vanguard of debates on land use, and, significantly, the giant and conservative Bank of America had signed on as one of the sponsors. This sponsorship instantly gave it a prominence and credibility it would not otherwise have enjoyed.[60]

To combat the influence of this report, the Building Industry Association of Northern California and the Home Ownership Advancement Foundation commissioned a response from two well-known free-market advocates, University of Southern California faculty members Peter Gordon and Harry Richardson. In their booklet *The Case for Suburban Development,* popularly nicknamed "Beyond beyond Sprawl," they examined, one after another, the diagnoses and prescriptions of the *Beyond Sprawl* report and argued that not only were the alleged problems not sufficient to warrant a wrenching reversal of the building patterns of the previous fifty years, but the proposed remedies would produce cities that were even less convenient and equitable.[61] They went on to engage in a very public debate about sprawl on the pages of the *Journal of the American Planning Association* in 1997 and in many subsequent publications.[62]

Resistance to the standard anti-sprawl arguments soon became a major interest of certain Libertarian think tanks like the Reason Foundation and the Heritage Foundation. Most of these organizations had previously been concerned with mining and grazing rights in the West but otherwise had rarely dealt with urban land-use issues, the environment or aesthetics. With the rapid growth in power of governmental agencies regulating in these areas, Libertarian groups became more engaged. They argued that what they characterized as top-down, "command-and-control" tactics of agencies like the federal Environmental Protection Agency or statewide growth management agencies often did more harm than good because they tended to provide standardized, one-size-fits-all remedies for situations that are very different one from another and very fast changing. These opponents of the anti-sprawl message further argued that big government agencies are rarely able to muster enough information quickly enough to respond to the complexities of actual life and, because they are governed by their own internal sets of incentives and priorities, are likely to ignore many of the negative consequences of their own acts even when these can outweigh the benefits.

The solution for dealing with the negative side effects of sprawl, as many Libertarians saw it, was to remove regulations and restrictions and unleash the power of the free market, which would give millions of individuals with specific and up-to-date local knowledge more power to experiment and deal with fast-changing circumstances. The proper response to things like traffic congestion or pollution, in their opinion, was to turn to market mechanisms that could allocate resources and environmental goods more efficiently and equitably than government agencies. Some of these ideas—particularly the use of emissions rights trading to curb pollution or "congestion pricing" to encourage a more efficient use of highway capacity and provide revenue for increasing mobility—have become popular in a wide political arena, even among many opponents of sprawl.[63] The Libertarian attacks on anti-sprawl advocacy, coupled with the problems that have become evident where anti-sprawl policies have been implemented, together seem to have caused a significant shift in opinion. Even among those who do not consider themselves Libertarians, doubts about the anti-sprawl campaign have become more common.[64]

In the wake of this criticism and in an effort to put a more positive spin on what could easily be seen as a negative message, many anti-sprawl reformers turned to concepts like sustainable growth. However, this term proved to be too fuzzy and too much associated with specifically environmental issues to serve as the banner anti-sprawl advocates were looking for. In the mid-1990s they found their motto in "smart growth."[65] This term had the great virtue of simultaneously incorporating the word "growth," which suggested that people using it were moderate individuals who had repudiated the kind of "no-growth" solutions favored by a previous generation of anti-sprawlers, and the word "smart," which was upbeat and general enough to include a wide variety of approaches. This strategy was so successful that even groups like the National Association of Home Builders and the National Association of Industrial and Office Parks signed on, although their own literature suggested a radically different agenda from the Sierra Club or National Trust.[66]

By the late 1990s the debate over sprawl was raging in print, on the Internet, in Congress, state legislatures and the council chambers of municipalities across the United States.[67] The surest sign that sprawl had finally made its way from technical jargon to popular catchphrase was its appearance on the cover of *Time* magazine on March 22, 1999. The report started with a punchy description of Atlanta: "Once a wilderness, it's now a 13-county eruption, one that has been called the fastest-spreading human settlement in history." The authors positioned Atlanta as a kind of new Los Angeles, contemporary America's prime example of sprawl. "Already more than 110 miles across, up from just 65 in 1990, it consumes an additional 500 acres of field and farmland every week," they continued, echoing the words of William Whyte in *The Exploding Metropolis* of 1958. "What it leaves behind is tract houses, access roads, strip malls, off ramps, industrial parks and billboards advertising more tract houses where the peach trees used to be."[68] Not surprising, given this punchy rhetoric, is the fact that the authors failed to notice, or at least to mention, the burgeoning countermovement attacking the claims of the anti-sprawlers. By 2000 sprawl had become a major issue in state and county elections, and it even made a prominent, if brief, appearance as an issue in the presidential campaign of Al Gore.

Anti-sprawl outside the United States

As the anti-sprawl lobby was coalescing in the United States in the 1990s, it was also increasingly in evidence elsewhere around the world. Where the agitation was mostly British during the first campaign and primarily American in the second, in its third incarnation the message spread across much of the rest of the affluent world. In the case of Europe this was not at all surprising given the enormous financial and emotional investment in the traditional historical urban centers, a long tradition of top-down land-use control and the historic tradition of aristocratic dominance in the countryside. European planners have been more insistent than those anywhere else about maintaining at all costs the supremacy of the historic centers and restricting any development that would seem to erode the urban patterns established before the widespread use of the automobile.[69] According to some authors, this fixation on the historical center has blinded planners and policymakers to the realities of life for most of the residents of the great metropolitan regions.[70]

The same debate is characteristic of Canada and Australia, whose planning systems resemble more closely those in European countries than those in the United States. Particularly in Australia during recent decades, there has been very little "unplanned" peripheral development because local authorities and the state government control development fairly tightly. Still, despite conditions very different from those in the United States, the campaign against it sounds strikingly similar. The reaction against this campaign, however, quite unlike the case in the United States, has more often than not come from the left side of the political spectrum. One of the most important critics of anti-sprawl remedies such as compaction has been Patrick Troy, a scholar interested in questions of urban environment, infrastructure, and equity. He has objected to the importation of anti-sprawl strategies from the United States on the grounds that Australia doesn't have sprawl in the same way the United States does. According to him, the popular anti-sprawl goal of compaction will primarily raise density in outlying settlements, and this will primarily work to cause further harm to those people at the lower end of the social scale by piling them up in the very areas that currently lack good infrastructure and amenities.[71]

Finally, in the 1990s, sprawl even came to be an issue in countries outside the Western world. Although Japan's system of "land readjustment" at the urban periphery is very different from Western practices, urban sprawl or *supuroru* entered the language as a term designating a fate to be avoided.[72] Similar anti-sprawl sentiments have surfaced in every other place that has witnessed a high degree of affluence and a good deal of development, from São Paolo to Singapore to Tel Aviv.[73] By the end of the twentieth century, the anti-sprawl coalition seemed to reach its apogee worldwide.

By the time any coalition becomes really successful in getting out its mes-

Why Has the Anti-sprawl Campaign Been So Successful?

I have argued that anti-sprawl alarmists have presented a picture that is at best a partial one. In some cases the diagnosis of problems caused by sprawl is based on tenuous evidence. In other cases it appears to be incomplete or even just wrong. In either case, such diagnoses rarely take into account the overwhelming evidence that sprawl has been beneficial for many people.

Even where sprawl has clearly created negative consequences, moreover, there seems to be very little evidence that for most people sprawl itself has precipitated any kind of crisis. The vast majority of Americans have responded to a whole battery of polls year after year by saying that they are quite happy with where they live, whether it is the city or a suburb, and they are optimistic about their future. Most objective indicators about American urban life are positive. Americans are more affluent than they have ever been. Home ownership is up. Life spans are up. Most indications of pollution are down. Crime in most cities has declined.

So what explains the current, undeniable popularity of the anti-sprawl crusade? How is it possible that in 1999 a prominent lawyer could open a book with the unqualified assertion that "sprawl is America's most lethal disease," suggesting that it is a problem worse than drug use, crime, unemployment, and poverty?[79] Why has a campaign that was led by a small group of professional people in a few cities during the first and second campaign against sprawl expanded into something that has become a major political force across America and much of the economically advanced world?

I would argue that worries about sprawl have become so important not because conditions are really bad, as the critics suggest, but precisely because conditions are so good.[80] What I mean by this apparent paradox is that during boom years expectations can easily run far ahead of any possibility of fulfilling them. A fast-rising economy can produce a revolution of expectations. I believe it is this revolution in expectations that is responsible for so many contemporary "problems" of all kinds. As Charles Rubin has observed in his history of American environmental reform, infant mortality was not a "problem" until people imagined something could be done about it.[81] No one liked air and water pollution in the nineteenth century, and most people had some idea that there was a strong link between pollution and health problems, but pollution wasn't a "problem," let alone a "crisis," until affluence created the conditions that made it possible for citizens to believe that they could stop it.

sage about a given problem, the original conditions will probably have changed. In the case of anti-sprawl campaign, the roaring economy of the 1990s that fueled the third campaign soon yielded to the economic downturn of the early years of the twenty-first century and, inevitably, some people started to blame the anti-sprawl and smart growth campaigns for this downturn.[74]

The Dynamics of the Anti-sprawl Coalition

When asked, most Americans familiar with the term declare themselves against sprawl just as they say they are against pollution or the destruction of historic buildings. As we have seen, though, the alliance against sprawl is actually more about a set of general attitudes than it is an agreement about any specific set of problems or solutions. This attitude is probably necessary for the anti-sprawl coalition to exist at all. After all, the very neighborhood that one individual targets as sprawl is another family's much loved community. Very few people believe that they themselves live in sprawl. Sprawl is where other people live, particularly people with less taste and good sense than themselves. Much anti-sprawl activism is based on a desire to reform these other people's lives.[75]

In many ways the diagnoses of the anti-sprawl movement mirror those of many other reform movements—the Progressive movement or the Prohibition movement in the early twentieth century, for example. In each case, most individuals and groups genuinely believed that the diagnoses and prescriptions they advocated would help everyone. However, these reformers often had specific targets in mind. For example, a businessman might be thinking primarily about the factory worker whose drinking made him miss work or cause a scene in public. For this reason, many discreet social drinkers, particularly those of high social status, felt justified in continuing to drink after Prohibition was enacted. After all, they weren't part of the problem that the laws were meant to address.

Likewise with sprawl. Although many opponents of sprawl believe their beliefs are based on a rational and disinterested diagnosis of urban problems, their actions often involve powerful, even if usually unacknowledged, self-interest. The self-interest is clear in the case of the New Yorker who owns a weekend home in the Hamptons and rails against the continuing development of Long Island. In similar fashion, families who have recently moved to the suburban periphery are often the most vociferous opponents of further development of exactly the same kind that created their own house because it would destroy their views or reduce their access to the countryside beyond their subdivision. The link with self-interest is often not as clear, as for example in the case of individuals advocating increased mass transit, for example, who are very unlikely to use it much if it is built. They assume that someone else will ride it and free up highway space for themselves.

Moreover, although it might not be a primary motivation, stopping or slowing the growth of new development and sprawl often provides great material advantage to existing residents. It can result in the preservation of open space near them without requiring its public purchase and possible higher taxes. It can work to limit the number of new cars that might drive on the roads that they use. It can, finally, increase the value of their house by limiting the supply of developable land at the periphery, thereby putting upward pressure on housing prices throughout the area. The behavior of a family of this kind provides a good example of what Canadian scholar Michael Poulton has called the incumbents' club. Members of an incumbents' club who have already achieved a great deal of what they want in the way of urban amenity will naturally fight to stop change that might erode their advantages.[76] American scholar William Fischel has made the same kind of argument in his book *The Homevoter Hypothesis*. Because a house often represents a large portion of the total wealth of any family, that family will spend a great deal of time and energy trying to avoid anything that could possibly diminish the value of the house.

Because self-interest is so much a part of almost any large reform effort, and because basic assumptions are so various and so subject to change, anti-sprawl alliances are often unexpected and ephemeral. The anti-sprawl campaign might bring together, if only temporarily, a conservative retired couple in Maine worried about a Wal-Mart outside their village with a young social worker of radical political inclinations living on the Upper West Side of New York, infuriated by what she perceives as the tilt of government funding away from transit riders in Manhattan in favor of suburban SUV owners. A small farmer worried that new suburban neighbors in Des Moines might complain about farm odors, crop spraying, and agricultural vehicles on local roads could easily find himself backing the same kind of stringent land controls as a large residential developer in San Diego who knows that this is politically the acceptable thing to say, that he will be able to pass on the costs of additional regulatory hurdles to the homebuyers, and that his lawyers will be able to negotiate the regulatory processes more efficiently than his smaller competitors. A belief that it is important to go

on record opposing sprawl could well be the only issue on which all of these people would agree.

There seems to be no strong correlation between political affiliation and anti-sprawl. As with the environmental movement or the preservation movement, individuals affronted by sprawl are just as likely to consider themselves conservative as liberal. It appears that the most important factor in pushing individuals toward an anti-sprawl position is class. In general, like the City Beautiful and Prohibition reform movements before it, the anti-sprawl movement has been heavily supported by individuals drawn from an upper-middle-class professional population. The leaders of the movement appear to come overwhelmingly from an elite group of academics, central-city business leaders, and employees of not-for-profit organizations.[77]

One of the oddest aspects of the anti-sprawl campaign is the way it has altered the relationship between progressive and conservative ideas. Many of the leaders of today's anti-sprawl movement came of age during the social and intellectual upheavals of the 1960s. At that time, they usually considered themselves to be progressive in their politics, by which they meant they were ready to expand civil liberties, like free speech, even at the expense of community rights, but at the same time, in the name of community rights like clean air and water, they were willing to advocate a tighter rein on individual property rights.[78] Through this formula, they believed, they could actually solve many centuries-old human problems.

This belief in progress, though, seems to have been short-lived, as heady optimism collided with the complex realities of human society. Within the past several decades, many of the people who still think of themselves as progressive have turned pessimistic and have concluded that things have actually gotten worse rather than better. Not surprisingly, they have looked to conservation and preservation rather than the development of new resources or new technologies, to limiting growth rather than aiding it, and to re-creating urban forms of previous eras rather than experimenting with new settlement patterns.

This position puts them squarely in the camp of many traditional conservatives, who have always been more interested in maintaining what exists than forging ahead with a strong belief in the possibilities of progress. The anti-sprawl movement is a powerful compound of this new progressivism and a traditional conservatism. It seems to be part of a widespread erosion of confidence in the future and an increased desire to create a utopia of the past.

Many Americans today crusade against urban conditions that even fifty years ago were considered perfectly normal and acceptable by most of the public. A half century ago, a substantial percentage of houses in many American cities lacked full indoor plumbing and central heating. Now that the vast majority of residents in virtually every major city in the developed world can take for granted so many things that were once luxuries and that we now consider necessities, from indoor plumbing to Internet service, many more people have been able to ratchet up their demands and expectations. Now they are able to mount major campaigns to stop the destruction of habitat of an endangered species of snake or the construction of a parking lot on a wetland area. To most observers fifty years ago, these would hardly have been considered problems, let alone things that required major corrective action.[82]

In the short history of sprawl diagnoses that we have just rehearsed, it has been conspicuous that the chorus of complaints about growth swelled during the boom periods, for example, in London in the eighteenth century, in Paris during the rebuilding by Napoléon III, or in the 1990s in Los Angeles or Atlanta. It is true, of course, that these boom periods did produce problems. Certainly the Parisian family displaced from an apartment in the path of a new boulevard in the 1860s would not have been happy about having to move to a tenement building in the suburbs. It is also indisputable that the wealth generated in all of these booms has tended to be very unevenly distributed. However, in all of these instances, even with vast inequalities, virtually everyone, even at the very bottom of the socioeconomic scale, eventually experienced an increased standard of living and a feeling of rising expectations. In fact, London in the eighteenth century or Paris in the mid-nineteenth century are today considered by many to have been golden ages.

Is it so inconceivable that in fifty years Los Angeles and Atlanta in the 1990s might not be seen in a similar way? Of course it is difficult to achieve any kind of perspective on long-term benefits in cities that are hurtling at breakneck speed into a future that no one can envision and where short-term annoyances loom so large. Consider, for a moment, the thunderous din of complaints about traffic in Los Angeles. From one perspective, this reaction is bizarre. Even when speeds on the freeway decline to twenty miles per hour, drivers throughout the Los Angeles area move much more quickly than they do by car or by public transportation at the center of almost any large, older industrial city in Europe or the United States. It is clearly not that congestion is objectively worse in Los Angeles; it is that the highway building program of the 1950s and 1960s was so successful in reducing congestion that people became used to being able drive across the entire metropolitan area at fifty miles per hour, dramatically expanding their choices in living, working, and recreational environments in the process. Since then, as the population and density continued to grow but road building slowed because of political pressures, this squeeze produced the inevitable result: more congestion. Some Los Angeles residents apparently now find themselves even more frustrated about traffic than residents of Paris or New York City. The reason for this has little to do with the traffic itself, however, and everything to do with the fact that residents of Paris or New York City never entertained the possibility that they would be able to drive through the center of the city at fifty miles per hour. The problem in Los Angeles is the sharp deflation of the greatly raised expectations.

The unprecedented concern about sprawl at the turn of the twenty-first century is an indication of how much expectations have risen for most ordinary urban dwellers. The most important reason that urban change has become such an issue in Los Angeles or Atlanta is not because these are inherently undesirable places to live. Quite the contrary. It has been because these places have been so attractive that so many new residents have flooded in and so much has changed so quickly. A great deal of this change has been beneficial for much of the population. These cities have generated enormous numbers of jobs and vast wealth for a tremendous number of people. Of course, as in all other cities throughout history, there have been problems. Jobs are lost as the economy changes. People are forced out of neighborhoods where they have lived for much of their lives.

For some of these problems there are solutions, and the problems will simply disappear as issues as boom periods fade and citizens adjust their lives to avoid the dislocations and imbalances. For other problems there are no real solutions because they involve a clash in goals and desires among different parts of the population. In these cases, most people will eventually learn to live with the consequences. The agitation against sprawl is evidence of a widespread feeling that many long-standing urban problems can be cured. This, by itself, is a positive development. What is far less positive is that so much of this energy is being directed toward things that may not be real problems or problems that can't be solved without causing severe unintended consequences and real losses for part of the population.[83] It is to these solutions and unintended consequences that we now turn.

PART 3

the prescription: remedies for sprawl

11 Early Remedies: *From Anti-blight to Anti-sprawl*

In parts 1 and 2 of this book as I traced the history of what we would now call sprawl and the changing nature of the complaints made against it, I noted in passing various attempts to control unplanned decentralization. These appear to go back in history as far as cities themselves, as kings and queens and municipal authorities tried, usually in vain, to halt the outward dispersal of people and activities from their cities. We know, for example, that already in the sixteenth century, Queen Elizabeth attempted to try to halt growth around London by issuing an edict prohibiting building at the edges of the city. In the seventeenth century, French kings likewise attempted to stop all further growth outside the walls around Paris. Like virtually every subsequent effort to halt sprawl, these attempts were largely a failure, and London and Paris continued to expand outward.[1]

It has only been in the twentieth century, in fact during the second half of the twentieth century, that any really sustained efforts have been mounted to stop sprawl. In this part of the book, I will consider some of these efforts. This history has been filled with curious twists and paradoxes. One of the most curious is the fact that many of the remedies to combat low-density sprawl in recent years are very similar to the remedies devised over a hundred years ago to combat high-density "blight." The word "blight" had its origins in horticulture, referring to a small, nearly microscopic insect that attacked plants. In the seventeenth century, the word had entered common speech as a more general term that meant a "baleful influence of mysterious or invisible origin."[2] By the end of the nineteenth century, it was commonly used to describe the way densely settled city neighborhoods seemed to breed physical and social pathologies, disease, social unrest, and crime. This was the assumption of American housing expert Lawrence Veiller when, at a planning conference in the 1920s, he called blight a "civic cancer that must be cut out by the surgeon's knife."[3] The implication was that blight was a kind of impersonal, external pathogen that had to be removed by a skilled practitioner, in this case a trained planner, to ensure the health of the rest of the organism.

In the early twentieth century the need to reduce densities at the center of the city was usually put at the top of the list of urban problems to be tackled by architects and practitioners of the new profession of city planning. In the most extreme version were the schemes of individuals who wished to see the old city disappear completely, to be replaced by highly decentralized landscapes.

By far the best known early advocate of radical dispersal was undoubtedly Ebenezer Howard, a minor British government bureaucrat at the turn of the previous century, who propounded the "garden city" concept.[4] Howard felt that the old industrial cities were obsolete. His relatively low-density garden cities would be constructed beyond the built-up area of the existing city as a way of alleviating the problems of booming but congested cities, on the one hand, and an economically struggling and culturally impoverished countryside, on the other. He envisioned new, self-contained communities of limited size, each strictly separated from adjoining settlements by a green agricultural belt and each connected back to the core city by roads and railroads. His ideal settlement unit would have contained 30,000 people living on 1,000 acres, surrounded by a 5,000-acre greenbelt housing another 2,000 people. The city would own all of the land and rent it to the citizens. It would be self-governed and self-managed, providing all kinds of social services for its citizens and financed by the rise in rents due to the rise in the value of the land.[5] It was a full-fledged and comprehensive utopia.

The text and diagrams that accompanied later editions of Howard's books have had a prodigious history in subsequent Western planning. The attack on the dense city was echoed by German architect Bruno Taut, who wrote a tract titled "Dissolution of the City"; the Russian "disurbanists," who wished to replace the older cities with new urban forms, for example, linear cities laid out along rail lines and highways; and perhaps the most radical of all, American architect Frank Lloyd Wright, who advocated a "Broadacre City," in which the population of the entire American nation would be dispersed at extraordinarily low densities across the landscape and rely heavily on the automobile and small flying vehicles that he envisioned as looking like personal helicopters.[6] Few of these radical schemes had much practical consequence.

More moderate variants of the garden city have thrived. The idea of the well-shaped utopian town, its form clearly defined by a greenbelt, with a careful balance of jobs and housing, buildings and green space, industry and agriculture, has inspired urban reformers ever since. It is the same kind of program seen in early twentieth-century British garden cities like Letchworth or Welwyn Garden City; American greenbelt cities of the interwar years, like Greenbelt, Maryland, or Greendale Wisconsin; American New Towns of the postwar years, like Columbia, Maryland, and Reston, Virginia; and the New Urbanist communities of the last two decades. Today it is accepted wisdom among many planners and smart growth advocates everywhere. That the remedies for high-density blight look very much like the remedies for low-density sprawl suggests that from the beginning many experts thought they had the answer to urban problems. They just needed to find the correct problem to solve with it.

In practice, none of the theories of good city form have worked out the way their advocates had hoped. If the Garden City Movement had been successful, for example, and new garden cities had actually been built to accommodate any substantial percentage of London's population, they would have produced a polka-dot pattern of hundreds of towns, each within its greenbelt, altogether covering thousands of square miles of countryside. A vast sprawl would have been inevitable given the overall low densities in Howard's scheme, a mere 5,000 people per square mile, about the same as a great many American suburbs. Because a town of 30,000 cannot support a very wide variety of employment, recreational, and cultural opportunities, moreover, residents of any given town would either have had to forgo most choices or they would have had to travel extensively between garden cities to obtain the kinds of opportunities offered by a large metropolis. The result would have been a low-density, discontinuous, multicentered metropolitan structure that might have looked different from typical American suburban regions today, but without drastic limits on affluence and mobility, it would probably have ended up functioning in distinctly similar ways.

This is not surprising since the reformers had no way of eliminating the tensions inherent in any community, between the desire for self-containment and clear urban form, on the one hand, and maximum opportunities and the ability to adapt to changing conditions, on the other. Neither the internal contradictions nor the practical problems seem to have daunted the generations of urban reformers across the globe who have tried to put Howard's ideas into practice. Despite all the efforts of garden city planners in the affluent Western world, the population has never really embraced garden cities and relatively few have ever been built. Those that have been built and have been successful have almost always done so not by functioning as self-contained places but by functioning essentially as suburbs for nearby cities.

Even if Howard's specific remedies were largely ineffective, his basic goal of reducing densities at the center of the existing cities and funneling the population into carefully controlled developments at the edge has remained the principal goal of most professional city planners at least until the end of the boom following World War II. Over this period, as we saw in part 1, densities did, in fact, decline dramatically in most central cities of the affluent world. As we also saw, planners probably had less to do with this than did many other factors—most important among them, a spectacular rise in affluence. This is apparent in the fact that densities declined faster in cities in the United States, which had a great deal of economic growth but comparatively little large-scale public land-use planning, than they did in Europe, where the reverse was the case. In either place, as soon as they could afford to do it, urban families poured out of the dense city neighborhoods and into lower-density settlements farther out.

12 Postwar Anti-sprawl Remedies

Despite the fact that almost all British planners in the early twentieth century advocated urban dispersal, when it really happened on a large scale in the inter-war years, they were horrified. The semidetached housing estates and residential and commercial strips that appeared along the many new urban bypass roads were not at all what they had had in mind. In an effort to control this kind of growth they pressured Parliament to pass legislation to deter ribbon (or strip) development, establish greenbelts around major cities, and permit various kinds of design review.[1]

This campaign was interrupted by the outbreak of World War II but not abandoned. In fact, it was during the darkest years of the war that a small group of planners created a series of splendidly produced reconstruction schemes that were intended to guide the rebuilding of postwar Britain (fig. 30). By far the most important example of these was the famous *Greater London Plan* of 1944, written by an austere and patrician British town planner named Patrick Abercrombie.[2] Following Ebenezer Howard and other garden city advocates, Abercrombie saw the crowding of the central city and sprawl at the edge of the metropolis as the twin evils of modern urbanization. His remedy, in great part derived from the Garden City Movement, called for massive clearance and thinning out at the center of London, a strengthened greenbelt around the already built-up area, and a series of new towns based on garden city principles in the "Outer Country."[3]

Shortly after the war, with the British economy in ruins, the Labour Party swept into power with an agenda for radical change. Labour leaders seized the

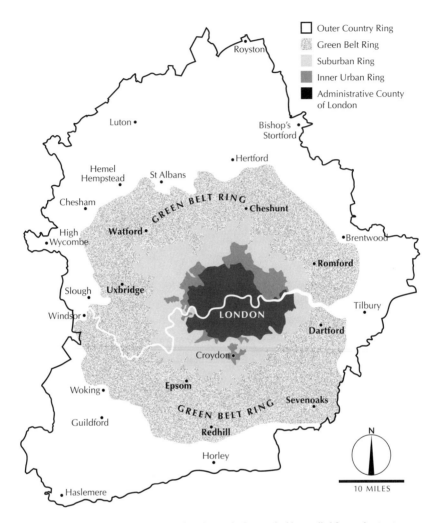

Figure 30. *Greater London Plan* of 1944. Although British planners had long called for a reduction in densities at the core of their cities, they were horrified at what they saw during the 1920s and 1930s when thousands of middle- and working-class London families poured out of the city and into suburban housing developments, particularly the semi-detached houses seen in figure 4. During the war these planners imagined a postwar urban Britain where government officials could curb this unsightly sprawl by the use of severe restrictions on development, greenbelts to stop the outward flow, and a series of new towns in the area beyond the greenbelt to accommodate the overflow population. The plan for greater London drawn up by Patrick Abercrombie, shown here, was the most famous of these. After World War II, the new Labour government gave the planners much of what they called for, including the remarkable step of nationalizing all development rights. Although this plan had a major effect on the landscape, it is very difficult to argue that it has reduced sprawl in Britain. Some observers have argued that it has actually pushed it farther out. (Redrawn by Dennis McClendon from Patrick Abercrombie, *Greater London Plan 1944* [London: HMSO, 1945], facing p. 30.)

opportunity to put into place dramatic new national land-use policies based on ideas long advocated by planners like Thomas Sharp and Patrick Abercrombie. The Town and Country Planning Act of 1947 and a barrage of related legislation completely changed the rules of the game for development in Britain. Most important, development rights on land were nationalized. This meant that existing owners would be allowed to use the land as they had in the past, but they were not allowed to develop it further without the express approval of local authorities. In return, they were paid for giving up the right to develop at will. This startling shift in the notion of property rights was made possible by what, at first glance, would appear to be an unlikely alliance between the Labour government, with its avowedly socialist policies, and the extremely conservative great landowners who had a large percentage of the land in the country under their control.

In reality, the deal made perfect sense for both parties. Many of the great landowners were in dire financial straits after World War II. When Parliament agreed on a plan that allowed them not only to continue to enjoy their rural estates but also to do so with much greater freedom from encroachment by ordinary middle-class citizens and, most remarkable of all, to receive payment from the government for the loss of development rights to boot, it was really one of the best things that had happened to them in an otherwise inhospitable century. The deal had consequences far less happy for ordinary middle-class and working-class families since any substantial amount of land removed from the market made it much more difficult and expensive for developers to create badly needed new housing.

This new legislation set the stage for the implementation of reconstruction plans like the one for London. Like the new land-use laws, the Abercrombie plan was at once highly conservative and quite radical. It was radical in the scope of government intervention into land use, reversing a centuries-long trend in which land ownership and land-use decisions had devolved from the central authority of kings and nobles to individuals and municipalities. This radical step was in the service of a program that was, at base, very conservative in its most basic notions about society, politics, and aesthetics. The city would remain the city, although reduced somewhat in density. The country would continue to serve, much as it had done in the past, as the preserve of wealth and privilege.[4] The overspill from the city and any growth would be accommodated in discreet new towns based on garden city principles and scattered around the area outside the greenbelt. This scheme assured that, as much as possible, the

most affluent residents of the city center and the countryside would be insu-
lated from change.

This was very much top-down planning. In fact, it is clear that Abercrombie
believed that the national government would not only dictate what would be
built but would itself do most of the actual building, presumably under the
watchful eye of high-minded and expert bureaucrats like himself. Free-market
development would be rendered inconsequential. This was greater discretion
than that enjoyed by even the most powerful European monarchs of the abso-
lutist era, and it was just as conservative. "Change was regarded in general as
a challenge to be resisted," according to Peter Hall, who collaborated in the
1970s on the most extensive analysis of the London growth management system. "The basic values were those of conservation of the existing order. Once-
for-all changes were in order, but once they were complete, the whole system
would settle down in a steady state."[5]

The London plan, like many anti-sprawl plans since, was based on a simple
and static view of the proper shape of the city. Although for a number of centuries London had actually leapfrogged outward in tentacle-like fashion along
transportation routes, in Abercrombie's diagrams the city was shown as a
series of concentric rings. Abercrombie's concentric circles suggested, probably
not altogether unconsciously, a desire to repudiate the untidiness of the democratic, industrial city of the nineteenth and twentieth centuries and return to
the order of the European city from medieval times through the era of absolut-
ist monarchs when city form was dictated by central authority and the building
of successive walls. Abercrombie's concentric circles may also have been based
in part on diagrams created to analyze the city, for example, the recent but
already famous diagrams of Chicago sociologists Park and Burgess. Even more
likely, the Abercrombie diagram was modeled after the diagrams of ideal urban
settlements as formulated by Ebenezer Howard and his garden city followers.

Like the commonly used schematic diagrams of an atom with electrons rac-
ing around a nucleus or the surprisingly similar diagrams used to model the
solar system with planets circling the sun, simple geometric diagrams of cities
can seem to mirror an eternal "natural" order. Of course, already by the time
Abercrombie was working, everyone knew that none of these natural phenomena were as tidy as the diagrams suggested. In fact, it had become increasingly
clear, as the twentieth century progressed, that most natural systems were infinitely complex and seemingly chaotic. But for Abercrombie, as for many plan-

ners and urban reformers before and since, planning was about rejecting the apparently chaotic in favor of a simple, easily comprehensible order.

Well before all of the basic legislation had been put into place, many of the assumptions on which Abercrombie's plan had been based were already out of date. Postwar growth turned out to be faster than anticipated. When Britain's economy started to rebound, the desire by middle-class residents for more personal space and for the increased personal mobility afforded by automobile ownership was greater than anticipated. Moreover, the population proved to be unwilling to leave all decisions in the hands of expert bureaucrats. When the conservatives regained power in 1951, they abandoned the attempt by the state to maintain the central role in real estate development that Abercrombie envisioned. After a checkered experience with new towns over the next two decades, including one remarkable attempt—at Milton Keynes, the last of the major new towns—to break with older traditions and emulate the patterns of Los Angeles, these were all but abandoned. [6]

In retrospect, the British system might be considered a success in many ways. It did lower densities at the core and it did stop uncontrolled low-density development at the edge. Americans visiting Britain to this day are often startled when they come to the last house or apartment building in a British suburb and see undisturbed fields beyond or they drive along the M25, the London Orbital Motorway, and see mostly pristine countryside even though they know they are nowhere near the edge of the London conurbation. Farther afield, many village centers have retained their rural charm. The British countryside today shows that reformers were able to achieve many of the things that they had campaigned for.

In the British planning system, however, as in any major urban reform effort, for every silver lining, there tends to be a dark cloud. Although the governmental regulations did stop building in many areas of the greenbelt, the British policies also strongly constrained the supply of land, which in turn drove prices up dramatically. Land prices in London, like those in Europe generally, rose very dramatically on the imposition of restrictive postwar planning mechanisms. While the greenbelt did stop the continuous wave of development pouring outward from central London, the combined capacity of the land within the greenbelt and the new towns was insufficient to house everyone at the densities that most people preferred. Many families were obliged to live at higher densities than they would have wished or else settle even farther out than they otherwise would have done. Because jobs did not move out as fast as the residential population, the result was probably even longer commutes than would have been the case if uncontrolled development had continued. In addition, because the vast majority of the residents of the relatively low-density outer reaches of the London metropolitan area soon bought and used automobiles for most of their travel needs, traffic congestion grew dramatically. By the end of the century and despite a massive public transportation system, the London urban area had some of the greatest traffic congestion among major cities in the world.[7] Also, despite a thicket of legislation designed to protect small shopkeepers in the historic urban centers, large shopping centers and enormous supermarkets have appeared within and at the periphery of almost all British cities.[8] Many former country towns, although well protected from physical change, have witnessed massive economic and demographic change as they have lost their intimate connection with the working agricultural landscape around them and have instead become gentrified exurban communities serving far-away cities.

Although it is notoriously difficult to prove or disprove an assertion of this kind, it is quite possible that the greenbelt and the planning system as a whole accelerated rather than slowed the decentralization and outward sprawl of London. It is also quite possible that tight planning control, by concentrating power in the hands of a relatively small professional elite group and tightly restraining physical change, may have slowed down social and economic change as well. What seems indisputable is that the British growth management system, like almost all anti-sprawl policies, was most favorable for what I have called the incumbents' club: those who were already well off and happy with their existing circumstances.[9]

Given all of these apparent contradictions, it is perhaps not surprising that even though planners had gotten most of the tools that they wanted, already by the mid-1950s dissatisfaction with British planning was widespread both inside and outside the planning profession.[10] On the one side, there was unhappiness in many families who were still warehoused in dense central neighborhoods and found themselves unable to move into new houses at the periphery because of the controls and the high land values. On the other side, many of those in the circle of the reformers who had pushed for the drastic measures in the first place looked at the results and were intensely unhappy with what they saw. A good example of this disenchantment can be seen in the writing of architect Ian Nairn. In a special issue of the most important British design journal,

Architectural Review, published in 1955, he decried exactly the conditions that the British planning system was supposed to have stopped. "The city today is not so much a growing as a spreading thing, fanning out over the land surface in the shape of suburban sprawl," Nairn wrote, calling it a "thing of terror" that had the power to "get you up sweating at night." [11]

Anti-sprawl Remedies on the Continent

The emphasis on state control of development patterns was a common theme in cities throughout the continent of Europe during the postwar years. In the interwar years, many affluent northern European cities had experienced, like Britain, an explosion in the scale of privately built suburban development, usually encouraged by national laws and incentives to aid dispersal of the overcrowded cities. After the war, in part to cope with the pressing demands of national reconstruction but perhaps also as a reversion to a long European tradition of top-down planning, many national governments seized important new planning powers. The force at the top of this planning system in the second half of the twentieth century was no longer a king or group of noblemen. Their place had been taken by upper-middle-class professional bureaucrats trained in elite national schools devoted to engineering, architecture, and governmental administration. This bureaucracy was at the apogee of its powers in the first two decades after World War II. [12]

In virtually every European country the result was the same. The production of private single-family houses was sharply curtailed in favor of large apartment blocks, often built by the state. In the Paris region, for example, government agencies presided over a gentrifying historic core that lost a great deal of its working-class population as this population was decanted into the burgeoning suburban belt. Within the inner suburbs arose a series of enormous housing projects, or *grands ensembles,* built using public moneys. [13] Beyond the inner suburbs, growth was channeled by a series of regional plans into a set of axes extending out from Paris and incorporating a new set of regional centers. [14]

Much of this top-down planning and management proved to be unacceptable as the European economies rebounded, however. By the end of the 1960s, this system was under attack. Critics derided the large publicly funded housing projects. The policies aimed at preserving the status quo in the countryside became more difficult to enforce given the demands of a newly affluent population. As European city dwellers became more affluent, they tended to buy cars and drive just as Americans had done earlier, and they were increasingly less willing to take jobs just because they were close to home or accessible by transit. Families started to move more frequently, both within cities and between cities. They were increasingly able to afford to live in single-family detached houses, and they increasingly demanded the convenience and low prices of outlying shopping centers.

The American City and the "Quiet Revolution"

Despite the paradoxes and unintended consequences that accompanied the British and European campaigns against sprawl, many American planners in the postwar decades looked on with envy. Compared with the furious pace and apparently chaotic form of development at the periphery of American cities, growth around British or Scandinavian cities seemed slower and more orderly. In contrast to the marginal role that planners felt they were able to play in the United States, European planners, particularly the Scandinavian and British planners, seemed to have much more influence on land-use decisions. During the second campaign against sprawl, a broad coalition of American reformers pushed for a system closer to the ones used in northern Europe. This inaugurated a tremendous burst of optimism about the possibilities for public planning and rational growth management.[15]

The desire to push land-use decisions upward in the governmental hierarchy met with resistance, though. The U.S. Constitution, by giving the federal government very little power over land use, reserved most of these rights to the states. In actual practice, the states had traditionally delegated day-to-day control to the counties and municipalities on the assumption that local residents were best able to understand and deal with the particular problems of their own area. Top-down land planning had long been considered by many Americans to be not only ineffective but also undemocratic. After the great bursts of reform activism of the 1960s, however, many reformers believed that the time was ripe to push land-use planning upward in the governmental hierarchy. For reformers, the advantage of planning at higher levels of government was twofold. First, they believed that the fragmentation of local government made planning difficult because of duplication of efforts and competitive and contradictory policies.[16] In addition, they assumed that at the higher levels of government it would be easier to legislate what reformers considered better land-use choices, and the states could afford more skilled professional planners who would, sup-posedly, be less swayed by local political pressures.[17]

It appeared for a while that this trend—soon dubbed the "quiet revolu-tion" because it was done state by state and apparently by many individuals and groups acting without any centralized command structure—would be suc-cessful. The first state to enact some kind of statewide land-use planning was Hawaii in 1961. Hawaii was quite different from the other states in its history and physical characteristics, however, and this legislation was primarily a kind of statewide zoning. With the enactment of more ambitious legislation in Ver-mont in 1970, Florida in 1972, and Oregon in 1973, however, the movement seemed to be well underway. By 1975, at least twenty states had environmental land-use planning laws and thirty-five states had statewide planning bodies or mechanisms in place to review local planning efforts.[18] This development was greeted with euphoria by some anti-sprawl reformers. Other observers were not impressed and saw in these initiatives just another tool for large business and government elites to impose their will.[19]

As we saw in chapter 9, anti-sprawl reformers believed that the culmina-tion of their attempts to push land-use planning upward in the governmental hierarchy would be a national land-use law, analogous to the national environ-mental legislation of the early 1970s. There was a flurry of activity in Congress in the 1970s to enact such a law, one that would, in the opinion of reformers, formalize a necessary and massive reorientation of American land-use practice. The law would ratify the assumption that individual property rights had to be more clearly subordinated to regional and national policies and to the practices specified by experts in reports like that of the Task Force on Land and Urban Growth.[20] It was also hoped that such a law would reduce considerably the ability of local citizens and groups to oppose "good" regional planning initia-tives. The optimism was short-lived. Resistance to national land-use policy, like resistance to national industrial policy, came from a wide range of individuals concerned with maintaining individual rights and local initiative against what they saw as their usurpation by big business and big government.[21] The pro-posed national land-use legislation finally died during the economic downturn of the mid-1970s. By this time, even though the national land-use policy had failed and only a few states had adapted statewide planning policies, the anti-sprawl forces could console themselves with large increases in federal funding during the 1960s and 1970s for local planning, public transportation, and open space acquisition.

Regional Planning Efforts and Washington, DC

If anti-sprawl reformers were only partly successful at the state and federal level, they seemed, at least at first, to be more effective in certain urban areas. At the conference on sprawl organized by William Whyte for *Fortune* magazine around 1957, the assembled experts had no trouble arriving at a remedy for sprawl.[22] The centerpiece of their program was a recommendation that local governments follow the example of certain European cities and get control of land around the existing built-up fabric. They could do this in several ways. The first was by simple regulation. This was the least expensive but the least attractive to reformers because there could be massive opposition from property owners and any such regulations could be altered. Better would be to follow the British example and have public authorities buy up development rights around every city or, even more attractive, the cities could actually buy the land itself.[23] The most important model here was Stockholm where, through much of the twentieth century, the municipal government had been buying peripheral land and directing growth by the extension of new "Tunnelbana" or subway lines to planned new settlements like Vällingby built around the stops (fig. 31).[24] American interest in cities like Stockholm and new towns like Vällingby and Tapiola, outside of Helsinki, was part of a vast wave of enthusiasm by reformers for all things Scandinavian and Nordic whether in matters of design or in the political and economic sphere where the Swedes were developing the notion of a "third way" between capitalism and socialism.[25]

Using the new federal funding for planning, a number of the nation's large metropolitan areas drafted plans for regional development. Like the 1944 *Greater London Plan,* the purpose was to renew and rebuild the center and impose an order on supposedly chaotic peripheral development. One of the earliest and most characteristic of these plans was a scheme proposed in the 1960s for Washington, DC.[26] A basic policy plan issued by the National Capitol Planning Commission in 1961 presented a series of alternative growth patterns. The first, "formless sprawl," was the one that the planners believed was actually happening at the time and one they rejected as being wholly unsatisfactory. A second, and better alternative, they believed, might be a highly compact metropolitan area interrupted only by a few green areas along streambeds—in other words, like many compact southern European cities. A third possibility was to maintain the current built-up area but to establish large new satellite cities located some thirty miles from central Washington, DC, on the model of British garden

Figure 31. The planners' dream. In the postwar decades, many American planners made pilgrimages to Sweden and Finland to see the ideal urban future. In Sweden they were thrilled to find a country with a high standard of living, an apparently solid national consensus to build a "third way" between capitalism and socialism, and what many considered to be the highest average design standards in the world. They also found a model for urban development. Vällingby was a compact master-planned town whose high-density center, pictured here, was located directly above the station of the "Tunnelbana," the underground rail link back to central Stockholm. Many of these towns are still tremendously attractive to planners and numerous other observers today, but as logical as the concept may have been, it turned out not to be the urban future in Stockholm or elsewhere in the world. With its freeways, shopping centers, and big-box Ikea stores, much of suburban Stockholm looks more like suburban America than like Vällingby. (Photograph by Robert Bruegmann, 2000.)

cities. The planners were dubious about the success of any of these schemes, however, so they settled on a fourth scheme that would mandate developments along transit lines radiating outward from downtown Washington, DC, like the spokes of a wheel (fig. 32). This scheme was further refined in a 1964 plan entitled *On Wedges and Corridors* prepared by the Maryland–National Capital Park and Planning Commission.[27]

The idea here was both an extrapolation into the future of the way the region had grown in the past along transit lines and a clear nod to the plans of Euro-

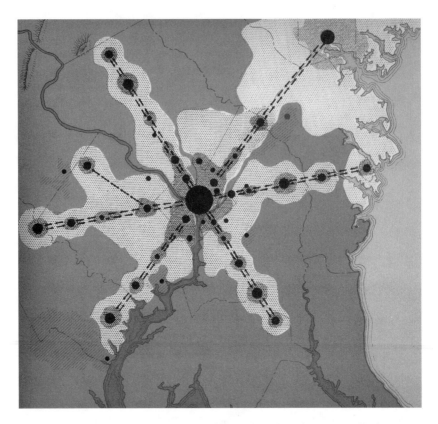

Figure 32. Fighting sprawl in America's Capitol. In this "radial corridor" scheme proposed by the National Capitol Planning Commission in 1961, growth in the Washington, DC, area would be confined to transportation corridors. This kind of plan, adapted from models developed by planners in European cities like Copenhagen, Stockholm, and Hamburg, was in many ways the opposite of the London scheme, in which growth was to be constrained by a roughly circular greenbelt. All of these proposals, however, whether concentric or radial, betray a strong preference for logical order and simple geometries over the messy realities of actual urban growth. And, of course, by the time this scheme was proposed, there was little likelihood that mass transit could ever again serve as the major determinant of metropolitan form as it had in the past. (National Capital Planning Commission, *A Policies Plan for the Year 2000* [Washington: U.S. Government Printing Office, 1961].)

pean cities such as Copenhagen, Stockholm, or Hamburg.[28] The *Wedges and Corridors* plan showed illustrations of suburban rail stations with urbane plazas in front of them, bounded by retail spaces and high apartment buildings, all of it looking very much like Vällingby or Tapiola. Although the report suggested areas of lower density beyond these centers, the authors clearly believed that a high percentage of residents in the metropolitan area would live in the dense concentrations around the transit stops and use public transit as their primary means of getting around the metropolitan area. Denser development in the corridors would, in turn, allow wedges of green to extend deep into the area between the corridors.

Enthusiasm ran high among the planners, particularly after 1965 when Congress approved initial funding for Metro, the massive new commuter rail system for the Washington, DC, metropolitan area. If any city in the United States had a chance to make this kind of plan work it was Washington. The federal government not only controlled the administration of the district but was by far the largest employer as well. It was in the unique position of being able to control the location of jobs and to provide the billions of dollars necessary for the new rail network that was expected to be the backbone of the system. However, the report acknowledged that in order for this scheme to succeed it would take a wholesale reworking of local governmental structures, a vast planning apparatus, and an unprecedented insertion of new regulations into the development process.

Although the plans for metropolitan Washington had some effect, particularly in the Maryland suburbs, it is fair to say that in any larger assessment that impact was not great. By the time the plans were issued, it was already clear that the old pattern, in which development had followed rail lines, was already a thing of the past. As soon as the automobile had freed developers and residents from clustering close to railroad stations, most development took place away from the transit corridors. This pattern had been established already in the 1920s. The plans for the Capitol region, like a great many attempts at planning in both Europe and America, were based on an attempt to turn the clock back. This sometimes worked, at least for a while, in Europe where there was a long history of top-down central planning extending back to the days of the absolute monarchs, but plans of this kind usually proved to be impractical in affluent, sprawling, middle-class America, and so it was in the Washington area. The Metro has had some influence on development around Washington. Dense new nodes have developed at some of the stops, for example, at Ballston in Virginia and some of the older suburban downtowns such as Silver Spring, Maryland, have witnessed considerable redevelopment. However, at most of these nodes, location near an expressway has probably been more important than the fact that there was a rail station. Maryland has had some success over the years in concentrating new development in designated radial fingers. The overall effect on the metropolitan area, however, has been surprisingly slight, given the high hopes of planners and the large expenditures of federal money.

The New Town Experiment

The Washington, DC, area did witness two of the most important American attempts to create garden cities along the lines proposed by Howard. Reston, Virginia, and Columbia, Maryland, were privately developed new towns intended to be compact and transit-oriented and with a balance of jobs and housing. In the end, Reston and Columbia did become successful communities and did attract a very enthusiastic resident population. What they did not do was to provide models for stopping sprawl. The fact that they were master planned did allow for coordination of infrastructure and a good many economies of scale. At the same time, the massive investments required up front in such master-planned communities made them more vulnerable to business downturns and to changes in the market. In both of these cases, the original development team failed financially, and the projects had to be reorganized.

Nor were these two communities notably successful in a number of other goals. The planners had hoped that if they achieved a balance of housing and jobs in the community, residents would take these jobs and drive less. They also proposed elaborate experiments in public transit. Neither effort was successful. As the British new town planners discovered decades earlier, ambitious residents of any given community are quite likely to find better jobs somewhere else in the region than in the town where they happen to live. The result was that a high percentage of the residents of Reston or Columbia found jobs elsewhere, and most of the jobs in these communities were taken by individuals who commuted from elsewhere. Given the overall low gross densities—no more than 6,500 people per square mile in Reston, the denser of the two in the initial plans, and just over 3,000 people per square mile for both in 2000—it is not surprising that residents of both places use the automobile much like suburbanites anywhere else. In the end, despite all of the careful planning and high-minded architectural design, these towns function much like any other middle-class suburbs.[29]

The federal government's involvement in new town development was even less successful. In legislation passed in 1968 and 1970, the federal government proposed to help private developers create large new towns. The legislation included highly optimistic wording that suggested that these new towns would demonstrate how to stop inefficient land use, prevent the loss of open space and natural resources, provide good housing, increase the choice of housing available to citizens, reduce segregation by class and race, and bolster public transportation. They were expected to house millions of people by the year 2000.[30]

In the end, this scheme turned out to be a near-total failure. Only one of the federally designated new towns, the Woodlands, outside Houston, was successful as a real estate venture. While it was undoubtedly important as an experiment in ecological design, it can hardly be said to have created an attractive alternative to standard development practices.[31] In fact, the location of the Woodlands, far north of the existing development in the Houston region, probably did more to abet than deter sprawl as it has acted like a magnet drawing a vast amount of new construction out from central Houston in its direction. Every single one of the other projects was either abandoned or drastically scaled back.[32] Not only did they not provide a model that developers everywhere wanted to emulate, but critics like Jane Jacobs charged that they were drawing resources away from the revitalization of town centers.[33] In short, large-scale efforts of the 1960s and the 1970s to channel growth on a metropolitan scale, revitalize the center, and provide compact new settlements on the edge, despite vast amounts of funding, never had much of an impact on overall growth patterns.

Local Efforts: No Growth and Slow Growth in Boulder, Colorado

Several local efforts had a far greater impact, although the results of these efforts were ultimately ambiguous at best. Most important was a set of local no-growth or slow-growth initiatives. The goals and methods were quite varied and were sometimes even contradictory, but all of them had in common a desire to stop sprawl or, at least, to slow it down.[34] Another thing that characterized almost all American local efforts to control sprawl in this era was a reluctance to follow the example of Sweden or Britain and buy land or at least development rights. Instead, almost all American attempts to stop sprawl have been based on government regulation.

One partial exception can be seen in what was perhaps the most ambitious attempt to control sprawl in the postwar decades, the one put into place by the municipal government of Boulder, Colorado, in the 1960s.[35] Boulder was a small affluent city enjoying a spectacular site at the foot of the Rocky Mountains, the presence of a large and reliable source of good jobs—the University of Colorado—and easy access to Denver, one of the most dynamic urban regions in the United States in the postwar era. Because of these advantages, and not surprisingly, a great many people wanted to move to Boulder, resulting in a dramatic population growth in the 1950s. This, in turn, led many existing residents to feel that the rapid growth, what they called "Denverization," had led to increased pollution, congestion, social problems, and a decline in the quality of life.

Citizens responded with a concerted campaign to slow or stop residential and commercial growth. In 1967, voters approved a greenbelt around the city and a sales tax increase to cover the costs of having the municipality acquire some of the necessary land. However, as in virtually all anti-sprawl strategies, efforts to stop sprawl tend to produce a chain reaction. If development is constrained at the edge but demand continues, the result is likely to be redevelopment at the center. However, the only thing that residents dislike more than low-density sprawl at the edge is higher density where they live. To forestall increased densities within the boundaries, in 1976 the city approved a height cap of fifty-five feet for all future buildings and a cap on building permits to limit population growth to 2 percent per year.

The city also increased commercial and industrial fees and residential fees for water and sewer hook-up. Although raising these fees was part of a national trend to transfer infrastructure costs from the local government to developers, it was especially attractive to affluent communities like Boulder.[36] Not only could they cut the cost of government but they were also able in this way to deflect unwanted growth from their community to neighboring municipalities that were not in a financial position to be as picky about the kind of growth that they would get. This arrangement was also acceptable to developers, who were able to pass the cost of the fees on to new homebuyers.[37] In Boulder, as elsewhere across the country, these fees soon came to represent a substantial part of the cost of a new house, raising to the bar dramatically for newcomers wishing to enter the community.[38]

Boulder was one of the largest and most complete examples of the slow-growth approach to anti-sprawl in America during the second campaign against sprawl. In some ways, the Boulder program was a success. It certainly slowed the pace of growth and preserved a belt of green around the city. As with the experience in London, however, it came at a cost. By reducing the supply of developable land and raising development fees, it drove up the price of land

and the cost of new housing. This was largely beneficial for existing owners but hurt potential new residents. The open space acquisition and greenbelt didn't stop growth in the area. In fact, by putting the land immediately around the town off-limits, it helped pushed growth out even farther in the county to nearby towns less affluent and less able to protect themselves.[39] Much the same results were visible in Ramapo, New York, and Petaluma, north of San Francisco, two other places that attempted to place strict curbs on growth during the slow-growth and no-growth era.[40]

Once again, it can be said that the principal beneficiaries were members of the incumbents' club. The growth control measures deflected the growth away from them and preserved the amenities that they valued. Best of all, these residents could claim to be doing all of this for the common good, for the sake of historic preservation and land conservation, all the while substantially raising the value of their own homes. Measures that benefit such an incumbents' club virtually always come at the expense of other people, however, especially poorer citizens, renters, and potential newcomers. From the perspective of these latter, these anti-sprawl efforts could be seen as just another version, vastly increased in scale, of NIMBYism (not in my backyard), a term that became common during the 1980s to describe the opposition of neighborhood groups against any change in their community that could have even the remotest possibility of diminishing their home prices.[41]

Not surprisingly, as soon as the economy started to slow in the 1970s and many communities started to worry about how to encourage economic growth, the no-growth and slow-growth movements no longer looked so attractive. A number of communities abandoned their efforts. Even when the economy eventually revived in the 1980s and, with it, anti-sprawl and anti-growth sentiments, most anti-sprawl activists were careful not to resurrect the terms "no growth" and "slow growth."

Zoning Techniques

Anti-sprawl reformers during the second campaign successfully lobbied for new zoning concepts that they believed would reduce sprawl.[42] One popular technique of the 1960s and 1970s was the creation of more flexible codes that would allow "cluster development."[43] Instead of the usual arrangement of similar-sized lots, a number of units could be clustered together, not only saving money on infrastructure and other costs but also leaving the remaining land as permanent open space. On a somewhat larger scale, there was a push to supplement or supplant traditional zoning with planned unit developments (PUDs), which were essentially special zoning provisions negotiated between the developer and the local government. The idea behind the PUD was that if developers and planners could be given more flexibility to negotiate the uses for a given piece of land they would be more likely to create high-density mixed-use development on one part of the site, allowing for open space elsewhere. These techniques, which produce, on a smaller scale, patterns akin to entire communities in many north European suburban regions, became quite popular, but neither clustering nor the use of PUDs necessarily had any effect on overall urban patterns since overall densities remained low. Most of the new developments using these techniques, like the suburbs of many European cities, could be seen as sprawl, just configured slightly differently.

Another reform effort was to mandate large-lot requirements in rural areas. The logic was that by forbidding the subdivision of rural areas into parcels smaller than, say, five or ten acres, these measures would discourage subdivision, and what development did occur would be at such low densities that it would not jeopardize the rural ambience. Like many of the measures aimed at curbing sprawl, this one eventually was judged to be counterproductive. As families became more affluent and farmland prices dropped, many more families were willing and able to buy large tracts of land and erect large suburban houses. This pushed what was essentially urban development even farther out and at even lower densities than would have occurred without these regulations.

Environmental Planning and the Environmental Impact Statement

Another important tool used by anti-sprawl activists in the second campaign against sprawl was the set of regulations contained in environmental laws. The massive package of environmental legislation of the late 1960s and early 1970s at all levels of government allowed reformers to put a great deal of land, including wetlands, hillsides, and coastlines, out of bounds for further development. Although most people were highly supportive of protecting particularly scenic or fragile parts of the environment, there was a great deal of concern among many individuals about the way this kind of legislation worked in practice and

how much land it might remove from development. Another important problem was the set of consequences that followed from the reluctance of voters to
pay for the land they wished to remain undeveloped. Many taxpayers understandably preferred to use the regulatory power of government to declare that
certain properties in private hands could not be developed rather than have the
municipality purchase the land because the latter could lead to increased taxes.
However, the use of regulation rather than purchase to preserve open space
led, also not surprisingly, to a strong reaction by the owners of the property
on whom the regulation fell, who argued that this process was unfair because
it required them as individuals to shoulder the economic burden of supplying a public good. They claimed that this constituted a regulatory "taking" by
the government, meaning that the government, even if it didn't occupy physi-
cally their land, effectively took from them part of the bundle of rights that
accompany land ownership. They pointed to horror stories in which government regulations, by putting land out of bounds for development, overnight
destroyed the majority of the value of that land and in so doing wiped out the
majority of the equity of the family that owned it. They took their case to the
courts, and the courts in some instances agreed with them that a regulatory
taking had occurred. The result has been a raging legal battle on the limits to
governmental regulation.[44]

In many cases even more important to anti-sprawl reformers than any specific environmental restriction has been the requirement of mandatory environmental impact statements (EISs). The point of departure here was quite reasonable—the notion that anyone wishing to develop land should be required
to disclose publicly all possible negative impacts. Environmental review for federal projects was a key feature of the 1969 National Environmental Protection
Act, and its use increased dramatically over the next several years as states and
municipalities adapted their own versions. Although these provisions undoubtedly blocked some environmentally destructive projects, it quickly became
apparent that the process was often clumsy, expensive, time consuming, and
easily manipulated by special-interest groups. Certainly the anti-sprawl activists
realized almost immediately that even when they could not stop projects on
the strength of the environmental case against it, they could often use the EIS
process to drive up costs and produce such lengthy delays that projects would
become uneconomical and die.[45] Needless to say, these regulations have also
contributed greatly to the cost of development (fig. 33).

Figure 33. The regulated landscape. Few large areas in the United States have witnessed a more extensive regime of regulation than the island of Nantucket. Between them, public and private restrictions used to protect historic structures and environmental features have removed large portions of the island from ordinary commercial development and sprawl. Few people would deny that the result has been an aesthetic triumph. Nantucket boasts some of the most spectacular natural and manmade scenery in America. It has come at a price, however. Nantucket was the first large area of the United States to see the average house price top $1 million, meaning that many people who would like to live on the island, including many individuals who work there, cannot afford to. A great many people would probably say that in this case it is a price worth paying. When entire metropolitan areas attempt to pile up environmental and other regulations to stop sprawl, however, it can lead to major inequities and to social and economic problems. (Photograph by Robert Bruegmann, 2003.)

The Anti-highway Crusade

As we have seen, the anti-car crusade of the 1960s and 1970s was unable to do much about the rising tide of automobile ownership or use in the United States, or in almost any other affluent nation, for that matter. The anti-automobile reformers were, however, quite successful in blocking certain roads, particularly urban freeways. Starting in the late 1950s, with the Embarcadero Freeway along the San Francisco waterfront, the anti-freeway forces, using slogans like "We can't build our way out of congestion," were able to stop the construction of many highways. Conspicuously, a large number of those blocked projects would have run through the most affluent parts of American cities where many of the fiercest anti-freeway opponents lived.

Although this movement undoubtedly was beneficial in stopping some of the most intrusive plans of highway engineers, along the San Francisco or New Orleans waterfronts, for example, it was far from an unalloyed blessing. In Chicago, for example, the great triumph of the reformers was the scrapping of the Crosstown Expressway, an inner "loop road." It is not clear that stopping this road, which was based on the most advanced design ideas of its day and was planned to minimize impact on the surrounding communities, actually benefited the neighborhoods it would have cut through. Although stopping the road did avoid some displacement, and it did avoid some disruption to these communities, many of them have seen a marked economic decline since the defeat of the road, a decline that easy access to a freeway might well have alleviated. Moreover, because the Crosstown wasn't built, much of the traffic that would have used the highway to bypass the center of the Chicago region has been obliged to use the freeways that actually were completed, notably the expressways that run into the very heart of the Chicago business district, on the one hand, or the region's outer beltway, the Tri-State Expressway, on the other. These roads soon came to be among the most congested in the country. So bad has the problem become that in recent years, there has been serious interest in reviving the Crosstown in Chicago, as well as other arrested freeways elsewhere in the nation. Many of the final, long-blocked, links of the interstate freeway system are being slowly built although often at huge cost due to the long delays and opposition.

One result of the anti-highway campaign has been that new road construction has lagged dramatically behind roadway use, and this has led to a marked increase in congestion.[46] Perhaps a greater negative effect of the anti-highway campaign was that, by pitting advocates for roads against advocates for public transportation, it created a zero-sum game. In the battles over the percentages allocated to public and private transportation from a fixed pot of money, neither the transit advocates nor road advocates have been successful in obtaining enough funds to maintain existing infrastructure, highway as well as transit, let alone build new infrastructure adequate to keep up with population growth.[47]

It is, moreover, quite likely that the success of the revolt against urban freeways has actually accelerated sprawl. As driving has increased faster than roadway construction, there has inevitably been a major increase in congestion and pollution. Congestion and pollution, in turn, are among the most important elements that make people want to move farther from the center.

The anti-road forces have had some notable success in appealing to Congress for additional funding for public transportation. Among other things, this money provided funding for several important new rail systems, for example, the Metro system in Washington, DC, and the BART system in San Francisco. These systems did provide enhanced accessibility for many people, and they were probably very important in boosting the image of their respective metropolitan areas. Like virtually every other new rail system in the country in recent decades, however, they cost more than projected and served fewer riders.[48] These expensive new systems were not able to capture any large percentage of travel, and they had very little effect on the sprawl of their urban regions. Despite vast expenditures on public transportation in cities across the country, automobile use continued to increase faster than public transit use during the rest of the twentieth century.[49]

The End of the Second Campaign

Despite the setbacks and the skepticism about many of their proposed remedies, by the early 1970s many anti-sprawl reformers in the United States thought that they stood on the brink of a momentous victory. With all of the new planning and environmental legislation and the success of the anti-highway lobby, it appeared that success was within reach. The best indication of the mood of these years is captured in the 1973 report of the Task Force on Land Use and Urban Growth discussed in chapter 2. In this report, author William Reilly wrote: "There is a new mood in America. Increasingly, citizens are asking what urban growth will add to the quality of their lives. They are questioning the way relatively unconstrained, piecemeal urbanization is changing their communities and are rebelling against the traditional processes of government and the marketplace which, they believe, have inadequately guided development in the past."[50]

Task force members were highly optimistic. They believed that Congress was on the verge of capping a long list of environmental measures by passing a sweeping national land-use act that would give planners in the federal government much more power. This measure, they believed, would allow well-trained professionals to step in, stop the unbridled development that had despoiled the American landscape, and perhaps make urban America look more like urban Europe. From their perspective this was merely the logical, indeed inevitable, next step in a process leading to a better urban environment for everyone.

This optimism proved to be short-lived. Within a few years the economy deteriorated, and in many areas where slow growth and no growth were most enthusiastically embraced, these very policies would be blamed for hurting business. They were also blamed, from both the right and left sides of the political spectrum, for being elitist and hurting the less affluent parts of the population while they aided entrenched interests.[51]

In retrospect, the legacy of the anti-sprawl, regional planning, and no-growth and anti-growth campaigns of the 1960s and 1970s was mixed at best. Large-scale planning aimed at protecting existing neighborhoods, preserving greenbelts, and concentrating new growth in satellite towns or along rail and public transportation corridors, had very little impact in most cities. This was partly because it would have required more stringent controls than were politically acceptable in the United States and partly because the use of public transportation as an ordering device for urban development was unlikely to be effective in cities already too low in density to support effective transit. The revolt against the automobile, while effective in stopping some highways, may actually have fueled further sprawl.

Successful Anti-sprawl: The Case of Moscow

Before leaving the postwar years, it is only fair to note that although the various schemes of growth management we have discussed were not able to stop sprawl in the liberal democracies of Europe and America, these same policies were much more successful elsewhere, notably in cities behind the iron curtain. Before the collapse of the communist regime, the planning system as it evolved in the Soviet Union, for example, was a model of fidelity to orthodox western European reform planning standards and anti-sprawl attitudes, and in many ways it was surprisingly successful.[52]

During the Stalinist era, after flirting with "urbanist" schemes to tear down and rebuild Moscow at much higher densities or, conversely, "disurbanist" projects largely to dismantle it and disperse the population across the countryside, planners in Moscow turned to a series of "progressive" Western planning ideals from the nineteenth and early twentieth centuries. Starting with the *General Plan* of 1935, they sketched out a series of new and vastly expanded boulevards in the manner of Haussmann's schemes for Paris.[53] They then lined these boulevards with impressive classical housing blocks and monumental public buildings as well as new parks and green spaces, all reminiscent of City Beautiful schemes in Europe and America at the turn of the century. In the 1950s, they added a set of seven skyscrapers along the city's garden boulevards, each in proximity to one of the city's railroad stations. These were intended as anchors for new regional subcenters. To accommodate most of the expected growth in population, they projected new housing in large tracts at the edge of the existing city in a large area annexed in 1960. To tie everything together they created one of the world's most extensive and efficient systems of public transportation, structured around the famous Moscow subway system, begun in 1935.

Beyond the built-up area, the planners laid out a circumferential roadway that ran around the city in a circle approximately eleven miles from the city center. This roadway, which opened in 1962, marked the inner edge of a ten-mile wide greenbelt that echoed English ideas of the 1920s and 1930s. Partially within the greenbelt but primarily beyond it they envisioned a set of satellite cities to house the population that could not be accommodated within the growth boundary. Also partly within and partly outside the greenbelt were large areas of countryside dotted with small allotment gardens, orchards, and dachas designated for weekend use by urban inhabitants. Although these allotment plots were hugely popular, as the population of Moscow ballooned, they threatened to eat up so much of the countryside that planners moved to discourage them in favor of more densely planned resorts and communal facilities.

Within a few decades, planners in Moscow could claim a fair measure of success. By 1980 a great deal of the population lived in safe and sanitary, if not particularly elegant, housing. Central densities were greatly reduced by moving much of the population to massive new apartment complexes at the periphery. In the area of the greenbelt and beyond, Soviet planners were largely able to stop large-scale developments outside the satellite communities. In almost every way, they were more successful in their efforts to stop sprawl than their Western counterparts. The visitor flying into one of Moscow's airports today can still clearly see the evidence: the concentric rings of the old historical core and Soviet boulevards with relatively low, classical housing blocks, all surrounded by new high-rise and high-density concrete apartment complexes, all of this in turn surrounded by a greenbelt with a vast rural hinterland beyond dotted with satellite communities and allotment gardens. By contrast with this relatively compact concentric scheme, Stockholm or London display a fabric with a consistency that looks on a map more like a slice of heavily perforated Swiss cheese.

The Moscow system worked in large part because government bureaucrats wielded considerable power not only to designate where factories and stores could be built but also who could work in them and where these employees could live. Although their power was always far from complete, still it allowed planners to proceed in a more orderly way than in Western cities. At the same time, it dramatically curtailed individual choice. It also seems to have fostered a system of bureaucratic corruption and favoritism, as individuals with power or influence sought to improve their own situation or those of friends and relatives. A great many of the most important cultural and social amenities in the region remained clustered at the center where they were most accessible to a privileged few. Many of the residents of the new developments on the urban periphery found themselves in quickly constructed barracks-like concrete apartment buildings, far from jobs and the lively urban life at the center.

It would be easy to dwell on these negative aspects of top-down central planning, on the waste and inflexibility in their industrial policy or on the bleak appearance of the massive barracks-like apartment buildings at the edge of Moscow. This seems to be the lesson that most people, particularly free-market enthusiasts, have drawn from the Soviet experiment just as they have drawn similar lessons from the concrete apartment blocks in the Paris suburbs or high-rise American public housing. However, in none of these cases is this conclusion entirely warranted. The record in Moscow, for example, is actually quite impressive in many ways. Much of Moscow in 1935 consisted of old wooden buildings lacking central heat, running water, or adequate municipal services. The streets were narrow and irregular and almost entirely paved in cobblestones. By the 1930s, the influx of families from the countryside had produced dangerously high densities at the center of the city and further strained the housing stock. Despite the devastation of World War II, and against all odds, the authorities were able to achieve a great deal in the postwar period. It is not a system most citizens of the Western democracies would have chosen to live under and clearly the leaders grossly abused it, but it did do many things well. As Russian citizens rush to embrace free-market systems and New Russians start covering the countryside with large suburban houses and sprawl, there will be those who look back at the Stalin years as a golden era of city planning.[54] A more realistic assessment would be that, as in any large-scale urban planning scheme, the benefits are almost always balanced by substantial costs and unintended consequences.

13 Anti-sprawl Remedies since the 1970s

The European Experience

As cities across Europe have become more affluent in the last decades of the twentieth century, they have witnessed a continuing decline in population densities in the historic core, a quickening of the pace of suburban and exurban development, a sharp rise in automobile ownership and use, and the proliferation of subdivisions of single-family houses and suburban shopping centers. All of these changes have been very beneficial for many urban inhabitants. But, predictably enough, for many highbrow observers, they are just more sprawl, and they need to be fought with every tool in the planner's arsenal.

At first glance it would appear that many of the cities in northern and western Europe had some success in stopping sprawl (fig. 15). In Hamburg, for example, a vibrant historic core still dominates the region. Much of the office space is still located there; there, as well, is the largest collection of retailers. Outside the core, residential neighborhoods are connected back to the center by an efficient transportation system. Beyond the contiguous built-up area, tidy farms and green forests are dotted with small, compact suburban settlements, often clustered around what used to be agricultural villages. Differences in wealth are much less obvious than in American cities. There is no widespread abandonment or urban decay and nothing resembling an American slum. To many American observers, a city like Hamburg, affluent but with a high level of car ownership, demonstrates that planning can accommodate a modern economy and still allow the preservation of an older urban pattern.

Of course, as noted in chapter 1, one of the most important reasons that Hamburg appears to sprawl less than American cities is that the population has not grown. The population there hit its peak in 1965 and has been declining since.[1] This is probably the single most important reason that much of the Hamburg region still has the kind of urban pattern that was developed during the railroad and streetcar era and was visible in almost all European and American cities before World War II. This pattern is actively reinforced by public planning. Planners have worked to protect the historic center from effective competition from outlying developments, and they have insisted that new suburban growth at the periphery be clustered, usually around what used to be old agricultural villages.

Still, the question remains whether the pattern in Hamburg couldn't be described as sprawl and, to the extent that it is not, what this effort has cost the citizens of Hamburg. The answer to the first question is not obvious. The residential density of the Hamburg region is quite low. The density of the city itself was about 5,900 people per square mile in the 1990s, less than that of the city of Los Angeles or the Los Angeles urbanized area and considerably less than that of a number of Los Angeles suburbs.[2] Of course, the population is arranged differently on the land, but if sprawl is about substantial areas of low-density settlement and high automobile usage, Hamburg would certainly qualify as sprawling. In fact, if sprawl is defined as scattered, discontinuous development, Hamburg could be called much more sprawling than Los Angeles.

There is no doubt that residents of Hamburg, unlike those in Los Angeles, enjoy many of the advantages of the nineteenth-century urban pattern. In Hamburg, as in many European cities, for example, a resident visiting the business core will find bustling stores and crowded sidewalks. In part this is due to the excellent transportation system that reinforces the center. It is also due to the fact that businesses and institutions of the central cities are protected and subsidized. Labor laws and legislation regulating store size, hours, and the number of employees help existing retailers and help ward off competition from chain and discount stores.

Conversely , residents of outlying areas of Hamburg do not enjoy the widely dispersed retail activity that makes shopping so convenient in suburban America. The restrictions on stores have also resulted in prices for household goods well above those seen in the United States.[3] All of the restrictions aimed at preserving open space and stopping scattered development have driven up the costs of residential land to levels much higher than in American cities. The residents of Hamburg and other European cities live in smaller residential units on smaller pieces of ground than their American counterparts.[4]

Many critics of American development suggest that the citizens of Hamburg and other European cities have happily accepted these costs as part of a package of amenities that they consider more important than mere retail convenience or lot size. In this view, Europeans are presumed to be more interested in community values and preserving commonly held open spaces than their counterparts in urban America, who are more interested in individual rights or personal mobility. It is possible that there is some truth to these stereotypes, but the trends in land use and car ownership seem to belie this explanation. The dense fabric of many European city centers, it appears, is due more to the fact that the settlement patterns for such a large portion of the urban region were fixed before World War I than because of any actual preference by the inhabitants. When many of these cities reached economic maturity more than a century ago, dense transit-oriented settlements were the only efficient way to house a large urban population. The fact that a large number of Europeans still live in apartments in high-density districts is not because Europeans necessarily prefer apartment living. Polls consistently confirm that most Europeans, like most Americans, and indeed most people worldwide, would prefer to live in single-family houses on their own piece of land rather than in apartment buildings.[5] Now that they are becoming affluent enough to do it, Europeans are doing exactly this in increasing numbers. The same is true with the dispersion of jobs and retail. The system of regulations that protected traditional European centers from competition is under siege. In country after country across Europe, consumers are demanding the convenience of longer store hours, shops closer to where they live, and easier access by automobile. The result is a proliferation of large supermarkets, shopping centers, discount centers, and big-box retail outlets like Wal-Mart or Target stores.

It is also highly unlikely that most European city dwellers prefer public transportation to driving. Outside the small central areas of European cities, it is almost always quicker to get from point A to point B by automobile than by public transportation. In the Paris area, for example, the average trip by car takes twenty-two minutes, whereas the average trip by public transportation lasts forty-six minutes. Most European city dwellers, moreover, like their American counterparts, appreciate the increased level of privacy and comfort that the private automobile allows.[6] For this reason, despite extremely high taxes imposed on automobiles and on fuel, city streets that are difficult to navigate, and a scarcity of parking, car ownership has been rising fast in urban Europe, faster, in fact, than in the United States (fig. 17). This is not surprising, actually, since in the United States there are now almost as many cars on the road as licensed drivers, meaning that the market may have reached a level of saturation. Additionally, the entry of women into the workplace that fueled so much of the expansion of driving over the past several decades in the United States has probably not yet peaked in Europe. Just as in America, European urban dwellers are using their cars more and using public transportation less. In Holland, the most densely populated country in Europe, cars now account for the vast majority of all vehicular trips; public transportation, in fact, accounts for less than 10 percent of commuting trips.[7] In charts illustrating transportation modes, the steeply rising lines indicating the increase in car ownership in Europe and the United States are very similar, simply starting later in Europe. It is possible that European planners will be able to convince urban dwellers not to follow the American example in transportation and land use as they move to the periphery, but nothing in the past suggests that this will be the case.

Even in Britain, the most important pioneer in public growth management, with over half a century of experience, there seems to be considerable debate about how well the regulations have actually worked.[8] The eminent British architect Sir Richard Rogers, currently the most conspicuous heir to the tradition of Thomas Sharp and other crusaders against sprawl, writes as though Britain had no growth management at all: "We continue to believe that the future belongs to the suburbs, or rather, to suburban sprawl. Over the past 20 years—under a free-market, laissez-faire planning regime—the built-up area in England has doubled, and we have allowed the development of four million square feet of out-of-town shopping centres."[9] Not the verdict one might have expected in a country that launched the anti-sprawl crusade and that today boasts one of the most stringent planning regimes in the world!

The American Experience: Portland, Oregon, and Regional Growth Management

As we have seen, some prominent anti-sprawl activists in the early and mid-1970s in the United States believed that they were on the verge of a historic victory over sprawl. A combination of new land-use and environmental laws at all levels of government, a sharp rise in energy costs, and the apparent success of activists in places like Boulder or San Francisco made it appear that the hardest part of the battle was over. As the boom of the 1980s and 1990s got underway, however, it soon became apparent that defeat had been snatched from the jaws of victory and that decentralization and sprawl were far from conquered.

During the next two decades of the twentieth century, anti-sprawl activists were very often successful in their demands for open space preservation, environmental restrictions, and an entire battery of other measures. Compared to the experience in European countries where many of these measures could simply be dictated by the national government, in the United States the power of thousands of units or local government, each with considerable power over land-use decisions within its jurisdiction, has resulted in what seems to be a crazy quilt of overlapping and even conflicting initiatives.[10] Rather than attempting to catalog and evaluate each of these efforts, it is perhaps more instructive to consider the experience of the urban area widely considered to be the leader in the fight against sprawl.

The longest-running, most extensive, best-documented, and most controversial assault on sprawl in this country has been the one launched by the state of Oregon and the Portland urban area (fig. 34). As we have seen, Oregon was one of the first states to set up statewide planning and growth management during the "quiet revolution" of the 1960s and 1970s. The campaign for this legislation, led by Tom McCall, the state's popular Republican governor, was a good example of the slow-growth and no-growth attitudes of that era. McCall fulminated against what he called the "grasping wastrels of the land," which most people in the state automatically assumed to be real estate developers who catered to newcomers, particularly Californians. He decried, with provocative alliteration, the "sagebrush subdivision, coastal condomania and the ravenous rampage of suburbia in the Willamette Valley."[11] McCall's speech made political hay of a widespread feeling among Oregonians that the wide open and loosely settled Oregon landscape—the reason many had moved there in the first place—would slip away if it had to be shared with many more newcomers. McCall quipped on television, "Come visit us again and again. This is a state of excitement. But for heaven's sake, don't come here to live."[12]

What many Oregonians wanted to avoid at all costs was becoming "another Los Angeles." The very mention of this city conjured up images of excessive growth, insufficient planning, pollution, and congestion. In many ways this was paradoxical, since Los Angelenos of an earlier period had used exactly the same rhetoric as they themselves had tried to avoid the problems of larger,

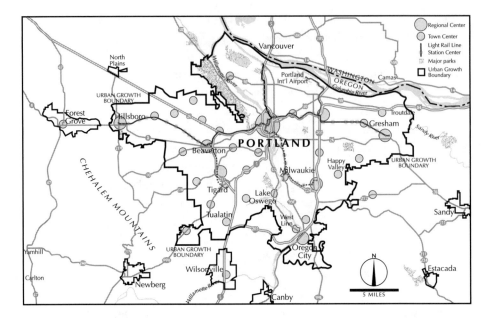

Figure 34. The Portland "planning system." The state of Oregon has conducted the longest-running and most extensive experiment in the United States in urban growth management. In the Portland region, a combination of a growth boundary with greenbelt beyond and a major campaign to downplay highway construction in favor of the creation of new transit has resulted in a place that is frequently lauded as one of the best example of large-scale "smart growth" in the country. Certainly the lively downtown and green hills around the city form one of the most attractive cityscapes in the nation. Critics have countered that despite all of these policies and billions of dollars invested in transit, Portland remains a low-density urban area with a rising automobile usage, a continuing decline in the market share of public transit, a continuing loss of agricultural lands, and a system that creates vast windfalls for some landowners and penalizes others. In addition, say the critics, the restrictions, to the extent that they constrain new construction, have exerted a heavy upward pressure on land prices, reducing home affordability. (Map redrawn by Dennis McClendon from the 2040 Concept Map produced by Metro, the Portland regional governmental body as part of the 2040 Growth Concept, issued 1995 and available on the www.metro-region.org Web site.)

more established places like New York or Chicago, which, in turn, had used the same language in relation to London and Paris.

The Portland System

Passed at the initiative of McCall, Oregon's 1973 Land Conservation and Development Act required that every city and county in the state adopt and enforce a comprehensive plan in accordance with a set of statewide goals. To supervise this process and ensure that the goals were met, the act set up a statewide Land Conservation and Development Commission (LCDC).[13] Perhaps the most important of the objectives was the desire to protect rural areas and agriculture. This goal was particularly attractive to voters in the Willamette Valley, containing Portland and most of the urban population of the state, because they were so keen on preserving open space and scenic amenities around their own cities. The most important tool in achieving these results was the urban growth boundary, a version of the greenbelt proposed by garden city reformers since the turn of the century and actually used for decades in London and other British cities.

After the legislation was passed, the task of drawing up the growth boundary fell to the Metropolitan Service District (known as Metro). Metro had started as an advisory "council of governments," but in 1979, the year it adopted the growth boundary, it became a regional governmental body with elected councilors. The original Portland boundary contained about 460 square miles of land. Unlike the case in London, the growth boundary for Portland and the other cities in Oregon was not supposed to remain static. By law, metropolitan areas were required to maintain a twenty-year supply of land. Once the boundary was initially established each of the three Oregon counties in the Portland metropolitan area—Clackamas, Washington, and Multnomah—along with each of the area's cities adopted its own comprehensive plan and implementing regulations in conformity with state guidelines and the urban growth boundary. Unlike the case in Britain but similar to the way most American cities have set up growth control programs, the principal tool to manage growth was not the purchase of land or development rights but regulations restricting private landowners.

The Oregon system of growth management was a striking innovation in American city planning. It had little effect on Portland during the 1970s or 1980s, however, because the original boundary contained so much land and because the region's economy and population grew so slowly. Development during most of those years continued to sprawl much as it had in the past. Especially in the suburbs of Washington county west of downtown, large areas of land were developed as low-density industrial parks and subdivisions. In the 1980s, the density of the Portland urbanized area, already quite low by American urban standards, declined even further, from over 4,000 people per square mile at the beginning of the decade to barely over 3,000 in 1990. This happened during the same years that other urbanized areas without any overall scheme of growth management, most notably Portland's great negative exemplar, Los Angeles, were becoming significantly denser.[14]

By the early 1990s, however, development started to pick up in Portland, sparking a new anti-sprawl push. The initial impetus for this development was opposition to a bypass highway planned for the western suburbs. A group that called itself the Thousand Friends of Oregon was successful in fighting the road, using what had become a standard, if dubious, argument that the new roads would only "induce traffic" and encourage development. They argued, in a study called LUTRAQ (Land Use, Transportation, Air Quality Connection) that a program of cutting back on highway construction, building new public transit, fostering mixed-use "transit-oriented design" at transit stops, and raising densities could break the cycle that had created sprawl. In the meantime Metro, which had gained considerable authority in 1992 when it was granted "home rule," meaning that it could exercise some of the powers usually reserved for cities, started its mandated review of the urban growth boundary. Ultimately, Metro enlarged the growth boundaries in accordance with Oregon law, but it also accepted many of the arguments of the Thousand Friends and incorporated these ideas in their Region 2040 Plan, which was finally passed in 1996.[15] The new motto, "Grow up not out," signaled new willingness to push densities higher within the growth boundary so that less land would be needed for future expansions. In fact, a good deal of the building in the past ten years, both in existing neighborhoods and at the suburban edge, has been denser and more compact than in previous decades.[16]

Measuring the Results of Growth Management

After more than twenty-five years in operation, the results of the Oregon experiment are controversial and puzzling. Growth control in Portland, like the text of the Bible, seems to provide almost anyone studying it evidence to bolster a preexisting viewpoint. According to proponents and many of the journalists writing for the national press, the Portland area growth management system has accomplished most of its goals. These individuals say that the Portland region today remains a highly livable, green metropolis that has managed to control its own destiny by careful planning. They claim that the Portland System has allowed the area to avoid excessive road building, introduce more public transportation, enhance the vitality of downtown, and conserve farmland at the urban periphery.[17]

Other observers range from skeptical of specific claims to adamant that the system as a whole has been a failure, and a fraud to boot.[18] There is no doubt that Portland is a beautiful and livable city, many of these individuals say, but much of this derives from its relatively small size, fairly homogenous population, mild climate, and magnificent natural setting. It also helps considerably that, economically, the city did so poorly in comparison with other American cities and many of its West Coast neighbors during much of the mid-twentieth century. Partly because of this, it has remained a small city with neither the pollution that heavy industry would have generated nor a large and poor minority population. None of this was the result of urban planning, these critics claim.

Skeptics of the Portland system also point out that not only has Portland not increased its density very much but the gap between the density of the Portland region and many other West Coast cities has actually increased (fig. 9). In the Portland region, both population and job growth have occurred much faster at the urban periphery than at the center, they say, and the massive efforts to create a new rail system have not increased transit's share of travel in the region. They even argue that in Portland, as elsewhere, the enormous sums of money spent for new rail systems have actually made matters worse for most citizens. This is because a substantial portion of the money needed to build and operate the rail system, used by relatively few people, was siphoned away from the roads and buses serving most of the population.

Why is this debate so acrimonious and how can the basic facts in the case be so much in doubt? Perhaps the most plausible answer is that because Portland has become the prime symbol of the anti-sprawl campaign, the question of whether the "Portland system" works or doesn't work has enormous ideological significance. Anyone advocating anti-sprawl measures, but also defenders of regional government or more public planning, are likely to seize on any statistics they can to bolster the case that the system is working. Libertarians and those opposed to regional government and top-down planning have been just as quick to make the opposite case. Let's review briefly the debate so far.

A reasonable first question about the Portland system might be whether it has stopped sprawl and decentralization. From one point of view the answer to this question is definitely yes. The growth boundaries have almost certainly kept a great deal of suburban growth out of the countryside around Portland. The impact of the boundary is very clear in many places from the ground or from the air. Flying out of the city at night, the bright lights of urban Portland stop abruptly in many places in a way rare in America except in cities in the American Southwest, where very scarce water supplies have strictly limited growth.

However, as we have seen, it was only in the 1990s that the urban growth boundary started to pinch, and it was only at this time that strong measures aimed at increasing density in already existing communities were put into place.[19] There is no doubt that densities have started to rise since the 1990s. How much of this rise has been caused by the growth management system is less easy to determine. As we have seen, the trend in cities across the country has been a lessening in decentralization or an increase in density, particularly at the developing edge. It is likely that Portland would have followed the example of Los Angeles or San Francisco in this trend with or without growth management. In 1990, the Los Angeles area counted some 5,800 people per square mile, or almost double the density seen in Portland. Although the figures for urbanized areas in 1990 and 2000 are not strictly comparable because the census bureau used some new methods to calculate the urbanized areas, it is clear that Los Angeles became much denser during this period, reaching over 7,000 people per square mile. During the same time period, Portland only edged upward from just over 3,000 to about 3,350 people per square mile. Critics of the Portland system have suggested that if Portland were able to double its density, which is what Metro's plans call for, the result would not be to keep Portland distinctly different from Los Angeles. Instead, they say, the result would actually make Portland much more like Los Angeles.

Assuming for a moment that the Portland system may eventually prove to be an effective way of making the central area more dense, there is still considerable debate over whether this is a good thing. Anti-sprawl advocates say that encouraging urban infill at higher densities not only reduces pressure to build on greenfield sites but also rejuvenates central neighborhoods. Critics of the system counter with the observation that across the country, the only thing that citizens dislike more than sprawl at the edge is higher density near themselves. Certainly in most American cities the zeal of community activists to preserve the character of their own neighborhood by stopping plans that would increase density and traffic at least equals the desire of citizens to fight low-density subdivision at the edge. The Portland system, if it is going to reach desired levels of density overall, will require sharply higher densities in some existing neighborhoods, and this means altering, some would say destroying, their character in the process. Critics of the system believe that there has already been considerable pressure in some neighborhoods to accept higher densities than residents nding, the percentage of Portland area residents taking public transportation as continued to decline. With transit use accounting for less than 2 percent of ll trips in the region, it remains a fairly negligible factor in the vast majority of he metropolitan area.

Critics further charge that the light rail system, like virtually every rail system in America in the last several decades, not only came in heavily over budget and failed to live up to ridership projections but also siphoned scarce transportation dollars from all other transportation modes, particularly the more heavily used, more flexible, and more cost-effective buses.[28] They also point to its slow speed and the fact that it was designed as a way to take commuters in and out of downtown, which houses a constantly declining percentage of the jobs in the metropolitan area. Finally, they charge, as the population has grown and the region has failed to keep up with the building of new roads, roadway congestion has gotten much worse even on the highways that parallel the new light rail lines.[29] They say that Metro's own projections show that there is little likelihood that most people will abandon their cars and use transit, meaning that congestion will necessarily get worse in the future if current policies continue.[30]

Agricultural Protection and the Perverse Consequences of Regulation

Agricultural protection, a critical element of the Oregon system from the beginning, provides a remarkable example of the complexities of apparently straightforward reform efforts.[31] Certainly from the point of view of food production, there is no evidence that the state was ever in any danger of running out of land. Cities and other urban areas have never occupied more than about 3 percent of the land in Oregon. The average cost of an acre of farmland in Oregon in 1995 was only $844 an acre and the average yearly income of an Oregon farm was only about $12,531, much of the latter from government subsidies.[32] This remarkably low level of land price and farm income in Oregon, as well as the declining real cost of food and fiber nationwide, suggests that considerably more land is being farmed than the market on its own would support.

In fact, despite all of the rhetoric to the contrary, it seems unlikely that agricultural production itself was ever the motivating force for the measures intended to preserve it in Oregon.[33] Much of what is grown in the Willamette Valley, in fact, as in many other metropolitan areas around the country, is not food but turf and ornamental plants, and most of the crops that are grown in

want and to short-circuit the local review processes that have been the principal mechanism many community residents have used to control the fate of their own neighborhoods.[20] They also charge that the process has been highly inequitable because more affluent communities have been able to maintain their low densities and deflect population growth to less affluent neighborhoods. All of these tensions have led to clashes between local communities and regional and state government agencies.[21]

Critics also point out that, as in the case of London, the growth control mechanisms have tended to push a good deal of the growth out beyond the boundaries altogether. While none of the three counties that make up the Oregon part of greater Portland grew by even 25 percent in the 1990s, Clark County in Washington, located across the Columbia River and outside the growth boundaries, grew 45 percent in the same period. By 2000, more than 60,000 of these residents, mostly living in the city of Vancouver, Washington, commuted daily into Portland. Among the reasons given by the new residents of Clark County for their move was that they wanted to escape from the high land prices and property taxes on the Oregon side of the river and also from the density, congestion, and land-use restrictions.[22] Also growing much more quickly than Portland itself are many small towns beyond the Portland growth boundaries on the Oregon side.

Driving around many of the newly created Portland suburbs, with their mix of single-family houses, apartment buildings, strip malls, and office parks, is like driving through the fast-growing suburbs of any other American city. Even the Northwest Environment Watch, a strong supporter of the growth system, tacitly acknowledged as much in a report prepared in 2002 by using language indistinguishable from that used by anti-sprawl reformers elsewhere. According to the report, growth in the Portland area in the 1990s "overran roughly 8 acres of farmland and open space each day" and "clogged the region's roads with worsening traffic congestion."[23]

Has Growth Management Driven up Prices?

An even more divisive debate surrounds the relationship between Portland's growth management measures and land prices. According to critics of the growth management system, the inevitable result of restricting the supply of land, while doing nothing about the demand for new houses, is a rise in prices. In fact, few individuals on either side of the debate deny that land prices have shot up in the Portland area. The city once had house prices below the national average; now these prices are well above. Defenders of the urban growth boundary argue that this was simply a result of high market demand and that other Western cities, San Francisco or Salt Lake City, for example, have either higher land prices or have seen prices rise even faster. According to them, moreover, the increase in land prices has been a relatively small factor in the increase in housing costs. All of this, they say, proves that it has been simple demand, particularly the increased demand due to smart growth, and not the urban growth limit, that has pushed up prices. In fact, some defenders of the system claim the Portland system has actually kept prices lower than they would have been otherwise by its policies expediting development reviews and encouraging higher-density units within the growth boundaries. This clash in views has led to a bewildering duel of statistics. It is hard to imagine that everyone is talking about the same place.[24]

It appears that the major reason the studies have been so inconclusive is that no one has found a way to sort out all of the variables. The urban growth boundary, which is the chief novelty in Portland, is only one element in a vast network of land-use regulations and not necessarily the most important. The comparison of Portland with San Francisco used by many advocates of the Portland system to prove the point that the growth boundary has not caused any undue rise in prices is particularly misguided. The San Francisco region, although lacking a single metropolitan-wide growth boundary, has had, since the early 1970s, some of the most rigorous regulatory laws in the country, including a number of local growth boundaries. Which of these growth management regulations are the main factors pushing up prices in the Bay Area is not clear, but to almost anyone connected with the real estate industry in that city, the combination of environmental regulations, growth management, and other governmental restrictions since about 1970 has exerted tremendous upward pressure on land prices.[25] In cities like San Francisco or Portland, land prices have risen far faster than in places like Phoenix or Houston or Las Vegas, which were growing at least as fast but with much less stringent regulation. In fact some believe that the country is increasingly dividing into a high-cost, regulation-heavy zone, particularly visible on the coasts, and a less expensive, less highly regulated zone inland.[26]

Interestingly, although both Portland and the Bay Area have been hotbeds of experimentation for all kinds of anti-sprawl methods, they have gone about this in quite different ways. In Portland, the system has been very central-

ized, set in motion by the state and administered by a re primary object has been to protect open space at the edg center denser, even if this means losing green space the cisco region, in contrast, efforts have been extremely decen ally every community trying to keep density down and pres its immediate vicinity. There has been little overall regulati the region as a whole. This has led to the preservation of m and vast areas of hilly terrain. No one denies that these a great deal toward making the Bay Area one of the most scen At the same time, protecting so much land from developme prisingly, contributed to the push of population outward, in t way into California's Central Valley around cities like Stockton Curiously, the Sierra Club, which has been active in the Portlan paigns leading to higher densities in established districts, has als in San Francisco campaigns to do just the opposite.[27] Even mo despite a lack of any specific regional plan to boost densities, the S area, like the Los Angeles area, has increased in density more o Portland has.

Has the Portland System Solved Transportation Problems?

In cities around the country, traffic congestion looms largest in man sions about sprawl. As we have seen, however, blaming sprawl for co may be completely wrong-headed. It is the denser urban areas worldw have the worst problems with congestion. The Portland experiment p interesting testimony on this issue. According to advocates of the s Portland turned the corner on transportation problems by diverting m the money that previously would have been allocated to roads into fundi public transportation instead. As the region and the new commercial r become denser, the percentage of transit riders will rise, they predict. Ac ing to critics of the system, however, this assumption is fundamentally flav and efforts to divert highway funds to transit, particularly rail transit, h already started to backfire. They say that voters were promised that the Po land light rail system, the crown jewel in the Portland planning system, wou relieve highway congestion, strengthen downtown, and help in the creation o new high-density mixed-used centers around the metropolitan area. However despite billions of dollars in construction costs, much of it subsidized by federal the valley, whether food or not, could be planted elsewhere in the state.[34] Moreover, the growth boundary all but guarantees that valuable farmland within the boundaries will be developed while a great deal of less-productive land outside the boundary will remain undeveloped. It seems likely that the real goal for most urban Oregonian voters was instead an aesthetic consideration: the preservation of countryside for its scenic and symbolic value. Even though most of Oregon is very thinly settled, it is the rural scenery in the Willamette Valley, the place where most Oregonians live and that most potential newcomers would like to live, that has been the emotional linchpin.[35]

There is nothing wrong with wanting to preserve open space for its scenic value, of course. Like many environmental regulations, however, the attempt to preserve farmland by regulation has had some very perverse consequences. A principal reason growth control regulations are so popular in Oregon, as elsewhere, is because of a perception that by simply mandating the growth boundary, rather than buying development rights the way the British did, citizens can secure open space and other public benefits without paying for them.[36] However, this kind of regulation often ends up disguising the real costs and creating major inequities. For example, it can produce a windfall for certain individuals, such as those with well-located land within the boundaries. It will simultaneously depress property values for others, notably those with land outside the boundaries. When millions of dollars hinge on the exact location of the urban growth boundary, moreover, it is almost certain to produce all kinds of attempts to manipulate the system that have nothing to do with rational planning. It also makes it more difficult for newcomers to enjoy the same freedom of choice that so many thousands of current residents took for granted when they bought land before the controls started to take effect.

Another consequence of the growth boundaries is the perverse way they actually enhance the value of living outside the boundaries. Around Portland, as around many cities, a considerable number of people want to protect the countryside, but they also want to live in it. Because there was some recognition of this at the time the Oregon growth system was inaugurated, Oregon's counties together set aside about 3 percent of the land outside the growth boundaries as "exception lands" for "hobby farms," noncommercial farming, ranchettes, and similar uses. The idea was to provide some space for these activities and divert potential urban dwellers away from prime farmland. A drive through some of the extensive exception lands in Clackamas County east of Tualatin provides a

remarkable view of large lots and "starter mansions" very much like those in
exurbia anywhere else.

Government agencies underestimated the demand for these exception lands,
moreover, and this demand has increased dramatically with rising affluence
and with every new regulation that makes living in the country more difficult. For several years Oregon led the country in the increase in the number
of hobby farms. Some of this happened in the areas set aside for this purpose.
However, many urban dwellers either weren't content with the land that was
set aside for this purpose or didn't want to pay the higher prices that resulted
from the removal of so much potential developable land from the market. So
they built their house on prime agricultural lands. Theoretically, this should not
have been possible since farmland outside the growth boundaries was zoned
exclusively for agriculture, and counties had put into place large minimum lot
requirements to discourage subdivision. However, urban residents could get
around these restrictions by buying land in pieces just large enough to satisfy
zoning requirements and calling their land a farm even if it never produced
any farm income. They were then free to erect enormous "farm" houses indistinguishable from suburban McMansions and eventually to abandon any effort
to maintain even the fiction that they were actually farming. A 1991 state study
showed that as many as 40 percent of the farm properties for which new dwellings had been approved in the previous years produced no farm income at all.

So widespread was this tactic that the state in 1994 instituted a policy that
required potential owners to prove that they had grossed at least $80,000 from
the products of their so-called farm for several years before they were allowed
to build a house. For the moment this policy has reduced the creation of hobby
farms. It will probably not stop wealthy Portlanders for long. As Portland grows,
an increasing number will become sufficiently affluent to plant just enough
strawberries or Christmas trees to meet the new requirements. They will then
be free to build large weekend houses on the property. They may also qualify
for Oregon agricultural tax breaks. Finally, in order to protect their alleged farm
from any other city dwellers, they are likely to become the most vociferous
proponents of tightening still further the growth management system.[37] This
would be an excellent example of the way a seemingly simple regulation can
unleash an entire series of unintended consequence.

It is possible that the bulk of the land around Portland could eventually
become an aristocratic preserve for the affluent like large parts of southeast
England or the Napa or Sonoma valleys north of San Francisco. As it is, the

Oregon Farm Bureau has estimated that nearly half of all farms in the state might already be hobby farms.[38] This may be an aesthetic victory and a desirable outcome, but it does not mean that the Portland system has stopped the diffusion of an urban population into the countryside.

Winners and Losers

As with any set of regulations affecting land, there are winners and losers. One good way to think about Portland is to look at the experience of a smaller, more contained region: the island of Nantucket. The beauty and character of Nantucket has been maintained by a dense network of private and public restrictions aimed at protecting the environment, preserving the old buildings, and conserving open space. While each of these is in itself a worthy goal, the net effect has been more or less to freeze large parts of the island, severely restraining the supply of land and pushing up house prices. In fact, Nantucket became the first place in the United States where the average house price topped 1 million dollars. All of this can obviously be very beneficial for existing landowners, but it can also be detrimental to the interests of many others, including those who work on Nantucket but can't afford to live there or those who might wish to live on the island but are priced out.[39] Nantucket is an example of what a similar set of regulations could do in any American urban area if pushed very far over a long period of time. It is likely that most Americans would say that in the case of Nantucket the benefits outweigh the costs. Whether this would be true for an entire metropolitan area is less clear (fig. 33).

The issues on Nantucket are similar to those seen in Portland, as are the groups that are winners and losers. Existing owners of land within the Portland growth boundary, for example, are clear winners, particularly those with undeveloped land.[40] In fact, because a good deal of land within the boundaries is not suitable for building and some parts of the region have much higher demand than others, some lucky landowners have obtained something approaching a monopolistic position in their part of the market. Within the built-up area, the winners in the Portland system will continue to be members of the incumbents' club, that is to say, those current homeowners who already have most of the amenities that want and have the political clout to shield their own neighborhoods from the increasing density and traffic that the system will almost certainly create elsewhere. They will reap the benefits of growth management with few of the burdens. They will see their property values soar but their taxes reigned in by tax caps.[41] In one memorable characterization, the Portland system was described as "a big, government-sanctioned homeowners association, with the UGB [urban growth boundary] serving as a metaphorical wall that rings a gated community." [42]

There have been several other important winners in this system, several of them quite unexpected. Although some homebuilders have understandably been unhappy, a number of others have actually privately cheered it on. Developers in Portland, as elsewhere, can make money whether development is compact or dispersed and whether there are tight governmental regulations or not. It actually doesn't much matter to them if government regulations add considerably to the expense of houses as long as there is good demand because they can pass on any added costs to homebuyers. In a place like Portland, local builders can also benefit from a reduction in competition due to the reluctance of outsiders to risk entering such a distinctive and highly regulated development environment. Small shop owners are likewise delighted that regulations against large chain stores protect them from larger, potentially more efficient retail operations. Transit enthusiasts are understandably pleased that the entire Portland system is designed to make driving less convenient and so might, they believe, force people out of their cars.

For every owner who has benefited from the system, there will be others who lose. Many owners of land outside the urban growth boundary, for example, have hardly benefited at all from the dramatic run-up in value of land around every other city on the American West Coast. In this case, the public good has been financed through the involuntary contributions of a relatively small group of individuals.

Probably the group that will be hurt the most by rising prices has hardly been mentioned in the voluminous literature on Portland to date. These are all of the potential future inhabitants of the city. Many of them will pay sharply higher prices for their houses than those who arrived before the growth management measures started to have an effect. They will in part be paying for the cost of benefits to currently existing residents. Many people will not be able to afford to come at all. They will instead move to Pocatello or Boise. We have no way to measure the impact of all of the things that will not happen because of attempts to control sprawl.[43]

Portland is the country's largest experiment with a kind of regulatory system that has been used extensively in Europe since World War II but rarely in the

United States on any scale. It can probably work in the United States only in places that have a coveted geographic location, extraordinary natural environment, or a set of large employers that can't easily relocate. These places have the luxury of imposing severe restrictions without the consequent loss of competitiveness that would be the result elsewhere. Nantucket Island, California's Napa Valley, or Boulder, Colorado, can do this because of their limited size, scenic beauty, large number of affluent citizens, and unique economic base. It is also possible in certain upscale suburbs like the towns of Marin County, outside San Francisco, or of western Connecticut, outside New York City, that have very good access to the nearby urban centers but are located just far enough outside them to provide attractive low-density living. Portland is the first large city to try this kind of regulatory strategy on the scale of a large metropolis.

It is easy to see, in any of these cases, why reporters will come away impressed. They will see places that seem to offer almost all of the amenities of urban life without having to deal with the drawbacks. Whether it is the pristine farmhouses, gentrified main street, or undisturbed fields in Nantucket, the pleasant small-town ambience of Santa Monica, or Portland's alluring downtown and surrounding green hillsides, each of these places is a kind of carefully constructed and minutely regulated paradise. In each, a group of residents has been able to impose standards through an entire battery of legal mechanisms like design review, preservation, conservation, and environmental regulations that in most cities in the United States would be considered excessively intrusive and subjective.

By comparison, the same reporters visiting Los Angeles, Atlanta, Phoenix, or Houston will probably end up writing less positive reviews. In place of Portland's spectacular natural setting of mountains and river and a marvelously equitable climate, Houston, set on a low, marshy plain and subject to a climate that is, by any estimate, uncomfortably hot and humid for a great deal of the year, will seem drab. Compared to the undeniable attractions of Portland's comfortable pedestrian-scaled downtown, Houston's downtown can strike visitors as unappealing since such a large part of the population during much of the year will be off the streets and in air-conditioned tunnels to avoid the sultry heat. Small wonder that the reporter will go back to the office and pound out yet another story about the Portland planning miracle.

This comparison is clearly unfair, however. It is, first of all, a tourist-eye view of the city, one that starts and ends with the things most tourists see, many of them in a small part of the downtown area. It fails to capture urban life as lived by most of its actual residents. It also ignores the fact that a city like Houston is larger and has had a faster growth in population and in its economy than Portland over the last several decades.[44]

A higher percentage of newcomers to Houston than to Portland have been poor and members of minority groups. The fact that Houston has somehow managed to accommodate all of these new citizens and provide for them a median family income only slightly below that of Portland is an extraordinary achievement. In part it has been able to do this because of a permissive attitude about growth and land use that has resulted in land and house prices in Houston below the American urban average. For many families, the economic and social mobility seen in Houston are more important than the benefits of smart growth, as seen in Portland.

Clearly the Portland system provides no silver bullet in the fight against sprawl. Any success will come with costs attached. None of the perverse consequences of the Portland system are either new or necessarily disastrous, however. Although it uses different methods, the Portland system is similar in kind to the systems of regulations used to control change in many other exclusive places, from the co-op apartment building on Fifth Avenue in New York to the streetscape in Beverly Hills. And, like the Upper East Side of Manhattan or Beverly Hills, it provides a distinct choice in the American urban system. It is quite possible that with increasing affluence, larger portions of the American population will demand the kinds of controls used today on Nantucket Island, in the Napa Valley, or in Portland. And it is likely that there will always be others who will consider these controls overly intrusive and a barrier to the kind of life that they would like to live. For them the relatively permissive regulatory climate seen today in Houston or Atlanta will be much more congenial. Fortunately, there is room for both Houston and Portland in country as large as the United States. Even if it is not the panacea claimed by its most ardent advocates, at very least, the Portland experience has been extremely useful as an experiment in alternative urban futures and in furthering a national debate on land use.[45]

The End of Smart Growth?

As in the previous campaigns, when the economy turned downward, in this case at the very end of the 1990s, enthusiasm for anti-sprawl reform efforts flagged. In a number of places across the country, a backlash to smart growth surfaced.[46] However, history suggests that as soon as the economy starts to roar again, the anti-sprawl campaign will pick up where it left off, jettisoning or amending some assumptions but retaining all of the core notions about the problems of sprawl and the benefits of increased planning, more compact development, and more stringent regulations.

SOME CONCLUSIONS

What can we conclude from this history of sprawl and the campaigns to stop it? It appears that sprawl has been a feature of urban life since time immemorial. In the past when cities reached a certain level of economic maturity and affluence, densities began to decline at the center as many people who had a choice moved farther out to escape the congestion and pollution of the city, reduce costs, or gain more space. This resulted in a corresponding rise in density at the edge as rural land became exurban or suburban. Within the last century this process has been visible in cities throughout the affluent industrialized world, producing a marked flattening and—until very recently—lowering of the density gradient (fig. 1).

This flattening of the density gradient seems to have happened because a more dispersed landscape has afforded many people greater levels of mobility, privacy, and choice than they were able to obtain in the densely settled large cities that were the norm through the end of the nineteenth century. A great many people have concluded from exactly this kind of analysis that sprawl is inevitable and that efforts to stop it are doomed.

However, in any analysis, it also pays to look at what we don't know or can't explain. For example, there is considerable evidence that—at least in the central city and regularly developed suburbs of many fast-growing American urban areas—the longstanding process of decentralization has actually reversed itself. The line on the chart that records density gradient is still flattening but it is no longer falling. Densities are actually rising sharply both at the center and at the edge in places like Los Angeles, Phoenix, or Las Vegas and more slowly elsewhere in the country. New suburban development at the edge of most American cities is now considerably denser than it was in the decades after World War II.

It is not clear why suburban densities are rising. It could be that this is in part a result of anti-sprawl policies that have removed a great deal of land from the market and have driven up prices on the land that remains. However, the rise was already underway in the 1950s, before there was any real campaign to stop sprawl. It is possible that, just as densities almost always fall after cities reach a certain point in their economic cycles, there may be another point at which densities will start to rise. It could also be that as individuals pass from affluent to extraordinarily affluent they are better able to enjoy the benefits of density without the negative side effects. After all, there have always been people willing to pay large amounts of money to live in very dense places like the Upper East Side of Manhattan or parts of central Paris.

It is quite possible that sprawl could recede everywhere as more citizens become affluent enough to live like the residents of the Upper East Side or the sixteenth arrondissement of Paris, and we will see more building at high densities in or near the existing cores. This could take development pressure off the countryside that will almost certainly become ever more important as a scenic and recreational amenity. It is also possible that this increase in density in the city might be counterbalanced by a growth in housing elsewhere as a larger number of citizens decide they would like two or three dwellings, for example, a condominium in a high-rise in the city, a house in the mountains, and a time-share unit at the beach. Or it could be that many families will instead choose to have their primary residence at the beach or mountains with an apartment in the city as their second house. Certainly this would not be totally unexpected if middle-income families continue to follow the lead of their wealthier counterparts. It is entirely possible that some attractive central cities will become essentially resort areas filled with second homes.

Most observers seem to have concluded that with increasing affluence and new communications technologies, more and more individuals will want the calm solitude of an isolated mountain peak in Montana. But our review of recent history suggests it is also possible that once they have enough money to live comfortably in a dense city many citizens might instead want the cultural and social stimulation of Manhattan or Tokyo. In fact, different people will probably want each of these alternatives and every other urban choice as well, for different reasons at different times in their lives. If so, the new technologies, like almost all earlier transportation and communications technologies, will have effects that are quite unpredictable.[1]

There is no way to guess what the future of urban growth and sprawl will be. The truth is that what we know about urban history is less important than what we don't know. Certainly history provides little in the way of guidance for any confident predictions about the future of sprawl, with or without efforts to stop it. Any observable pattern of urban development is a result of a great many different forces acting on each other in ways that are very hard to measure, explain, or predict. Any strong movement in one direction is likely to generate a reaction in another. Short-term trends that suggest one scenario often disguise larger trends that would suggest another. All of this makes formulations like "business as usual," "current trend," or other stock phrases used in discussing urban growth patterns almost useless. By the time social scientists have discovered a current trend, it is likely that other trends, quite possibly leading in very different directions, are in the process of overtaking it.

In theory, public policy ought to be based on an attempt to draw up a balance sheet showing which kinds of environment achieve the most benefits for the most people without unduly harming any group. Because of the complexity of urban systems, however, it is often difficult to draw up such a balance sheet. Information available at the time of any assessment is usually out of date by the time it is fully collected and analyzed. Conclusions are almost invariably based on the evidence of an insufficiently long time span and on too few variables. The way data are collected, moreover, is inevitably colored by preexisting assumptions about the conditions that are being studied.

When it comes to setting public policy about anything as complex as sprawl, this problem is compounded by the fact that the "solution" to any given problem depends on the vantage point of the person doing the proposing. Although certain factors—for example, a desire for mobility, privacy, and choice—seem to remain fairly constant over long periods of history and across cultures, there has been considerable variation in preferences even within specific groups, with a result that the physical forms produced over the years have been astonishingly varied. At very least, the simple fact that none of our existing models of thought can explain this variety should, I think, make us wary of making any sweeping generalizations about the so-called problems of sprawl, let alone remedies for them.

Does this mean that all efforts to understand urban change and to plan for the future are futile? Of course not. Planning is exactly what every individual and every group does all the time, each according to specific sets of expectations and assumptions. The question is really at what level and through what means should planning and decision making take place. Should this be intensely local, at the level of the family or municipality or county, or should these decisions be pushed upward to a region or a state or an entire country? Is it best done by governmental regulation or do market forces provide a more flexible and better informed process of decision making? I don't think that history provides any simple answers to questions like these, and there is ample reason to think that different problems are best dealt with at different levels and in different ways. It does suggest that the inevitable response of sprawl reformers to push for more public planning and more regulations at constantly higher levels of government might not be wise. It also suggests that since everything—the basic urban patterns, our evaluations of them, even our political and social institutions—are constantly changing, we should be very wary of any sweeping diagnoses or remedies. We should also be constantly alert to the unintended consequences and harm that any of these remedies might do to some part of the population.

With any luck, when the fourth wave of anti-sprawl agitation gets underway during the next major economic boom we will have more information about existing conditions, more flexibility of thought, and a more nuanced assessment of the benefits as well as the problems of sprawl. We might even have decided by then that the use of the word "sprawl" itself is confusing and divisive, hopeless as an objective description of the infinitely complex and fast-changing urban world around us and counterproductive as an analytical concept. Then again, if history is any guide, "sprawl" will survive, shorn of some of its negative polemical overtones just as phrases like "Gothic" or "Baroque"—originally derogatory terms but now standards in the history of art—have done. The fate of the term "sprawl" is as uncertain as the slippery urban reality it seeks to describe.

We started this book flying into New York City in the morning. We will end with an evening flight out of Los Angeles, that paragon of sprawl for several generations of urban reformers. Departing from LAX at dusk on a cloudless day, the plane will take off to the west, rising up sharply over the blue-black ocean, punctuated only by the faint lights of boats far below and the almost imperceptible outline of the Channel Islands, which, only slightly darker than the sky itself, loom against the horizon. As the plane banks to the south and then again to the east, the lights of the Los Angeles basin come into view.

Even for people who have seen it a hundred times before, this view can take one's breath away. Marking off a vast grid are the great arterial highways with their regular punctuation of yellowish sodium vapor lamps and the pools of colored light created by electric store signs at the major intersections. Snaking across the arterials are the dark linear voids of the river beds and the brightly lit freeways with their shimmering ribbon of white headlights and red tail lights. Between these brilliantly lit lines of motion are the darker residential neighborhoods with a fainter and more irregular block pattern. Only the streetlights flickering through the tree canopy and the occasional sweep of a car headlight turning into a driveway illuminate these territories.

Perhaps the most remarkable thing about this panorama is its size. Even at four hundred miles per hour it takes the plane a full fifteen minutes to fly from the beach at Redondo to the place where the city lights stop in the desert beyond Palm Springs. The great city of today is so large and complex that it defies our attempts to describe, let alone to comprehend it.

Almost everyone at one time or another has pondered the question of who provided the real force, for better or for worse, behind a great urban panorama like this one. Some people will say that it happened this way because of planning, because of those individuals who imagined the grid and those who platted all of the subdivisions. Others instinctively counter that, in fact, developers, uninterested in planning but with a steadfast eye to the bottom line, had the upper hand. This in turn, will lead the next person to argue that, since the developers needed money, it was the owners of capital that pulled the strings. Then someone will come back with the thought that governmental organizations like Fannie Mae or the FHA set out the rules that guided the bankers. The urban historian then might observe that these regulations were put in place based on an analysis of what already worked in the private financial market place. Very few people seem to complete the circle by observing that what worked and what didn't in the market was, in turn, based, at least in part, on the choices of millions of individuals and families about where and how they wanted to live.

Many people, especially academics, have resisted the notion that ordinary citizens have played a major role in the creation of the great cities of the world. They would argue that the average urban family actually has few choices because these choices are so heavily controlled by vast economic, political, and social systems. The family can only buy what the merchant offers or the developer builds or the government allows. They will say that it is those with power who make all the important decisions. Of course, in one sense they are correct. Everyone is constrained by what is available to them, whether by governmental decree, the marketplace, or societal pressure. But it seems fair to say that the average family in the affluent world today has more choices available to it than a similar family in any other society or era in history. Moreover, even a little reflection will suggest that very few individuals, no matter how wealthy or powerful, have much ability to change fundamentally any large piece of our built environment on their own. Even if the wealthiest family of any large American city devoted its entire fortune to creating change, this money would not go very far unless that family was able to mobilize support from many other individuals or institutions. A billion dollars, for example, in most cities would buy only about 2,000 moderately expensive houses.

At the same time, every individual has some role in determining how the city looks and functions. If I shop at a suburban Wal-Mart rather than a downtown department store or choose to live in an apartment near the old downtown rather than in a single-family house on five acres in exurbia, these choices have an effect on urban form. If my choices are echoed by those of many other people, they can have a profound effect. More than any other human artifact in the world today, our urban areas are the result of the actions of every citizen, every group, and every institution, every day. In its immense complexity and constant change, the city—whether dense and concentrated at the core, looser and more sprawling in suburbia, or in the vast tracts of exurban penumbra that extend dozens, even hundreds, of miles into what appears to be rural land—is the grandest and most marvelous work of mankind.

ACKNOWLEDGMENTS

I have been working on this project on decentralization and sprawl for some fifteen years. Over the course of those years, I have learned a vast amount from a great many people, some of whom I list below. I apologize for the omissions and the very brief mention of many individuals who spent considerable amounts of their time offering me information and advice, poring over maps with me, driving me around cities, suburbs, and exurbs, and, above all, listening to me try to explain what I was doing. Despite the necessarily terse quality of this list, I am deeply grateful to all.

Among my many guides were Carl Abbot and Gerard Mildner of Portland State and Jim Jacks, a city planner in Tualatin, Oregon, all of whom tried to explain Portland to me; Robin Bachin, Peter Muller, and Greg Castillo of the University of Miami; architect, critic, and historian Aaron Betsky, formerly of Yale University, Los Angeles, San Francisco, and now living in the Netherlands; Christine Boyer of Princeton University; the late Gordon Cherry, a great pioneer in the field of international planning history; British historian Mark Clapson, who helped me understand some of the social dynamics of the English urban landscape; geographer Michael Conzen of the University of Chicago; Wendell Cox, consultant of Belleville, Illinois, whose Demographia Web site provides a model for the display of statistical information; Margaret Crawford, who has been a keen observer of the everyday landscape; Timothy Davis, who helped me understand Texas cities; Timothy Duane of the University of California, Berkeley, who has enlightened me on matters environmental and legal, particularly in relation to the settlements of the Sierra region of California; Alan Ehrenhalt of *Governing* magazine; Robert Fishman and Edward Dimendberg of the University of Michigan; Marcial Echenique and Andrew Saint of Cambridge University; Nnamdi Elleh of the University of Cincinnati;

Annie Fourcaut of the Centre d'Histoire Urbaine in Paris; Thomas Hines of the University of California at Los Angeles and Diane Favro, from the same institution, who helped me understand the geography of ancient Rome; Rob Freestone of the University of New South Wales; William Fulton, editor of *California Planning and Development Report*, president of Solimar Research Group, one of the most reliable sources of information on subjects related to land use and planning, as well as my guide to Ventura County, California; Genevieve Giuliano, Peter Gordon, Harry Richardson, Greg Hise, and Philip Ethington, a remarkably diverse and interesting set of individuals who all find themselves at the University of Southern California; Isabelle Gournay and Mary Corbin Sies at the University of Maryland, both of whom are experts on various aspects of suburban history; urban economic policy consultants Claude, Nina, and Aaron Gruen of Gruen, Gruen and Associates of San Francisco and Chicago; Timothy Hagan; Richard Harris of McMaster University, a leader in the recent reevaluation of suburban history; Neil Harris of the University of Chicago; Steven Hayward; Richard Ingersoll; Joel Kotkin; Reed Kroloff and his father Kirk Kroloff and Grady Gammage, Jr., all of whom helped me understand Phoenix; Charles Lave; Ned Levine; Peirce Lewis and Wilbur Zelinsky of Pennsylvania State University; Richard Longstreth of George Washington University; John McKinney, who showed me the landscape of AT&T in central New Jersey; Francisco Javier Monclús of Barcelona; Pietro S. Nivola of the Brookings Institution; William Richards, through whose eyes I saw the real estate landscape of Washington's Virginia suburbs; Matthew Roth of the Automobile Club of Southern California and architectural critic and author Alan Hess, both of whom have been excellent guides to the automobile landscapes of Southern California; Charles Rubin of Duquesne University, who started me thinking about environmental history; Lynn Scarlett and Virginia Postrel, both formerly of the Reason Foundation, who gave me new ways to think about the environment and about aesthetics, respectively; André Sorensen, who taught me about Japanese sprawl; and Jacqueline Tatom of Washington University in Saint Louis.

I would like to give special thanks to Anthony Alofsin, who invited me to organize a small conference on the cities of Texas at the University of Texas in 1991, and to Robin Bachin and Alison Isenberg, who invited me to do something similar in Miami in 1997. I learned a vast amount from these events and these colleagues as I did from all of the speakers and participants at a National Institute of the Humanities Summer Institute that I led in 1999. I would also like to give special thanks to Sam Staley, formerly of the Reason Foundation and now of the Buckeye Institute, for hours of useful discussion about the role of planning, the market, and government in urban settlement.

I have been very fortunate in my colleagues and students at the University of Illinois at Chicago. Among the present or former colleagues from whom I learned a great deal about cities are, in the Department of Art History, Deborah Fausch, Peter Hales, and Mitchell Schwarzer. Elsewhere at the University of Illinois at Chicago were Anthony Orum in sociology; Evan McKenzie and Dennis Judd in political science: Richard John in history; David Perry, Martin Jaffe, and Wim Wiewel in urban planning; and Joseph DiJohn and Siim Soot of the Urban Transportation Center. Among present and former students, Bet Alabern, Tamsen Anderson, Adrian Calvo, Philip Gruen, Michael Kowsky showed me parts of the world that they had come to know well. I was also fortunate to spend several extended periods of time at Columbia University, where I found a great deal to discuss with Barry Bergdoll, Owen Gutfreund, Kenneth Jackson, and Mary McLeod. I am particularly grateful for the hospitality of the Buell Center for the Study of American Architecture, which awarded me a fellowship in 1989 and much hospitality and help subsequently, and I am glad to acknowledge the wise counsel of two of its directors, Gwendolyn Wright and Joan Ockman.

Several friends and colleagues went well beyond the call of duty and read all or parts of the manuscript at one point or another. These include the irrepressible Joseph Bigott of Purdue University Calumet; Sally Chappell, architectural and landscape historian formerly at DePaul University, who has long served as a reliable sounding board; Harold Henderson, journalist and judicious judge of writings on land-use planning and environmental matters; Peter Hales and Richard John of the University of Illinois at Chicago, both of them expert in identifying problems with arguments and evidence; Gerrit Knaap, formerly of the University of Illinois at Urbana-Champaign and now at the National Center for Smart Growth Research, who was very helpful on Portland; Matthew Lasner, who offered several key suggestions at the very end of the process; Charles Rubin of Duquesne University; and Patrick Wirtz.

For help in getting this book published I would like to thank agent Carl Brandt and Susan Bielstein, my editor at the University of Chicago Press, and Yvonne Zipter, copy editor. I would also like to thank two reviewers of the manuscript, one of whom, William Fischel of Dartmouth College, deserves my special thanks for his seven-page review, a small masterpiece of penetrating observation and useful suggestion. I would also like to thank the Graham Foundation for Advanced Studies in the Visual Arts for a grant made early in the process of writing this book; the Institute for the Humanities and the Great Cities Institute at the University of Illinois at Chicago, which offered fellowships at critical moments in its preparation; and the National Endowment for the Humanities, which funded a summer institute on American cities at the Institute for the Humanities at UIC in 1999.

Finally, I would like to thank a handful of people who had the most profound impact on this project: David Van Zanten, my adviser at the University of Pennsylvania, who has followed my work from Evanston, where he is professor of art history at Northwestern University; the late Spiro Kostof who, although never my teacher, taught me by example how to look at cities and write about urban processes; James Russell, architect and journalist of New York City, who has never agreed with me about anything connected with sprawl but was always been willing to talk about it; Dennis McClendon, formerly managing editor of *Planning Magazine* and today the owner of the firm Chicago Cartographics, who spent hundreds of hours driving around Chicago and other cities with me as well as preparing most of the maps and charts I have published over the years; Jack Schafer, formerly an architect in San Francisco and now an industrialist in Ravenna, Ohio, who has accompanied me in the pursuit of sprawl from Boston to Bellingham and from Buenos Aires to Bangkok; Alexander Garvin, architect, planner, author, professor, and probably the most knowledgeable person I know on the subject of American cities; my brother William Bruegmann, an attorney in Walnut Creek, California, specializing in real estate practice, who helped me see the question of sprawl through the eyes of a generous Libertarian point of view; and my partner Scott Jorgenson, who lived through the last dozen years of this project offering judicious advice at every stage.

NOTES

Chapter 1

1. For a demonstration of the difficulties in defining sprawl, see the exhaustive, and sometimes exhausting, essay by George Galster, Royce Hanson, Michael R. Ratcliffe, Harold Wolman, Stephen Coleman, and Jason Freihage, "Wrestling Sprawl to the Ground: Defining and Measuring an Elusive Concept," *Housing Policy Debate* 12, no. 4 (2001): 681–709. In this study, the authors try to show that sprawl can be measured using levels of density, continuity, concentration, clustering, centrality, nuclearity, mixed uses, and proximity. Despite the heroic effort, however, this definition is not very useful. Many of these elements appear to be independent variables, and they often move in opposite directions. Thus, for example, a metropolitan area like Los Angeles or Miami that is very multinucleated, a pattern suggesting sprawl, is also very dense, which suggests the opposite. At the same time, a relatively centralized place like the Portland area might have a very low density. In any case, as I will argue in this book, it has been the nonmeasurable, especially aesthetic, aspects of sprawl that have constituted the emotional heart of the debate on the subject. Among the attempts to collect the various meanings of the term are Robert Burchell et al., *Costs of Sprawl Revisited* (Washington, DC: Transportation Research Board, National Research Council, 1998), 5–7, and *Costs of Sprawl 2000* (Washington, DC: Transportation Research Board, National Research Council, 2002); Nancy Chin, "Unearthing the Roots of Urban Sprawl: A Critical Analysis of Form, Function and Methodology" (paper 47, Center for Advanced Spatial Analysis, London, 2002); Reid Ewing, "Is Los Angeles–Style Sprawl Desirable?" *Journal of the American Planning Association* (Winter 1997): 107–9; Anthony Downs, "Some Realities about Sprawl and Urban Decline," *Housing Policy Debate* 10, no. 4 (1999): 956; and Oliver Gillham, *The Limitless City* (Washington, DC: Island Press, 2002). Both the Burchell and the Gillham works, although they end up ratifying most of the accepted wisdom on sprawl, do represent some attempt to present opposing views. To my mind, the best analysis of why none of these attempts to define sprawl really work can be found in Kenneth A. Small, "Urban Sprawl: A Non-Diagnosis of Real Problems," in *Metropolitan Development Patterns*, ed. Ann LeRoyer, Annual Roundtable, 2000 (Cambridge, MA: Lincoln Institute of Land Policy, 2000), 26–29. For an important study of sprawl and its causes that appeared too late for me to use in this work, see Marcy Burchfield, Henry G. Overman, Diego Puga, and Matthew A. Turner, "The Determinants of Urban Sprawl: A Portrait from Space" (working paper, October 2004, dpuga.economics.utoronto.ca/papers/sprawl.pdf).

2. For a discussion of the coining of the word, its various meanings over time, and the anti-sprawl crusade, see pt. 2.

3. A good source of information on current urban densities and other statistics can be found on a Web site maintained by Wendell Cox, demographia.com. Similar information is available in two books by Peter W. G. Newman and Jeffrey R. Kenworthy, *Cities and Automobile Dependence: A Sourcebook* (Aldershot: Gower Publishing, 1989), and *Sustainability and Cities: Overcoming Automobile Dependence* (Washington, DC: Island Press, 1999).

4. Density gradient charts have been popular, particularly with geographers, since the 1950s. It appears that their greatest exponent was the British geographer Colin Clark. See, for example, Colin Clark, "Urban Population Densities," *Journal of the Royal Statistical Society* 114 (1951): 490–94; D. Edmonston, *Population Distribution in American Cities* (Lexington, MA: Lexington Books, 1975); and Ivan Light, *Cities in World Perspective* (New York: Macmillan, 1983).

Chapter 2

1. In this book, unless otherwise specified, for large areas I use gross densities, meaning the number of residences or people divided by the total land area. When I refer to small areas I use net residential densities, meaning the density of residences in the residential part of the area. So a city of 100,000 occupying forty square miles would have a gross density of 2,500 people per square mile. Typically, half the land in any large urban area would be nonresidential, so a typical residential subdivision might have a residential density of 5,000 people per square mile. Unless otherwise indicated I also use the words "city" or "urban" in their largest sense, meaning an entire urban territory.

2. On Rome, see Ludwig Friedlaender, *Darstellungen aus der Sittensgeschichte Roms in der Zeit von August bis zum Ausgang der Antonine* (Leipzig: S. Hirzel, 1910); and Neville Morley, *Metropolis and Hinterland: The City of Rome and the Italian Economy, 200 B.C.–A.D. 200* (Cambridge: Cambridge University Press, 1996). I am grateful to Diane Favro of the University of California, Los Angeles, for her help on Roman urban geography.

3. On the Chinese preference for rural, exurban, and suburban life, see Yi-Fu Tuan, *Passing Strange and Wonderful: Aesthetics, Nature and Culture* (Washington, DC: Island Press, 1993), 111, 131. For suburbanization in pre-Columbian Mexico, see John Noble Wilford, "In Maya Ruins, Scholars See Evidence of Urban Sprawl," *New York Times*, December 19, 2001, D1.

4. On city cycles, see the short discussion and bibliography in Anthony M Orum, *City-Building in America* (Boulder, CO: Westview Press, 1995), 20–21.

5. For the eighteenth-century expansion of London, see Peter Hall, *Cities in Civilization* (New York: Pantheon Books, 1998), 1066; and Donald Olsen, *Town Planning in London: The Eighteenth and Nineteenth Centuries* (New Haven, CT: Yale University Press, 1982).

6. In this book, I have chosen the somewhat unfamiliar term "exurban" because there has been no consensus among observers what to call the exceedingly low-density area beyond the suburbs that is still an integral part of the urban system. Some of the possible alternatives—for example, the "countrified city," "postsuburbs," "urban fringe," "rural-urban interface," "rural-urban fringe," and "metropolitan fringe"—are discussed in Tom Daniels, *When City and Country Collide: Manag-*

ing Growth in the Metropolitan Fringe (Washington DC: Island Press, 1999). See also R. E. Pahl, "The Rural-Urban Continuum," in *Readings in Urban Sociology* (Oxford: Pergamon Press, 1968), 263–97. There are also variations on the term "peri-urban" used primarily in southern Europe but also occasionally in English and "rurbanisation," used in France. The first prominent use of the term "exurban" was apparently made by Auguste C. Spectorsky in his book *The Exurbanites* (Philadelphia: Lippincott, 1955), a light-hearted look at affluent commuters in the New York area. A much more pessimistic view was put forward by John J. Tarrant, *The End of Exurbia: Who Are All Those People and Why Do They Want to Ruin Our Town?* (New York: Stein & Day, 1976). An interesting analysis of the phenomenon, although not using the term "exurbia" in any prominent way, can be found in a book by John Herbers, a *New York Times* correspondent, entitled *The New Heartland: American's Flight beyond the Suburbs and How It Is Changing Our Future* (New York: Times Books, 1978). At least as interesting is another journalistic treatment in Richard Louv, *America II* (New York: Penguin Viking, 1985). Interesting comments can also be found in Jack Lessinger, *Penturbia: Where Real Estate Will Boom after the Crash of Suburbia* (Seattle, WA: Socio-Economics Inc., 1990). Unfortunately, academic writing on this topic has been amazingly thin. Probably the most useful recent work has been a series of studies by Arthur C. Nelson, for example, in his "Characterizing Exurbia," *Journal of Planning Literature* 6, no. 4 (May 1992): 350–68; Judy S. Davis, Arthur C. Nelson, and Kenneth J. Dueker, "The New 'Burbs, the Exurbs and Their Implications for Planning Policy" *Journal of the American Planning Association* 60, no. 1 (Winter 1994): 45–59; Arthur C. Nelson and Thomas Sanchez, "Exurban and Suburban Households: A Departure from Traditional Location Theory," *Journal of Housing Research* 8, no. 2 (1997): 249–76, and "Debunking the Exurban Myth: A Comparison of Suburban Households," *Housing Policy Debate* 10, no. 3 (1999): 689–709; and Arthur C. Nelson, "The Planning of Exurban America: Lessons from Frank Lloyd Wright's Broadacre City," *Journal of Architectural Planning Research* 12, no. 4 (1995): 337–56. See also the very useful essay and maps by David. M. Theobald, "Land-Use Dynamics beyond the American Urban Fringe," *Geographical Review* 91, no. 3 (July 2001): 544–64.

7. Daniel Defoe, *A Tour through England and Wales* (London: Everyman's Edition, 1928), 1:168. See also Pahl, "The Rural-Urban Continuum," 269.

8. A single New York City block, measuring 200 × 400 feet or about two acres, could house as many as 3,000 people. Richard Plunz, *A History of Housing in New York City* (New York: Columbia University Press, 1990), 45.

9. A classic study of suburban Britain is H. J. Dyos's classic *Victorian Suburb: A Study of the Growth of Camberwell* (Leicester: Leicester University Press, 1961). This was followed by F. M. L. Thompson, *The Rise of Suburbia* (Leicester: Leicester University Press, 1982); and A. E. Edwards, *The Design of Suburbia* (London: Pembridge Press, 1981). For France there was the remarkably precocious study by Jean Bastié, *La Croissance de la banlieue Parisienne* (Paris: Presses universitaires de France, 1964).

10. For a very good study of the decentralization of business from the late nineteenth century to the Second World War, see Robert Lewis, *Manufacturing Montreal: The Making of an Industrial Landscape, 1850 to 1930* (Baltimore: Johns Hopkins University Press, 2000).

11. Friedrich Engels, *The Housing Question* (New York: International Publishers, 1935), 84–85.

12. This landscape of chateaus or country houses, with its carefully preserved "rural" feel, was called "seasonal suburban" by Hugh Clout because its inhabitants moved back and forth from Paris

("The Growth of Second-Home Ownership: An Example of Seasonal Suburbanization," in *Suburban Growth: Geographical Processes at the Edge of the Western City,* edited by James Johnson [New York: John Wiley, 1974], 101–28). Because it was at such low density I have chosen to call this part of the landscape exurban rather than suburban.

13. For a brief but useful glimpse of the history of exurbanization around Paris, see Henri Raymond et al., *L'Habitat pavillonnaire* 2d ed. (Paris: Centre de Recherche d'Urbanisme, 1971), 35–36.

14. On the Cocktail Belt, see J. W. R. Whitehand, "The Settlement Morphology of London's Cocktail Belt," in *Tijdshrift voor Economische en Sociale Geografie* 58 (January–February 1967): 20–27.

15. There is an odd lack of serious study of these resort landscapes, particularly the Riviera. Some information can be gleaned from Michael Nelson, *Queen Victoria and the Discovery of the Riviera* (London: I. B. Tauris, 2001); and Robert Kangil, *High Season: How One French Town Has Seduced Travelers for 2000 Years* (New York: Viking, 2002).

16. H. G. Wells, *Anticipations of the Reactions of Scientific and Mechanical Progress upon Human Life and Thought* (New York: Harper's, 1902), 52.

17. Ibid., 70–71.

Chapter 3

1. For an excellent analysis of suburban development in the twentieth century, see J. W. R. Whitehand and C. M. H. Carr, *Twentieth-Century Suburbs: A Morphological Approach* (London: Routledge, 2001).

2. Where builders in the region of London had constructed only 6,000 houses yearly in the early 1920s, the figure soared to over 34,000 before the end of the decade and to nearly 73,000 at the peak in 1934. Alan A. Jackson, *Semi-Detached London: Suburban Development, Life and Transport, 1900–39* (London: George Allen & Unwin, 1973), 99–120.

3. J. E. Martin, *Greater London: An Industrial Geography* (Chicago: University of Chicago Press, 1966).

4. Jackson, *Semi-Detached London,* 315. For Britain as a whole, urban population increased from 37.9 million in 1920 to 41.5 million in 1939, an increase of about 9.5 percent, but urban land increased from 2.2 million acres to 3.2 million acres or nearly 50 percent. Peter Hall et al., *The Containment of Urban England,* 2 vols. (London: PEP, 1973), 1:69, 83.

5. Information about work trips along with a great deal of detail about urban Britain at the end of the 1930s can be found in the famous "Barlow Report," the *Report of the Royal Commission on the Geographical Distribution of the Industrial Population* (London: HMSO, 1940). The work trip figures are cited in Hall et al., *Containment of Urban England* 2:380.

6. On the plotlands, see Dennis Hardy and Colin Ward, *Arcadia for All: The Legacy of a Makeshift Landscape* (London: Mansell, 1984).

7. Although the term "gentrification" is relatively new, apparently coined by the sociologist Ruth Glass in the 1960s to describe the invasion of middle-class residents into working-class areas of London, the phenomenon it identifies probably has a very long history. There is, however, only a very scant literature on the early history. One example, although without the "gentrification" label

is Isabelle Backouche, *La trace du fleuve: La Seine et Paris (1750–1850)* (Paris: Editions de l'Ecole des hautes études en sciences sociales, 2000). One of the first substantial texts to discuss the term itself was *Gentrification of the City*, ed. Neil Smith and Peter Williams (Winchester, MA: Allen & Unwin Inc., 1986). Neil Smith, in his *The New Urban Frontier: Gentrification and the Revanchist City* (London: Routledge, 1966), concentrates on what he considers the negative aspects, particularly displacement. Like most urban issues of this kind, there is considerable controversy surrounding even the most basic notions. See, for example, the very different views on the issue of displacement in Lance Freeman and Frank Braconi, "Gentrification and Displacement," *Journal of the American Planning Association* 70, no. 1 (Winter 2004): 39–53.

8. A classic work on the growth of the Paris suburbs is Jean Bastié, *La Croissance de la banlieue Parisienne* (Paris: Presses universitaires de France, 1964). On the creation of the new suburban single-family houses or *pavillons*, see Françoise Dubost, "Le Choix du pavillonnaire," and Annie Fourcaut, "Naissance d'un quartier ordinaire en banlieue parisienne: Le Nouveau Domont (1923–1938)," both in *Les Premiers banlieusards: Aux origines des banlieues de Paris, 1860–1940*, ed. Alain Faure (Paris: Editions Créaphis, 1991). Annie Fourcaut has been one of the most prolific commentators on the history of twentieth-century French suburbs. See, for example, her bibliographic essay "L'Histoire urbaine de la France contemporaine: Etat des lieux," *Histoire Urbaine*, no. 8 (December 2003): 171–85.

9. On the rise, decline, and then resurgence of Greenwich Village, see Caroline F. Ware, *Greenwich Village, 1920–30* (New York: Houghton-Mifflin Co., 1935). One of the interesting results of the recent flood of books on gay history has been a new awareness of the history of many of the early gentrified neighborhoods. See, for example, the now-classic essay by Manuel Castells, "Cultural Identity, Sexual Liberation and Urban Structure: The Gay Community in San Francisco," in *The City and the Grassroots* (Berkeley: University of California Press, 1983), 138–69.

10. Among the best recent books describing working-class suburbia are Joseph Bigott, *From Cottage to Bungalow: Houses and the Working Class in Metropolitan Chicago, 1869–1929* (Chicago: University of Chicago Press, 2001); and Betsy M. Nicolaides, *My Blue Heaven: Life and Politics in the Working-Class Suburbs of Los Angeles, 1920–1965* (Chicago: University of Chicago Press, 2002).

11. On the way that less affluent families were able to afford to live in the suburbs, there is the interesting work of Richard Harris—for example, *Unplanned Suburbs: Toronto's American Tragedy, 1901–1951* (Baltimore: Johns Hopkins University Press, 1996). For a summary of suburban developments in the United States, see Harris's "The Making of American Suburbs, 1900–1950s: A Reconstruction," in *Changing Suburbs: Foundation, Form and Function*, ed. Richard Harris and Peter J. Larkham (London: Spon Press, 1999).

12. On automobile ownership and the percentage of people living in single-family homes, see Robert Fogelson, *The Fragmented Metropolis: Los Angeles, 1850–1930* (Berkeley: University of California Press, 1967), 146.

13. The development of what we think of as postwar trends in Los Angeles in the interwar years is one of the themes of an admirable book by Greg Hise, *Magnetic Los Angeles: Planning the Twentieth-Century Metropolis* (Baltimore: Johns Hopkins University Press, 1997). On Detroit, see Heather Barrow "The Automobile in the Garden: Henry Ford, Suburbanization and the Detroit Metropolis, 1919–1945," a 2005 dissertation for the History Department of the University of Chicago on the way the suburb of Dearborn anticipated later developments.

14. Harris, *Unplanned Suburbs.*

15. The earliest industrial parks, for example, the Trafford Park Industrial Estate outside Manchester or the Central Manufacturing District in Chicago, date to the turn of the twentieth century. On the role of industry in the decentralization of American cities, see Robert Lewis, *Manufacturing Montreal: The Making of an Industrial Landscape, 1850 to 1930* (Baltimore: Johns Hopkins University Press, 2000), and "Running Rings around the City: North American Industrial Suburbs, 1850–1950," in *Changing Suburbs*, ed. Harris and Lewis. For San Francisco, there is Richard Walker, "Industry Builds the City: The Suburbanization of Manufacturing in the San Francisco Bay Area, 1850–1940," *Journal of Historical Geography* 27, no. 1 (2001): 3–19. An excellent study of the decentralization of industry in Los Angeles can be found in Hise, *Magnetic Los Angeles.* For Chicago, see Robert Bruegmann, "Schaumburg, Oak Brook, Rosemont and the Restructuring of the Chicago Metropolitan Area," in *Chicago Architecture and Design, 1923–1993*, ed. John Zukowsky (Chicago: Art Institute of Chicago, 1993), 159–78.

16. Richard Harris and Robert Lewis "The Geography of North American Cities and Suburbs, 1900–1950: A New Synthesis," *Journal of Urban History* 27, no. 3 (March 2001): 265.

17. On commercial decentralization, perhaps the best recent studies are by Richard Longstreth, notably his *City Center to Regional Mall: Architecture, the Automobile and Retailing in Los Angeles, 1920–1950* (Cambridge, MA: MIT Press, 1997), and *The Drive In, the Supermarket and the Transformation of Commercial Space in Los Angeles, 1914–1941* (Cambridge, MA: MIT Press, 1999).

18. Harris and Lewis "The Geography of North American Cities and Suburbs," 271.

19. Although many books on urban history persist in describing the interstate highway system as a product of the postwar era, it had already been prefigured in the great parkways of the New York City and Washington, DC, areas. The outline of the system that eventually was constructed was already clearly described in documents produced by almost every large metropolitan area as well as in national studies such as U.S. Public Roads Administration, *Toll Roads and Free Roads: Message from the President of the United States . . . on the Feasibility of a System of Transcontinental Toll Roads and a Master Plan for Free Highway Development* (Washington, DC: Government Printing Office, 1939); and U.S. National Interregional Highway Committee, *Interregional Highways: Message from the President of the United States Transmitting a Report of the National Interregional Highway Committee* (Washington, DC: Government Printing Office, 1944).

20. Ernest W. Burgess, "The Growth of the City: An Introduction to a Research Project," in Robert E. Park, Ernest W. Burgess, and Roderick D. McKenzie, *The City* (Chicago: University of Chicago Press, 1925).

21. Park, Burgess, and MacKenzie, *The City,* 47–62.

22. For example, Harris and Lewis in "Geography of North American Cities and Suburbs," 273, have shown that there were as many suburbs with rents below the metropolitan average as there were high-rent suburbs.

23. The Homer Hoyt model is described in Homer Hoyt, *The Structure and Growth of Residential Neighborhoods in American Cities* (Washington, DC: Federal Housing Administration, 1939).

24. For a summary of the various models of urban growth, along with theoretical and critical positions on this growth, see W. Parker Frisbie and John D. Kasarda, "Spatial Processes," in *Handbook of Sociology*, ed. Neil J. Smelser (Newbury Park, CA: Sage Publications, 1988).

Chapter 4

1. The population of the Paris region expanded from 5.5 to 8.3 million people in the period 1950–70. Greater Hamburg, which had 1.7 million inhabitants in 1939, in contrast, reached only 1.85 million by 1965 and then declined back to 1.7 million by the end of the century.

2. Household size in the United States, which had been nearly five people at the end of the nineteenth century and was still over four people in 1930, fell to 3.37 persons in 1950 and by the 1970s had reached 3.14. The figure in 2000 stood at 2.62 persons.

3. The book usually described as the standard history of suburbanization in the United States is Kenneth Jackson's *Crabgrass Frontier: The Suburbanization of the United States* (Oxford: Oxford University Press, 1985). Other major treatments include Robert Fishman, *Bourgeois Utopias: The Rise and Fall of Suburbia* (New York: Basic Books, 1987); and Dolores Hayden, *Building Suburbia: Green Fields and Urban Growth, 1820–2000* (New York: Pantheon Books, 2003). These books, although valuable in telling some part of the story, tend to share a number of standard academic assumptions about the suburbs and, for this reason, dwell on many of the same episodes, usually atypical developments and reform efforts, rather than talking about the growth of typical, ordinary suburbs. They also suggest that American suburbia is inherently different from suburbia elsewhere, and there is often a negative tone, particularly as the story approaches the present. What is still lacking is a body of work that describes history of the development of the average suburb both in the United States and elsewhere without jumping so quickly to value judgments. In recent years, there has been a steady outpouring of new work that starts to do this: Richard Harris and Robert Lewis "The Geography of North American Cities and Suburbs, 1900–1950: A New Synthesis," *Journal of Urban History* 27, no. 3 (March 2001): 262–93; several of the essays in Kiril Stanilov and Brenda Case Scheer, eds., *Suburban Form: An International Perspective* (New York: Routledge, 2004); and Greg Hise, *Magnetic Los Angeles: Planning the Twentieth-Century Metropolis* (Baltimore: Johns Hopkins University Press, 1997). There has also been a recent literature that is more positive about the average suburban experience, for example, Tom Martinson, *American Dreamscape: The Pursuit of Happiness in Postwar Suburbia* (New York: Carroll and Graf, 2000).

4. On large-scale suburban development before World War II, see Harris and Lewis, "Geography of North American Cities," 279; Greg Hise, *Magnetic Los Angeles*, 1997.

5. Harris and Lewis "Geography of North American Cities," 280. On the ways working-class ethnic families were able to acquire their own houses, see also Joseph Bigott *From Cottage to Bungalow: Houses and the Working Class in Metropolitan Chicago, 1869–1929* (Chicago: University of Chicago Press, 2001); and Betsy Nicolaides, *My Blue Heaven: Life and Politics in the Working-Class Suburbs of Los Angeles, 1920–1965* (Chicago: University of Chicago Press, 2002). Homeownership rates are discussed in Mason C. Doan, *American Housing Production, 1880–2000: A Concise History* (Lanham, MD: University Press of America, 1997).

6. One of the reasons that the history of residential decentralization has been so obscure is that most scholars have used the set of statistics that was most easily available to them—that is, population figures by municipal boundaries. But these boundaries have shifted constantly in many cities, at least through the earlier part of the century, so trying to compile any reasonable set of statistics about degree of suburbanization at different eras has been very difficult. What we would really need to get

a good picture would be a set of Geographic Information System (GIS) historical databases with all census data indicated by graduated colors for each census tract every decade.

7. For the origins and development of suburban industrial parks and office parks, see chap. 5, n. 33.

8. Where 32 percent of all metropolitan manufacturing jobs were located beyond city limits in 1900, by 1947 this figure had grown to 41 percent, according to Harris and Lewis ("Geography of American Cities and Towns," 265). It is likely that even more jobs had moved outward but because they stayed within city boundaries they were less visible to the statisticians. Clearly, industrial moves took place on a larger scale after the war than before because the country was larger and more prosperous, but the apparent jump in the rate was probably just a statistical artifact, a result of the fact that cities in the North and East of the United States that earlier were regularly able to annex large adjacent land areas could no longer do so because of opposition by suburbanites. This meant that outward relocations of industrial plants crossed municipal boundaries and were easier to spot in statistics. A good study showing the continuity of industrial decentralization can be found in Robert Lewis, *Manufacturing Montreal: The Making of an Industrial Landscape, 1850 to 1930* (Baltimore: Johns Hopkins University Press, 2000).

9. On black suburbs, see, for example, Andrew Wiese, "Places of Our Own: Suburban Black Towns before 1960s," *Journal of Urban History* 19 (1992): 3–54, and "Stubborn Diversity: A Commentary on Middle-Class Influence in Working-Class Suburbs," *Journal of Urban History* 27, no. 3 (March 2001): 347–54.

10. On the proliferation of suburban governments and their diversity, see Harris and Lewis "Geography of North American Cities," 280–83.

11. On the work of the Levitt firm in France, see Isabelle Gournay, "Levitt France et la banlieue à l'américaine: premier bilan," *Histoire Urbaine*, no. 5 (June 2002), 167–87.

12. The comment that did occur was largely negative, particularly when it concerned the single-family house, *le cancer des banlieues*. On this, see Henri Raymond et al., *L'Habitat pavillonnaire*, 2d ed. (Paris: Centre de Recherche d'Urbanisme, 1971), 27.

13. On the decline of the dowtown before World War II, see Alison Isenberg, *Downtown: A History of the Place and the People Who Made It* (Chicago: University of Chicago Press, 2004), chap.4. On the suburban shopping center, see remarkable work by Lizabeth Cohen, "From Town Center to Shopping Center: The Reconfiguration of Community Marketplaces in Postwar," *Historical Review* 101, no. 4 (October 1996): 1050–80.

14. Charles Jones and Layne Hoppe, *The Urban Crisis in America* (Washington, DC: Washington National Press, 1969); Jeanne R. Lowe, *Cities in a Race for Time* (New York: Random House, 1967); and Mitchell Gordon, *Sick Cities* (Baltimore: Penguin Books, 1965).

15. For an excellent study of the idea of the "urban crisis" and the debate that surrounded it, see Robert Beauregard, *Voices of Decline: The Postwar Fate of U.S. Cities*, 2d ed. (New York: Routledge, 2003). The classic attempt to refute the accepted wisdom on the urban crisis was Edward Banfield's *The Unheavenly City: The Nature and Future of Our Urban Crisis* (Boston: Little, Brown & Co., 1968).

16. On "back to the city," see, for example, Shirley Laska and Daphne Spain, *Back to the City: Issues in Neighborhood Renovation* (New York: Pergamon, 1980). This concept was hotly contested by

many other writers, who claimed that the trickle of people moving in was dwarfed by the flood of people moving out. Unfortunately there is no good study of the history of gentrification, particularly gentrification before the late 1960s. Osman Suleiman, a graduate student in American studies at Harvard University, is doing an important study on the gentrification in Brooklyn in his dissertation "The Birth of Postmodern New York: Gentrification, Postindustrialization and Race in South Brooklyn, 1950–1980."

17. On the multinucleation of industry, see Harris and Lewis, "Geography of American Cities and Towns," 268–69. For the Harris-Ullman model, see Chauncey D. Harris and Edward L. Ullman, "The Nature of Cities," *Annals of the American Academy of Political and Social Science* 42 (November 1945): 7–17.

18. On the Ruhrgebiet, see Ursula von Petz, "The German Metropolitan Region," in *Mastering the City: North European City Planning, 1900–2000,* ed. Koos Bosma and Helma Hellinga (Rotterdam: NAi Publishers, 1998), 56–65.

19. Jean Gottmann, *Megalopolis: The Urbanized Northeast Seaboard of the United States* (New York: Twentieth Century Fund, 1961).

Chapter 5

1. Deyan Sudjic, *The 100 Mile City* (San Diego, CA: Harcourt Brace, 1992).

2. The difficulty in understanding contemporary urban systems is one of the major themes of *Sprawltown: Cercando la città in periferia* by Richard Ingersoll (Rome: Meltemi, 2004). This book was unavailable at the time I finished this volume, but I was able to see some draft chapters of the forthcoming English version generously sent to me by the author.

3. Christophe de Chenay, "Les industries quittent aussi l'Ile de France," *Le Monde,* January 18, 2003.

4. For an overview of the jobs in central business districts compared to their metropolitan area, see Peter Gordon and Harry Richardson, "The Geography of Transportation and Land Use," in *Smarter Growth: Market-Based Strategies for Land Use Planning in the Twenty-first Century,* ed. Randall Holcombe et al. (Westport, CT: Greenwood Press, 2001), 36–39.

5. On the Dutch Randstad, see Harm Tilman, "The Dutch Metropolitan Region," in *Mastering the City: North European City Planning, 1900–2000,* ed. Koos Bosma and Helma Hellinga (Rotterdam: NAi Publishers, 1998), 76–85.

6. Much conventional thinking about the relationship between center and edge is encapsulated in the title of an essay in a recent book on urban change: "Exurbia or Islington." In this essay Anita Summers suggests that continued decentralization and gentrification are two different urban fates (Anita A. Summers, Paul C. Cheshire, and Lanfranco Senn, eds., *Urban Change in the United States and Western Europe* [Washington, DC: Urban Land Institute, 1999]).

7. The rise of condominium ownership in the city has been surprisingly little studied. Matt Lasner at the Graduate School of Design at Harvard is writing a dissertation on the subject.

8. For the way Paris has dominated French governmental attention, see Jean-Francois Gravier, *Paris et le désert francais,* 2d ed. (Paris: Flammarion, 1958).

9. Figures for Paris and its region here and elsewhere are taken from Philippe Louchart and Jean-Jacques Ronsac, *Atlas des Franciliens: Recensement de la population de 1990*, vol. 1, *Population et Logements* (Paris: Institut d'Aménagement et d'Urbanisme de la Région d'Ile-de-France & Institut national de la statistique et des études économiques, 1991), and from the very handy charts in Wendell Cox's Web site www.demographia.com. The peak population for the city of Chicago, slightly over 3.5 million, was recorded in the 1950 census. Since then it declined to just under 3 million before rebounding slightly.

10. On densities, see Robert Bruegmann, "Urban Sprawl and Density," in *Smarter Growth: Market-Based Strategies for Land-Use Planning in the Twenty-first Century*, ed. Sam Staley and Randall Holcombe (Westport, CT: Greenwood Press, 2001). Robert Bruegmann, "The Paradoxes of Sprawl Reform," in *Urban Planning in a Changing World: The Twentieth-Century Experience*, ed. Robert Freestone (London: Spon Press, 2000), 158–74. As mentioned earlier, almost all of the figures I cite in this book for large areas are "gross densities," meaning the total population of a given area divided by the total amount of land. They are simple to calculate and useful in giving an idea of the general order of magnitude of density. So, for example, the gross population density for the United States is seventy people per square mile. This includes densely populated states like New Jersey, which, at just over 1,000 people per square mile, is the densest state, to the largest and most loosely populated state, Alaska, with less than five people per square mile. In this book, the set of figures I will use for American urban areas is most often what the Census Bureau calls "urbanized areas." Unlike other census categories, for example, the figures associated with "metropolitan areas," the urbanized areas classification defines cities functionally, including all of the area that clearly belongs to one urban system. The metropolitan area definitions, by way of contrast, because they follow governmental boundaries, are all but useless in computing densities. When I talk about density in small areas, for a block, for example, I use "net" densities that measure the number of houses or people only on residential land and factor out all of the uninhabited land or land used for other purposes such as parks or industry. So, for example, a subdivision composed of houses with 9,000-square-foot lots would have a net density of five units to the acre, or a "net residential density" of 3,200 people per square mile. Net densities could range from four hundred dwelling units per net residential acre in new apartment buildings on New York's Upper East Side to one unit for every five acres at the far reaches of the New York metropolitan area.

11. These secondary or "occasional" residences are mapped in Louchart and Ronsac, *Atlas des Franciliens*, 1:70.

12. Matthew Power and Daniel Guido, "Downtown Rebound: Downtown Residential Development Swells," *Builder* 25, no. 1 (January 2002): 182.

13. Starting with residential neighborhoods near the city core, like Nob Hill and Russian Hill and then with larger adjacent areas like North Beach, the tide of gentrification started to sweep across the very large Western Addition and Castro Valley in the 1960s. Since then gentrification has reached into almost every part of the city. On racial change in the city, see Evelyn Nieves, "Blacks, Hit by Housing Costs, Leave San Francisco Behind," *New York Times*, August 2, 2001. For some information on population growth, see Rebecca Sohmer and Robert Lang, "Downtown Rebound," *Fannie Mae Foundation and Brookings Institution Center on Urban and Metropolitan Policy Census Note*, May 2001 (http://www.brookings.edu/es/urban/census/downtownrebound.pdf). The social science literature on gentrification is largely unsatisfactory. As recently as the early 1990s, there was

doubt about whether it was really an important trend; see, for example, L. S. Bourne, "The Myth and Reality of Gentrification: A Commentary on Emerging Urban Forms," *Urban Studies* 30, no. 1 (1993): 183–89. By the end of the 1990s it was clear that it was a very important trend. A good summary of some of the current thought on it can be found in a special issue of *Housing Policy Debate*, vol. 10, no. 4 (1999). See also Neil Smith, *The New Urban Frontier: Gentrification and the Revanchist City* (London: Routledge, 1966).

14. See, for example, the testimony in Paul S. Grogan and Tony Proscio, *Comeback Cities: A Blueprint for Urban Neighborhood Revival* (Boulder, CO: Westview Press, 2000).

15. In Chicago, for example, the 1957 zoning ordinance would have allowed a city many times larger than the 3 million people it then housed. Since the 1960s, along with gentrification has come a nearly continual pressure for downzonings and other restrictions. A recent study has shown that a small area of Lakeview that seems congested to many residents with its current population of about 100,000, was actually zoned in 1957 to accommodate nearly half a million people. Successive zoning changes have removed much of this capacity. Chicago, Mayor's Zoning Reform Commission, *Principles for Chicago's New Zoning Ordinance: Recommendations for Preserving, Protecting, and Strengthening Chicago's Neighborhoods*, 2004, p. 17. As far as I know, there has been no comprehensive study of the cumulative effect of downzoning efforts in American central cities.

16. For some of the objections to homeowner associations, see Evan McKenzie, *Privatopia: Homeowner Associations and the Rise of Residential Private Government* (New Haven, CT: Yale University Press, 1996). For objections to the gated community, see Mary Gail Snyder and Edward J. Blakely, *Fortress America: Gated Communities in the United States* (Washington, DC: Brookings Institution Press, 1996).

17. A strong defense of the mobile home against the charges against it can be found in Allan D. Wallis, *Wheel Estate: The Rise and Decline of Mobile Homes*, rev. ed. (Baltimore: Johns Hopkins University Press, 1997).

18. For an attempt to describe the reordering of the suburban landscape in one American city, see Robert Bruegmann "Schaumburg, Oak Brook, Rosemont and the Restructuring of the Chicago Metropolitan Area," in *Chicago Architecture and Design, 1923–1993*, ed. John Zukowsky (Chicago: Art Institute of Chicago, 1993), 159–78.

19. The original figure came from the Northeastern Illinois Planning Commission, *Strategic Plan for Land Resource Management* (Chicago: The Commission, 1992), 4. This figure appears over and over again in local literature and in national publications. See, for example, F. Kaid Benfield et al., *Once There Were Greenfields: How Urban Sprawl Is Undermining America's Environment, Economy and Social Fabric* (New York: National Resources Defense Fund, 1999), 18; Constance E. Beaumont, *How Superstore Sprawl Can Harm Communities and What Citizens Can Do about It* (Washington, DC: National Trust for Historic Preservation, 1994), 3; Bruce Katz, ed., *Reflections on Regionalism* (Washington, DC: Brookings Institution Press, 2000), 16, Ton Daniels, *When City and Country Collide: Managing Growth in the Metropolitan Fringe* (Washington, DC: Island Press, 1999), 12.

20. Researchers at this organization, the Northeastern Illinois Planning Commission (NIPC), arrived at the new figures by using more accurate measuring techniques and excluding parks and other open space preserved within the newly urbanized area. Northeastern Illinois Planning Commission, *1990 Land Use in Northeastern Illinois Counties, Minor Civil Divisions and Chicago Community Areas*, NIPC Data Bulletin 95–1 (Chicago: Northeastern Illinois Planning Commission, June 1995).

21. This story is summarized in an excellent article by Harold Henderson, "Up against the Sprawl," *Reader* 25, no. 48 (September 6, 1996), 1 ff.

22. For an excellent compilation of these figures, see Wendell Cox's Web site, Demographia (http://www.demographia.com/).

23. For a discussion of density and sprawl, see Witold Rybczynski, "Measuring Sprawl," *Zell/ Lurie Real Estate Center Review* (Spring 2002), 94–103.

24. As defined by the census, the "urbanized area" contains a "central place" and an adjacent densely settled "urban fringe" that together contain at least 50,000 inhabitants. The urban fringe generally consists of contiguous territory with a density of over 1,000 people per square mile but in some cases islands of lower density surrounded by higher density settlement are included as are noncontiguous densely settled areas separated by a body of water or mountain.

25. Already in the mid-1990s, the Northeastern Illinois Planning Commission calculated that several of the fast-growing counties on the periphery were growing in population faster than they were growing in land area (John Paige, NIPC, e-mail correspondence with author, February 2000).

26. In this Urban Transportation Center model of the Chicago region, for each census since the 1950s, the population for each census tract was loaded into the appropriate area on a GIS map so that researchers could calculate the average distance between any two pairs of individuals in the metropolitan area. The resulting set of figures constituted an effective "index of decentralization," and it clearly showed that the pace of decentralization had slowed since the 1960s (Ashish Sen et al., *Highways and Urban Decentralization* [Chicago: Urban Transportation Center, University of Illinois at Chicago], 1998).

27. Real estate analyst Tracy Cross reported that in late 1999 the ratio of detached to attached houses in the Chicago area stood at 50/50 ("Four Perspectives on Shaping Community," presented at the "Shaping Community: The Choices We Make," a conference held at DePaul University, November 12, 1999).

28. "Crowding Now Way of Life in California," *Los Angeles Times,* June 10, 2001, B-1.

29. For a good recent survey and analysis of densities and sprawl, see William Fulton, Rolf Pendall, Mai Nguyen, and Alicia Harrison, *Who Sprawls Most? How Growth Patterns Differ across the U.S.,* Survey Series (Washington, DC: Brookings Institution, Center on Urban and Metropolitan Policy, July 2001). This report uses figures from the National Resources Inventory, which gives a much higher estimate of urbanized land than the census because it also counts what we have called exurban land.

30. In this book, the figures on lot sizes have been taken from the U.S. Census, Construction Statistics, part of the Manufacturing, Mining and Construction Statistics. They are available on the department's Web site.

31. Peter Mieskowski and Edwin C. Mills, "The Causes of Suburbanization," *Journal of Economic Perspectives* 7, no. 3 (September 1993): 135–47; Marlow Vesterby and Ralph Heimlich, "Land Use and Demographic Change: Results from the Fast-Growth Counties," *Land Economics* 67, no. 3 (August 1991): 279–91.

32. There is a startling lack of good information about the teardown phenomenon. I am grateful to Michael Kowski, a student in a seminar I taught on cities, suburbs, and exurbs for alerting me to the fact that his own working-class suburb of Burbank, Illinois, shows the same patterns of gentrification and teardowns as some of the wealthiest communities. There are some good comments on

teardowns in Karen A. Danielsen, Robert E. Lang, and William Fulton, "Retracting Suburbia: Smart Growth and the Future of Housing," *Housing Policy Debate* 10, no. 3 (1999): 526–27.

33. For some history of the industrial park, see John M. Findley, *Magic Lands: Western Cityscapes and American Culture after 1940* (Berkeley: University of California Press, 1998), 117–59; and Margaret O'Mara, *Cities of Knowledge: Cold War Science and the Search for the Next Silicon Valley* (Princeton, NJ: Princeton University Press, 2004). For a discussion of this building type in the Chicago region, see Bruegmann "Schaumburg, Oak Brook, Rosemont and the Restructuring of the Chicago Metropolitan Area," 159–78. There has been extremely little research on the office park, which seems to have developed around cities in the American South in the 1950s.

34. The north Italian plain has been called the *Megalopoli Padana*, or megalopolis of the Po Valley, by the Italian geographer Eugenio Turri in his important study *La Megalopoli Padana* (Venice: Marsilio, 2000). A good description of the kinds of fabric found in the urban area of Milan can be found in Stefano Boeri, Arturo Lanzani, and Edoardo Marini, "Le tre città della regione milanese" (with an English summary), *Casabella*, no. 607 (1993), 18–23.

35. The term "edge city" was coined by journalist Joel Garreau in his book *Edge City: Life on the New Frontier* (New York: Doubleday, 1991). Although there is a great deal of wonderful material in this book, and it deserved the very large readership it enjoyed because it explained a good deal about decentralization in simple language, the term itself has not proven to be useful.

36. Perhaps the most direct response to Joel Garreau has been Robert E. Lang, *Edgeless Cities: Exploring the Elusive Metropolis* (Washington, DC: Brookings Institution Press, 2003). On the continuing decentralization of jobs, see Edward L. Glaeser, Matthew Kahn, and Chenghuan Chu, *Job Sprawl: Employment Location in U.S. Metropolitan Areas*, Survey Series (Washington, DC: Brookings Institution, May 2001). For Los Angeles, see Peter Gordon and Harry Richardson, "Beyond Polycentricity: The Dispersed Metropolis, Los Angeles, 1970–1990," *Journal of the American Planning Association* 62, no. 3 (Summer 1996): 289–95; and Genevieve Giuliano and Kenneth Small, "Subcenters in the Los Angeles Region," *Regional Science and Urban Economics* 21 (1991): 163–82.

37. A good example of this is the original scheme for what became Old Orchard Shopping Center in Skokie. Developed by the owners of Marshall Field's, the center was to contain branches of the two large State Street department stores, Field's and Carson Pirie Scott, with a group of other merchants that would replicate in part the spatial arrangements of the Loop.

38. Louchart and Ronsac, *Atlas des Franciliens*, 1:32.

39. For a good review of efforts to write the history of the French city in the twentieth century, see Annie Fourcaut, "L'histoire urbaine de la France contemporaine: Etat des lieux," *Histoire Urbaine*, no. 8 (December 2003): 171–85. In this and her other important works on French urban history, Fourcaut describes the French city in the same way that many American authors describe American cities. She writes (175) that by the end of the twentieth century a generalized urban sprawl had rendered the old distinctions between urban and rural in France obsolete and had created a diffuse mode of life founded on mobility and the single-family house. See also Vincent Fouchier, *Les densités urbaines et le développement durable: Le cas de l'Ile de France et des villes nouvelles* (Paris: Édition du SGVN, 1997), 73.

40. On the social problems of the French suburbs, see Henri Rey, *La peur des banlieues* (Paris: Presses de la fondation nationale des sciences politiques, 1996). Some examples of recent reports in English: "Burning 'Burbs," *Economist*, January 27, 1996; Anne Swardson, "France Watches Warily

as Violent Protests Mount; Unemployment, Racial Issues Prompt Disorder," *Washington Post*, January 3, 1998; Chris Hedges, "In Suburban Squalor Near Paris, Echoes of Jihad." *New York Times*, October 16, 2001.

41. On the French preference for single-family houses or *pavillons*, see, for example, the chapter "La satisfaction residentielle," in Yvonne Bernard's *La France au logis: Étude sociologique des pratiques domestiques* (Mardaga: Architecture & Recherches, 1992); Henri Raymond et al., *L'habitat Pavillonnaire*, 2d ed. (Paris: Centre de Recherche d'Urbanisme, 1971), 135; and Norma Evenson, *Paris: A Century of Change, 1878–1978* (New Haven, CT: Yale University Press, 1979), 249–55.

42. Guenter Haag, *Sprawling Cities in Germany* (Milan: FrancoAngeli, 2002).

43. Thomas Sieverts's use of the term *Zwischenstadt* is complex, suggesting not just the physical layout of cities but also the way they are positioned economically in a local and international context. For example, in one place he defines *Zwischenstadt* as the "type of built-up area that is between the old historical city centres and the open countryside, between the place as a living space and the nonplaces of movement, between small local economic cycles and the dependency of the world market" (*Cities without Cities: An Interpretation of the Zwischenstadt* [London: Spon Press, 2003], xi). The first edition of this work, *Zwischenstadt: Zwischen ort und welt, Raum und Zeit, Stadt und Land* (Zurich: Birkhäuser Verlag, 1999), attracted a good deal of attention and was republished several times before the English edition appeared in 2003.

44. Sievert, *Cities without Cities*.

45. On the urban region of northern Italy, see n. 34 above, this chap.

46. On Barcelona, see Francisco Javier Monclús, "Estrategias ubánisticas y crecimiento suburbano en las ciudades espanolas: El caso de Barcelona," in *La ciudad dispersa, suburbanización y neuvas periferias*, ed. Francisco Javier Monclús (Barcelona: Centre de Culture Contemporània de Barcelona, 1998). For a particularly graphic illustration of the dramatic dispersion of the city since the 1960s, see the chart of population figures for the various parts of the metropolitan area (164). On Barcelona, there is also the very interesting work of Antonio Font, Carles Llop, and Josep Maria Vilanova, *La constucció del territory metropolità: Morfogènsi de la region de Barcelona* (Barcelona: Mancomunitat de municips de l'Area metropolitana de Barcelona, 1999), with a summary in English. An extremely good graphic presentation of the dispersion of Barcelona can be found in *Peninsula Iberica*, vol. 15 of *Atlas histórico de ciudades europeas*, ed. Manuel Guàrdia, Francisco Javier Monclús, and José Luis Oyón (Barcelona: Centre de Cultura Contemporània, 1994).

47. This is confirmed, for example, by two of the most vocal critics of excessive automobile use, Peter Newman and Jeffrey Kenworthy, in their *Sustainability and Cities* (Washington, DC: Island Press, 1999), 82.

48. Christian Gerondeau, *Transport in Europe* (Boston: Artec House, 1997), 85.

49. For an eloquent statement about the connection between affluence and mobility, see Charles Lave, "Cars and Demographics," *Access* 1 (Fall 1992): 4–11.

50. For a good review of international trends in automobile ownership and use, see Genevieve Giuliano, "Urban Travel Patterns," in *Modern Transport Geography*, ed. Brian Hoyle and Richard Knowles, 2d ed. (New York: John Wiley & Sons, 1998), 115–33.

51. Gerondeau, *Transport in Europe*, 226–27, 314–16.

52. A number of commentators have seen Australia as the quintessential suburban nation. On suburban Australia, see the summary by Tony Dingle, "'Gloria Soame': The Spread of Suburbia

in Post-War Australia," in *Changing Suburbs: Foundation, Form and Function*, ed. Richard Harris and Peter J. Larkham (London: Spon Press, 1999). For Canadian suburbs, there is also a summary by Larry McCann in the same volume: "Suburbs of Desire: The Suburban Landscape of Canadian Cities, c. 1900–1950," 111–45.

53. For a recent collection of essays on suburbanization in Europe, America, and elsewhere, see Kiril Stanilov and Brenda Case Scheer, eds., *Suburban Form: An International Perspective* (New York: Routledge, 2004).

54. The exact amount of this new "exurban" land is hard to quantify. The major surveys that attempt to give some kind of picture are the National Resources Inventory (NRI) and the American Housing Survey. The NRI survey is conducted by the U.S. Department of Agriculture and relies on aerial surveying and sampling from small areas. It is probably adequate for recording agricultural lands, but it seems to be wholly unreliable for any precise estimates of developed land. The other major survey, the American Housing Survey conducted by Housing and Urban Development and the Bureau of the Census, relies instead on census materials.

55. According to Arthur C. Nelson of the Georgia Institute of Technology, exurbia houses something like 60 million Americans and is the fastest growing segment of the country ("Characterizing Exurbia," *Journal of Planning Literature* 6, no. 4 [May 1992]: 350–68; Arthur C. Nelson and Kenneth J. Dueker, "The Exurbanization of America and Its Planning Policy Implications," *Journal of Planning Education and Research* 9, no. 2 [1990]: 91–100). For a graphic demonstration of the importance of large exurban lots, see Tom Peterson, "Changes in American Housing Acres Used," paper presented at the "Keep America Growing Workshop: What Is Happening to the Land?" Washington, DC, May 9, 2000. Some excellent information on exurbia, although not using the term, can be found in Ralph E. Heimlich and William D. Anderson, *Development at the Urban Fringe and Beyond: Impacts on Agriculture and Rural Land*, Agricultural Economic Report no. 803 (Washington, DC: U.S. Department of Agriculture, Economic Research Service, 2001); and in David M. Theobald, "Land-Use Dynamics beyond the American Urban Fringe," *Geographical Review* 91, no. 3 (July 2001): 544–64.

56. Judy S. Davis, Arthur C. Nelson, and Kenneth J. Dueker, "The New 'Burbs, the Exurbs and Their Implications for Planning Policy" *Journal of the American Planning Association* 60, no. 1 (Winter 1994): 45–59.

57. On the Carolinas Piedmont there is an interesting old paper by Charles R. Hayes, *The Dispersed City: The Case of Piedmont, North Carolina*, Research Paper no. 173 (Chicago: University of Chicago Department of Geography, 1976). An excellent and prescient study of the Charlotte area of the Piedmont can be found in James W. Clay and Douglas M. Orr, Jr., *Metrolina Atlas* (Chapel Hill: University of North Carolina Press, 1972).

58. For commentary on the California gold rush country as exurbia, see a remarkable book by Timothy Duane, *Shaping the Sierra: Nature, Culture and Conflict in the Changing West* (Berkeley: University of California Press, 1999).

59. For a description and analysis of these decentralizing businesses, see Robert Cervero, *Suburban Gridlock* (New Brunswick, NJ: Rutgers Center for Urban Policy, 1986). See also Truman A Hartshorn and Peter O. Muller, *Suburban Business Centers: Employment Implications* (Washington, DC: U.S. Department of Commerce, Economic Development Administration, Technical Assistance and Research Division, 1986); and Brenda Case Scheer and Mitcho Petkov, "Edge City Morphology:

A Comparison of Commercial Centers," *Journal of the American Planning Association* 64, no. 3 (Summer 1998): 298–310.

60. Some of the best descriptions of what I am calling exurbia come from the pen of geographer John Fraser Hart. He has coined the phrase the "perimetropolitan bow wave" to describe the zone at the edge of the regularly built-up suburbs. This striking metaphor captures a sense of the heightened activity on land at the very edge of the urban region where the forward march of development abuts a zone of intensive agricultural production. The "bow wave" is created where "the least intensive urban land uses are steadily displacing the most intensive agricultural uses" (John Fraser Hart, "The Perimetropolitan Bow Wave," *Geographical Review* 81, no. 1 [January 1991]: 35–51).

61. On the urban fate of Youngstown, see two articles from *Planning* magazine: "Youngstown: Can This Steel City Forge a Comeback?" *Planning* (January 1978); and Thomas A. Finnerty, Jr., "Youngstown Embraces Its Future," *Planning* (August–September 2003): 124–19. A good overview of sprawl in Ohio, from a primarily free-market viewpoint, can be found in Samuel Staley and Matthew Hirsch, *Urban Sprawl and Quality Growth in Ohio* (Columbus: Buckeye Institute for Public Policy Solutions, December 2001).

62. On the extent of "recreational farming," see Heimlich and Anderson, *Development at the Urban Fringe and Beyond.*

63. The mobile home (or "manufactured home") has been one of the largest and fastest growing parts of the American residential market. However, as with so much else in our contemporary landscape, there has been very little real research into the history and dynamics of this building type.

64. Two important French studies include G. Bauer and J. M. Roux, *La rurbanisation ou la ville éparpillée* (Paris: Éditions du seuil, 1976); B. Dézert et al., *La périurbanisation en France* (Paris: SEDES, 1991). The term "periurban" has also been used occasionally in English, for example, in A. B. Cruickshank *Where Town Meets Country: Problems of Peri-Urban Areas in Scotland* (Aberdeen: Aberdeen University Press, 1982).

65. For an excellent analysis and set of maps showing the distribution of second houses in the Paris region, see Louchart and Ronsac, *Atlas des Franciliens*, 1:68. The figures I have given are for the French basin outside the heavily urbanized area of the Île-de-France.

66. Much of the literature comparing American and European cities has simply taken the statistics collected at a given moment and then has drawn conclusions based on these rather than attempting to compare overall trends over a longer time period. Not surprisingly, this has resulted in a literature that emphasizes the differences between the two places. This problem compromises even the best of attempts to compare European and American cities, for example, the essays in Summers, Cheshire, and Senn, eds., *Urban Change in the United States and Western Europe.*

67. Lewis Mumford, *The City in History: Its Origins, Its Metamorphoses and Its Prospects* (New York: Harcourt, Brace Jovanovich, 1961), 540.

68. Lewis's "galactic metropolis" was prefigured by Hans Blumenfeld, who already in the 1980s used an astronomical metaphor when he observed that by the early twenty-first century the entire continental United States would be a "mosaic of contiguous metropolitan orbits" (Hans Blumenfeld, "Metropolis Extended," *Journal of the American Planning Association* 52, no. 3 [1986]: 348).

69. The "galactic metropolis" is described in Peirce Lewis, "The Galactic Metropolis," in *Beyond the Urban Fringe*, ed. Rutherford H. Platt and George Macinko (Minneapolis: University of Minnesota Press, 1983), "The Geographic Roots of America's Urban Troubles," *Earth and Mineral Sciences*

52, no. 3 (Spring 1983): 25–29, and "The Urban Invasion of Rural America: The Emergence of the Galactic Metropolis," in *The Changing American Countryside: Rural People and Places*, ed. Emery Castle (Lawrence: University of Kansas Press, 1995), 39–62.

70. For a striking collection of these images for American cities, see Roger Auch, Janis Taylor, and William Acevedo, *Urban Growth in American Cities: Glimpses of U.S. Urbanization*, U.S. Geological Survey Circular 1252 (Denver, CO: U.S. Geological Survey, EROS Data Center, 2004).

71. Farm prices are from Margot Anderson and Richard Magleby, *Agricultural Resources and Environmental Indicators, 1996–97*, Agricultural Handbook no. 712 (Washington, DC: U.S. Department of Agriculture, Economic Research Service, Natural Resources and Environment Division, July 1997). This publication is available on the Economic Research Service Web site (http://www.ers.usda.gov/publications/arei/Ah712/).

Chapter 6

1. On the supposed anti-urban bias of Americans, see, for example, Kenneth Jackson, *Crabgrass Frontier: The Suburbanization of the United States* (Oxford: Oxford University Press, 1985), 68–69. This view is countered effectively by Andrew Lees, *Cities Perceived: Urban Society in European and American Thought, 1820–1940* (New York: Columbia University Press, 1985), particularly in his conclusions on pp. 305–13.

2. A good example of this nostalgic view of urbanity can be found in the works of Richard Sennett, for example, his *The Fall of Public Man* (New York: Knopf, 1976).

3. Attempts to explain sprawl as the result of the unregulated market economy can be found, for example, in a pioneering American work on sprawl, William H. Whyte, Jr., "Urban Sprawl" in *The Exploding Metropolis*, ed. the editors of *Fortune* (Garden City, NY: Doubleday, 1958).

4. A good postwar example of the point of view that governments must restrain markets in land-use matters can be found in J. William Kapp, *The Social Costs of Private Enterprise* (Cambridge, MA: Harvard University Press, 1950).

5. Marsh ridiculed claims that "sociability increases in proportion to the number of people living on the acre" (in his "Can Land Be Overcrowded? How Little Land Do People Need to Live On?" *Annals of the American Academy of Political and Social Sciences* 51 [January 1914]: 54–58).

6. For some good commentary on the history of the British regulatory system, see Philip Booth, *Planning by Consent: The Origins and Nature of British Planning Control* (London: Routledge, 2003); and Jules Lubbock, *The Tyranny of Taste: The Politics of Architecture and Design in Britain, 1550–1960* (New Haven, CT: Yale University Press, 1995), 338–48.

7. For an argument about the flaws in the concept of market failure, see Richard O. Zerbe and H. E. McCurdy, "The Failure of Market Failure," *Journal of Policy Analysis and Management* 18 (Fall 1999): 558–78.

8. A good exposition of the General Motors myth and refutation of it can be found in David Brodsly's *L.A. Freeway: An Appreciative Essay* (Berkeley: University of California Press, 1981), 95; and in Scott C. Bottles, *Los Angeles and the Automobile: The Making of the Modern City* (Berkeley: University of California Press, 1987), 1–4.

9. Richard Peiser, in his essay "Decomposing Urban Sprawl," *Town Planning Review* 73, no. 1

(2001): 275–99, does a good job refuting the notion that speculators or developers have an inherent interest in promoting low-density development.

10. Attempts to explain sprawl primarily as a consequence of governmental intervention from opposite ends of the political spectrum include Mark Gottdiener, *Planned Sprawl* (Beverly Hills, CA: Sage Publications, 1977); and Michael Lewyn, "Suburban Sprawl: Not Just an Environmental Issue," *Marquette Law Review* 84 (Winter 2000): 301. See also H. V. Savitch, "Encourage, Then Cope: Washington and the Sprawl Machine" in *Urban Sprawl: Causes, Consequences and Policy Responses*, ed. Gregory D. Squires (Washington, DC: Urban Institute Press, 2002). To my mind the most convincing argument that governmental regulations, particularly zoning, have caused "excessive suburbanization" has been made by William Fischel in his essay "Does the American Way of Zoning Cause the Suburbs of Metropolitan Areas to Be Too Spread Out?" in *Governance and Opportunity in Metropolitan America*, ed. Alan Altshuler et al. (Washington, DC: National Academy Press, 1999), 151–91.

11. The most powerful arguments of this kind are found in Jackson's *Crabgrass Frontier*, chap. 11. A major corrective can be found in Robert A. Beauregard, "Federal Policy and Postwar Urban Decline: A Case of Government Complicity," *Housing Policy Debate* 17, no. 1 (2001): 129–51.

12. For Kenneth Jackson's attempt to demonstrate how federal programs of the 1930s helped to doom central neighborhoods though agencies like the Home Owners' Loan Corporation, see *Crabgrass Frontier*, 195–218. On the self-amortized mortgage, see Richard Harris and Robert Lewis, "The Geography of North American Cities and Suburbs: A New Synthesis," *Journal of Urban History* 27, no. 3 (2001): 279. An important corrective to Kenneth Jackson's work on redlining can be found in Amy E. Hillier, "Redlining and the Home Owners' Loan Corporation," *Journal of Urban History* 29, no. 4 (May 2003): 394–420. Hillier shows that the government maps were probably much less influential than Jackson believed because they were not widely available to mortgage lenders.

13. For an example of the way some observers have blamed federal income tax policies for low-density suburbia, see Jackson, *Crabgrass Frontier*, 294.

14. For a discussion of American and foreign incentives for home ownership as well as for an excellent treatment of urban policies generally in the United States and Europe, see Pietro Nivola, *Laws of the Landscape: How Policies Shape Cities in Europe and America* (Washington, DC: Brookings Institution, 1999).

15. For a succinct analysis of the concept of "imputed" rent, see Henry J. Aaron, *Shelter and Subsidies: Who Benefits from Federal Housing Policies?* (Washington, DC: Brookings Institution, 1972), chap. 4.

16. Encouraging homeownership has been a long-standing American policy, one that has attracted very little real dissent and one that is shared by a great many countries worldwide. The estimates of the extent of the subsidy to homeowners has probably been grossly exaggerated, however. One reason is that they typically fail to factor in the value of the standard deduction that is lost when taxpayers itemize expenses. Another is the failure to account for the way this advantage has been capitalized into the costs of the homes producing higher prices and higher taxes. Much of the supposed advantage of the tax incentive can disappear when potential owners bid up the purchase price of a home to reflect at least some of the savings they will receive over time from the deduction because this, in turn, results in higher property taxes, with the result that some of the advantages bestowed by Uncle Sam are merely taken back in subsequent years by the municipalities. This is a very complicated subject, and estimates about how the capitalization of the mortgage interest deduc-

tion benefits translates into home price have been hotly debated. See, for example, Joseph Gyourko and Richard Voith, "Does the U.S. Tax Treatment of Housing Promote Suburbanization and Central City Decline?" (working paper no. 97-13, Federal Reserve Bank of Philadelphia, 1997); Richard Voith, "Does the Federal Tax Treatment of Housing Affect the Pattern of Metropolitan Development?" *Business Review* (March–April 1999), 7; Jesse Abraham and Patric Hendershott, "Patterns and Determinants of Metropolitan House Prices, 1987–91" (NBER working paper 4196, National Bureau of Economic Research, Cambridge, MA, October 1992, http://www.nber.org/papers/w4196); and William A. Fischel, "Sprawl and the Federal Government," *Cato Policy Report* 21, no. 5 (September–October 1999), where Fischel argues that the deduction can be seen as a reward to homeowners for managing their own properties and that the effect of the subsidy is more to increase the size of new houses than it is to increase the amount of land.

17. The role of the condominium in recent urban development is the subject of "Cooperatives, Condominiums, and the Re-Shaping of the American City," a doctoral dissertation by Matthew Lasner currently underway at the Graduate School of Design at Harvard.

18. Even without this wider accounting, the U.S. General Accounting Office recently concluded that there is little conclusive evidence that federal dollars have been a major cause of sprawl (U.S. General Accounting Office, "Community Development: Extent of Federal Influence on 'Urban Sprawl' is Unclear," GAO/RCED-99-87, Washington, DC, April 1999).

19. Joseph J. Persky, Haydar Kurban, and Thomas W. Lester, "Impact of Expenditures on Residential Land Absorption," in *Suburban Sprawl*, ed. Wim Wiewel and Joseph J. Persky (Armonk, NY: M. E. Sharp, 2002), 237–38.

20. This appears to be a major theme in Joel Hirschhorn's *Sprawl Kills: How Blandburbs Steal Your Time, Health and Money* (Revolution Publishing, 2005), forthcoming, at least as indicated in his essay "Sprawl Politics Traps Americans in Blandburbs," *Newtopia Magazine*, no. 17 (2004), http://www.newtopiamagazine.net/content/issue17/features/sprawlpolitics.php.

21. William Fischel, in his essay "Does the American Way of Zoning Cause the Suburbs of Metropolitan Areas to Be Too Spread Out?" makes a strong case that zoning has caused lower densities than the market itself would have dictated.

22. A source of information on land-use controls in Houston as well as an argument that zoning could be replaced by private controls can be found in Bernard Siegan, *Land Use without Zoning* (Houston: Bartholdi & Lazarus, 1972).

23. As we will see in pt. 3, large-lot zoning was much used in the second campaign against sprawl to slow growth and to maintain the appearance of a "rural" environment. For an argument about how low-density zoning fueled "excessive suburbanization," see William Fischel, *The Homevoter Hypothesis* (Cambridge, MA: Harvard University Press, 2001), 230.

24. A statement of this position can be seen in Marc Gottdiener's *Planned Sprawl: Public and Private Interests in Suburbia* (Beverly Hills, CA: Sage Publications, 1977), a study of Suffolk County, Long Island, and one of the best early descriptions of sprawl.

25. For a powerful recent statement of this position, see Edward L. Glaeser and Matthew Kahn, "Sprawl and Urban Growth" (NBER working paper no. w9733, National Bureau of Economic Research, Cambridge, MA, May 2003). The impact of the automobile and roadways on cities and towns is a primary theme of Owen Gutfreund, *Highways and the Reshaping of the American Landscape* (London: Oxford University Press, 2004).

26. A study by David Hartgen in North Carolina suggests only a very weak link between road improvements and construction and growth ("Highway and Sprawl in North Carolina" [Policy Report, John Locke Foundation, Raleigh, NC, 2003]).

27. Thomas Sieverts, *Cities without Cities: An Interpretation of the Zwischenstadt* (London: Spon Press, 2003), 1.

28. Individuals nostalgic for the transit era often claim that people were able to get around as easily by transit and traveled as much then as they do now by automobiles. For a refutation of this argument and an excellent analysis of how the amount of travel has increased, see Randal O'Toole, *The Vanishing Automobile and Other Myths* (Bandon, OR: Thoreau Institute, 2001), 85–92, 301–2. For eloquent arguments on the importance of increased mobility for ordinary citizens, see Marcial Echenique, "Mobility and Space in Metropolitan Areas," in *Cities for the New Millennium*, ed. Marcial Echenique and Andrew Saint (London: Spon Press, 2001); Charles Lave, "Cars and Demographics," *Access* 1 (Fall 1997): 4–11; and Melvin M. Webber, "The Joys of Spread-City," *Urban Design International* 3, no. 4 (1998): 201–6.

Chapter 7

1. Quoted in Patrick Abercrombie, *Town and Country Planning* (London: Thornton Butterworth, 1933), 177.

Chapter 8

1. Anthony D. King, *The Bungalow: The Production of a Global Culture*, 2d ed. (Oxford: Oxford University Press, 1995), 177–92. See also Mark Clapson, *Invincible Green Suburbs, Brave New Towns* (Manchester: Manchester University Press, 1998), for some excellent commentary on class-based suburb bashing before and after the Second World War (5–13).

2. Howard Marshall, "The Rake's Progress," in *Britain and the Beast*, ed. Clough Williams-Ellis (London: J. M. Dent & Sons, 1937), 164. This volume was a collection of some of Britain's most spirited warriors against the suburbs and the working-class inhabitants of them.

3. Clough Williams-Ellis, *England and the Octopus*, reprint ed. (Portmeirion: Penrhyndeudraeth, 1975), 26.

4. Ibid., 40.

5. Peter Hall, *Cities of Tomorrow* (London: Basil-Blackwell, 1988), 80–85; Anthony King, "Historical Patterns of Reaction to Urbanism: The Case of Britain, 1880–1939," *International Journal of Urban and Regional Research* 4 (1980): 453–69.

6. Thomas Sharp, *Town and Countryside: Some Aspects of Urban and Rural Development* (London: Oxford University Press, 1932), 149.

7. Ibid., 218–24.

8. Ibid., 11.

9. On the use of the term in the nineteenth century, *Oxford English Dictionary*, compact ed., s.v. "sprawl." David Halton, a postgraduate student at the Glasgow School of Art in a forthcoming article on the use of the word "sprawl" reports that the earliest usage of the term as a noun referring to

the built environment that he could find in the *London Times* date to 1919 but that the term, usually modified by the word "urban" or "suburban," appeared in the newspaper over two dozen times between then and 1950.

10. Lewis Mumford, *The Culture of Cities* (New York: Harcourt, Brace & Co., 1938), 234. Further testimony that neither the term nor the concept were new can be found in H. Myles Wright, "The Next Thirty Years: Notes on Some Probable Trends in Civic Design," *Town Planning Review* 27, no. 3 (1956): 103–23.

Chapter 9

1. For a compendium of information about attitudes about growth during the second campaign against sprawl, see Randall W. Scott, ed., *Management and Control of Growth*, 4 vols. (Washington, DC: Urban Land Institute, 1975).

2. Among those attending *Fortune*'s conference on sprawl were the venerable New York planner Charles Abrams, Philadelphia planner Edmund Bacon, housing reformer Catherine Bauer, landscape architect Charles W. Eliot of Harvard University, Charles Haar of the Harvard Law School, Wilfred Owen of the Brookings Institution, and Douglas Haskell, editor of *Architectural Forum*.

3. The editors of *Fortune* magazine, eds., *The Exploding Metropolis* (Garden City, NY: Doubleday, 1958), 131.

4. William Whyte, "Urban Sprawl," in ibid., 115.

5. On Los Angeles bashing, see Mark Peel, "The Urban Debate: From Los Angeles to the Urban Village," in *Australian Cities: Issues, Strategies, Policies for Urban Australia in the 1950s*, ed. Patrick Troy (London: Cambridge University Press,1995), 39-64; Mitchell Gordon, *Sick Cities* (Baltimore: Penguin Books, 1965), 1 ff.; Jane Jacobs, *Death and Life of Great American Cities* (New York: Vintage Books, 1961), 12, 73, 119.

6. Real Estate Research Corporation, *The Costs of Sprawl: Environmental and Economic Costs of Alternative Residential Development Patterns at the Urban Fringe*, vol. 1, *Detailed Cost Analysis;* vol. 2, *Literature Review;* vol. 3, *Executive Summary* (Washington, DC: Government Printing Office, 1974).

7. For some critics of *The Costs of Sprawl Report*, the major problem was methodological, that the researchers failed to account for differences in size between houses and apartments, meaning that the purported savings were really not due at all to differences in planning or density but almost entirely to simple construction costs. On this, see Alan Altshuler's review of *The Costs of Sprawl*, by Real Estate Research Corporation, *Journal of the American Institute of Planners* 43, no. 2 (1977): 207–9; Duane Windsor, "A Critique of the Costs of Sprawl," *Journal of the American Planning Association* 45, no. 3 (July 1979): 279–92. For other critics, the chief problem was that the assumptions made in the computer programs were unrealistic because they only considered first costs and failed to account for whatever might have happened after that. Richard Peiser, for example, showed that master-planned communities very often turned out not to be more economical because they were less adaptable to changes in market demand ("Does It Pay to Plan Suburban Growth?" *Journal of the American Planning Association* 50 [1984]: 419–33, and "Density and Urban Sprawl," *Land Economics* 65, no. 3, [August 1989]: 193–204).

8. John R. Seeley, *Crestwood Heights: A Study of the Culture of Suburban Life* (New York: Basic

Books, 1956); David Riesman, *The Lonely Crowd: A Study of the Changing American Character* (New Haven, CT: Yale University Press, 1950).

9. John Keats, *The Crack in the Picture Window* (Boston: Houghton-Mifflin, 1957); Richard Gordon et al., *The Split-Level Trap* (New York: Random House, 1961

10. Herbert Gans, *The Levittowners: Ways of Life and Politics in a New Suburban Community* (New York: Vintage Books, 1967). The quote is taken from a new preface to a later edition (New York: Columbia Univeristy Press, 1982), xviii.

11. Gans's comments were part of a "Symposium on the State of the Nation's Cities," *Urban Affairs Quarterly* 18, no. 2 (December 1982): 177.

12. Thomas L. Blair, *International Urban Crisis* (New York: Hill & Wang, 1974); Jean R. Lowe, *Cities in a Race with Time* (New York: Random House, 1967); Jeffrey Hadden, Louis Masotti, and Kevin Larson, *Metropolis in Crisis* (Itasca, IL: F. E. Peacock, 1967); and Charles O. James and Layre D. Hoppe, *Urban Crisis in America: The Remarkable Ribicoff Hearings* (Washington, DC: National Press, 1969).

13. On the environmental movement, see the major study by Samuel P. Hays, *Beauty Health and Permanence: Environmental Politics in the United States, 1955–1985* (Cambridge: Cambridge University Press, 1987). For the relation of this movement to suburbanization, see Adam Rome *The Bulldozer in the Landscape* (Cambridge: Cambridge University Press, 2001). A very good analysis of the history of key strains of environmental thought as well as their limitations can be found in Charles Rubin, *The Green Crusade* (New York: Free Press, 1994); and Hal K. Rothman, *Saving the Planet* (Chicago: Ivan R. Dee, 2000).

14. On attempts to control pollution, see Martin Melosi, *Pollution and Reform in American Cities, 1870–1930* (Austin: University of Texas Press, 1980); and Joel Tarr, *The Search for the Ultimate Sink: Urban Pollution in Historical Perspective* (Akron, OH: University of Akron Press, 1996).

15. Rachel Carson, *Silent Spring* (Boston: Houghton Mifflin, 1962); Barry Commoner, *The Closing Circle: Nature, Man and Technology* (New York: Knopf, 1971); and Robert Rienow and Leona Train Rienow, *Moment in the Sun: A Dial Report on the Deteriorating Quality of the American Environment* (New York: Dial Press, 1967).

16. On the suburban support for the environmental movement, see the fascinating testimony in Rome, *The Bulldozer in the Landscape.*

17. On the Nixon administration and environmental legislation, see Russell E. Train, "The Environmental Record of the Nixon Administration," *Presidential Studies Quarterly* 26 (Winter 1996): 185–95; and, from a very different perspective, John Brooks Flippen, "Containing the Urban Sprawl: The Nixon Administration's Land Use Policy," *Presidential Studies Quarterly* 26 (Winter 1996): 197–207.

18. Paul Ehrlich, *The Population Bomb* (New York: Ballantine Books, 1968), 69–80.

19. There had been many earlier examples of this kind of thinking—see, for example, Fairfield Osborn, *Our Plundered Planet* (Boston: Little, Brown, 1948); William Vogt, *Road to Survival* (New York: W. Sloane Assoc., 1948)—but it was in the late 1960s that they took hold of the popular imagination.

20. The most conspicuous critic of Ehrlich was Julian Simon. His *The Resourceful Earth* (Oxford: Oxford University Press, 1984), was a massive assault on the entire philosophical as well as quantitative edifice of the limits to growth enterprise. A more recent book that explores the weaknesses of limits to growth is Greg Easterbrook, *A Moment on the Earth* (New York: Viking, 1995), a book that,

among other things, investigates the long history of environmental "crises," many of which turn out to be false alarms.

21. Fred Hirsch, *The Social Limits to Growth* (Cambridge, MA: Harvard University Press, 1976).

22. Among the more important anti-automobile titles were Lewis Mumford, *The Highway and the City* (New York: Mentor Books, 1964); John Keats, *Insolent Charioteers* (Philadelphia: Lippincott, 1958); Alpheus Quinley Mowbray, *Road to Ruin* (Philadelphia: Lippincott, 1969); Helen Leavitt, *Superhighway-Superhoax* (Garden City, NY: Doubleday, 1970); Richard R. Schneider, *Autokind vs. Mankind* (New York: Schocken Books, 1972); and Ronald A. Buel, *Dead End: The Automobile in Mass Transportation* (New York: Prentice Hall, 1972). A recent book in the same genre is Jane Holtz Kay, *Asphalt Nation: How the Highway Took over America and How We Can Get It Back* (New York: Crown Books, 1997). Still highly negative but somewhat more reliable is Elmer Johnson, *Avoiding the Collision of Cities and Cars* (Chicago: The Academy, 1993). For a good corrective, see James Dunn, Jr., *Driving Forces: The Automobile, Its Enemies and the Politics of Mobility* (Washington, DC: Brookings Institution, 1998).

23. A powerful polemic against freeways was one of the major elements in journalist Robert Caro's massive biography of New York's great highway builder, Robert Moses. Although *The Power Broker* (New York: Knopf, 1974) received much praise when it was issued, it was a fundamentally one-sided portrayal and fails to give any indication of why Moses was so successful for such a long time and how he was able to do what planners and engineers all over the country were doing but typically with more success and skill. A major reappraisal of Moses is long overdue.

24. For a listing of some of the studies that purport to show "induced traffic," see the Sierra Club Web site (http://www.sierraclub.org/sprawl/transportation/seven.asp). For a short rebuttal from the critics of anti-sprawl, see Randal O'Toole, *The Vanishing Automobile and Other Myths* (Bandon, OR: Thoreau Institute, 2001), 397–99. A good recent survey can be found in Robert Cervero, "Road Expansion, Urban Growth, and Induced Travel: A Path Analysis," *Journal of the American Planning Association* 69, no. 2 (Spring 2003): 145–65.

25. In most cities, the early freeways had a very obvious effect on cutting travel times and reducing congestion. People came from all over the world to witness the way residents of Los Angeles or San Diego could drive around their metropolitan areas at fifty miles per hour. Some more recent examples of building out of congestion are Phoenix, Atlanta, and Houston in the 1980s and 1990s (Robert T. Dunphy, "Passing Gridlock," *Urban Land* 56, no. 11 [November 1997]: 58–61, 83; Robert Dunphy et al., *Moving beyond Gridlock: Traffic and Development* [Washington, DC: Urban Land Institute, 1997]; and Wendell Cox, "Performance Indicators in Urban Transport Planning," paper delivered to eighth International Conference on Competition and Ownership in Passenger Transport in Rio De Janeiro, September 2003, reprinted on Cox's Web site, www.demographia.com).

26. For a very useful analysis of this sort with a number of interesting challenges to conventional wisdom, see Brian D. Taylor, "Rethinking Traffic Congestion," *Access*, no. 21 (Fall 2002), 8–16.

27. Quoted in Kenneth Jackson, *Crabgrass Frontier: The Suburbanization of the United States* (Oxford: Oxford University Press, 1985), 42.

28. "Big Yellow Taxi," written and originally performed by Joni Mitchell in 1970.

29. Twentieth Century Fund report quoted by Walter A. Tucker, ed., *The Crisis in Open Land* (Wheeling, WV: American Institute of Park Executives, 1959). This quote also appears in Rome, *The Bulldozer in the Landscape*, which is a good source on the campaign for open space.

30. Aldo Leopold, *Sand County Almanac* (New York: Oxford University Press, 1949). Rome, *The Bulldozer in the Landscape*, 153–88, does an excellent job chronicling some of these revisions in aesthetic notions about landscape.

31. Stewart Udall, *The Quiet Crisis*, with an introduction by John F. Kennedy (New York: Holt Rinehart & Winston, 1963); Ian McHarg, *Design with Nature* (Garden City, NY: Nature Press, 1969).

32. Peter Blake, *God's Own Junkyard: The Planned Deterioration of America's Landscape* (New York: Holt, Rinehart & Winston, 1964).

33. Lewis Mumford, *The City in History: Its Origins, Its Metamorphoses and Its Prospects* (New York: Harcourt, Brace Jovanovich, 1961), 506.

34. "Little Boxes," words and music by Malvina Reynolds, 1963.

35. There has been a massive upsurge in interest in the middle-class suburban landscape of the 1950s as the growing literature on Googie coffee shops, Eichler homes, and drive-in restaurants attests.

36. William Reilly, *The Use of Land: A Citizen's Policy Guide to Urban Growth* (New York: Thomas Y. Crowell Co., 1973.

37. Ibid., 47.

38. Bay Area geographer James Vance was particularly eloquent in his argument that the anti-sprawl campaign was fueled by a coalition of downtown business people, artists, and academics who wanted to impose their own aesthetic ideas on the population at large (*Geography and Urban Evolution in the San Francisco Bay Area* [Berkeley: University of California Institute for Governmental Affairs, 1964], 68–69).

Chapter 10

1. Robert Burchell et al., *Costs of Sprawl—2000*, Transit Cooperative Research Program Report 74 (Washington, DC: Transportation Research Board, National Research Council, 2002). This report was a follow-up to a literature survey: Robert Burchell et al., *Costs of Sprawl Revisited* (Washington, DC: National Academies Press, 1998).

2. Burchell et al., *Costs of Sprawl—2000*, 58–59.

3. For a broadside attack on *The Costs of Sprawl*, see Wendell Cox and Joshua Utt, "The Costs of Sprawl Reconsidered: What the Data Really Show" (Backgrounder, no. 1770, Heritage Foundation, Washington, DC, June 25, 2004), on the Heritage Foundation Web site. For a sensible analysis of the costs of sprawl in New Jersey, see Anthony Downs, "The Impacts of Smart Growth upon the Economy" (paper presented to Land Use Institute of the New Jersey Institute for Continuing Legal Education, New Brunswick, NJ, April 2003; available at www.anthonydowns.com).

4. For example, Burchell et al.'s *Costs of Sprawl—2000* and *Costs of Sprawl Revisited* both list many of the studies of Harry Richardson and Peter Gordon, perhaps the most prominent academic critics of the anti-sprawl campaign, but there is no real effort to engage with their arguments. For an interesting and characteristically pragmatic retrospective analysis of the *Costs of Sprawl* reports, see Anthony Downs, "The Costs of Sprawl Revisited" (paper presented to the Urban Land Institute District Council Meeting, Washington, DC, April 15, 2004; available at www.anthonydowns.com).

5. Peter Newman and Jeffrey Kenworthy, *Cities and Automobile Dependence: An International*

Sourcebook (Aldershot: Gower Publishing, 1989). This book was expanded and updated in Jeffrey Kenworthy and Felix Laube with Peter Newman, *An International Sourcebook of Automobile Dependence in Cities, 1960–1990* (Boulder: University of Colorado Press, 1999). The same authors proposed ways to reduce automobile dependence in Peter Newman and Jeffrey Kenworthy, *Sustainability and Cities: Overcoming Automobile Dependence* (Washington, DC: Island Press, 1999).

6. For a succinct review of the problems of these anti-automobile books, see Randal O'Toole, *The Vanishing Automobile and Other Myths* (Bandon, OR: Thoreau Institute, 2001).

7. For a recent summary of the views of Peter Gordon and Harry Richardson, see their "Compactness or Sprawl: America's Future vs. the Present," in *Cities for the New Millennium,* ed. Marcial Echenique and Andrew Saint (London: Spon Press, 2001), 53–64.

8. When the Texas Transportation Institute calculated the amount of time lost to congestion in 2000, Los Angeles, America's densest urbanized area, came in at eighty-two hours per year, Boston at sixty-six, and Kansas City at just twenty-eight hours.

9. For a good presentation of issues surrounding travel and density, see Brian D. Taylor, "Rethinking Traffic Congestion," *Access,* no. 21 (Fall 2002), 8–16. For an interesting graphic display, see Wendell Cox, "Smart Growth and Housing Affordability" (paper commissioned by the Millennial Housing Commission, Washington, DC, March 2002, on www.dmographia.com Web site, 61).

10. For a good, short exposition of the correlation between affluence and mobility, see Marcial Echenique, "Mobility and Space in Metropolitan Areas," in *Cities for the New Millennium,* ed. Echenique and Saint, 30–37. See also Randall Crane and Daniel G. Chatman, "Traffic and Sprawl: Evidence from U.S. Commuting, 1985 to 1997," *Planning and Markets* 6, no. 1 (2003), 14–22 (www.pam.usc.edu), who argue that commutes would, in fact, be longer, rather than shorter, if development had been more compact. They also demonstrate how complicated and little understood are the connections between sprawl and transportation.

11. For the arguments about farmland loss during the second campaign against sprawl, see Robert Rienow and Leona Train Rienow, *Moment in the Sun: A Dial Report on the Deteriorating Quality of the American Environment* (New York: Dial Press, 1967), chap. 4, "Stoking Stomachs." A good summary of issues as seen from the anti-sprawl side can be found in American Farmland Trust, *Farming on the Edge: A New Look at the Importance and Vulnerability of Agriculture near American Cities* (Washington, DC: American Farmland Trust, 1994). See also Tom Daniels, *Holding Our Ground* (Washington, DC: Island Press, 1997).

12. Bill McKibben, "An Explosion of Green," *Atlantic Monthly* 275, no. 4 (April 1995): 65–83. Ironically, some writers have suggested that this increase in forested area is due, in part, to increases in housing construction that, in turn, cause an increase in demand for wood, and this in turn drives the planting of trees.

13. For a response from anti-sprawl skeptics on farmland, see Peter Gordon and Harry W. Richardson, "Farmland Preservation and Ecological Footprints: A Critique," *Planning and Markets* 1, no. 1 (September 1998): 1–7; Samuel Staley, *The Sprawling of America: In Defense of the Dynamic City,* Policy Study no. 251 (Los Angeles: Reason Public Policy Institute, 1996), and and "The Vanishing Farmland Myth and the Smart Growth Agenda" (Policy Brief No. 12, Reason Public Policy Institute, Los Angeles, January 2000); Samuel R. Staley and Matthew Hisrich, "Urban Sprawl and Quality Growth in Ohio" (Buckeye Institute for Public Policy Solutions, Columbus, OH; Reason Public Policy Institute, Los Angeles, December 2001). See also the insightful comments on the geography

of the fringe between urban and rural uses in John Fraser Hart, "The Perimetropolitan Bow Wave," *Geographical Review* 81, no. 1 (January 1991): 35–51. There is excellent material on agriculture in Ralph E. Heimlich and William D. Anderson, *Development at the Urban Fringe and Beyond: Impacts on Agriculture and Rural Land,* Agricultural Economic Report no. 803 (Washington, DC: U.S. Department of Agriculture, Economic Research Service, 2001). The authors report that a staggering percentage of farm income, as much as 90 percent, actually comes from nonfarm sources (38).

14. The notion that sprawl causes obesity is a particularly good example of the way apparently authoritative statistical reports, endlessly recycled on Web sites and in the media, have been used to sway public opinion. It appears that the opening salvo was an undated study, apparently put out about 2002 by Richard J. Jackson and Chris Kochititsky, "Creating a Healthy Environment" (Sprawl Watch Clearinghouse Monograph Series, Sprawl Watch Clearinghouse, Washington, DC), www.sprawlwatch.org. This was followed by Barbara A. McCann and Reid Ewing, "Measuring the Health Effects of Sprawl" (Smart Growth America and Surface Transportation Policy Project, September 2003), www.smartgrowthamerica.org; and Reid Ewing et al., "Relationships between Urban Sprawl and Physical Activity, Obesity, and Morbidity," *American Journal of Health Promotion* 18, no. 1 (September–October 2003): 47–57, www.smartgrowthamerica.org. At first glance it would appear that these are important and objective medical studies. But it appears that few, if any, of the authors were actually medical professionals involved in obesity research. The statistical correlation between sprawl and obesity presented in these studies seems hardly conclusive, and the proof of causal link is even less convincing. In fact, it appears that ethnic and racial characteristics and low income are much more closely associated with obesity than any particular land-use pattern. For a mass of contrary evidence and some biting criticism, see Randal O'Toole, "Fake CDC Study Full of Holes" (Myth of the Vanishing Automobile Update 22, Thoreau Institute, Bandon, OR), http://www.ti.org/vaupdate22.html, and "The Myth of the Fat Suburbanites" (Myth of the Vanishing Automobile Update 25, Thoreau Institute, Bandon, OR, April 1, 2002), http://www.ti.org/vaupdate25.html. I am grateful to William Fischel for suggesting the link between Paul Ehrlich's predictions of famine and the current rush to blame sprawl for obesity.

15. One might have thought that one of the few things that everyone in the debates over sprawl could agree on was the total amount of existing developed land in the United States, but even this is hotly contested, with figures ranging from 2 percent to over 10 percent. For some discussion of this debate and the 5.2 percent figure estimated by the National Resources Inventory, see Oliver Gillham, *The Limitless City* (Washington, DC: Island Press, 2002), 84–85. See also Staley, *The Sprawling of America.*

16. Staley, *The Sprawling of America,* 14–17.

17. Edward Glaeser, Matthew Kahn, and Jordan Rappaport, "Why Do the Poor Live in Cities?" (NBER working paper 7636, National Bureau of Economic Research, Cambridge, MA, April 2000); and David M. Cutler, Edward L. Glaeser, and Jacob L. Vigdor, "The Rise and Decline of the American Ghetto," *Journal of Political Economy* 107, no. 3 (1999): 455–506.

18. On this topic, see Pietro S. Nivola, *Laws of the Landscape: How Policies Shape Cities in Europe and America* (Washington, DC: Brookings Institution, 1999), 9; and H. D. Forbes, *Ethnic Conflict: Commerce, Culture and the Contact Hypothesis* (New Haven, CT: Yale University Press, 1997).

19. The decline in "civic engagement" was the theme of a famous essay by Robert Putnam that

was reprinted in *Bowling Alone: The Collapse and Revival of American Community* (New York: Simon & Schuster, 2000). This theme has been taken over by many critics of the suburbs and sprawl.

20. A classic exposition of the theme of "community without propinquity" was articulated by Melvin M. Webber "Order in Diversity: Community without Propinquity," in *Cities and Space*, ed. Lowdon Wingo (Baltimore: Johns Hopkins Press, 1963), 25–54. Webber, one of the most prescient of urbanists, expanded his observations in "The Post-City Age," *Daedalus* 99, no. 4 (Fall 1968): 1091–1110.

21. Myron W. Orfield, *Metropolitics: A Regional Agenda for Community and Stability* (Washington, DC: Brookings Institution Press, 1997), and *American Metropolitics: The New Suburban Reality* (Washington, DC: Brookings Institution Press, 2002); David Rusk, *Cities without Suburbs*, 2d ed. (Washington, DC: Woodrow Wilson Center Press, 1995). A compendium of essays on the ills caused by sprawl concentrating on its supposed role in heightening inequities can be found in Gregory D. Squires, ed., *Urban Sprawl: Causes, Consequences and Policy Responses* (Washington, DC: Urban Institute Press, 2002). By contrast, other authors have explored the benefits sprawl offers to minorities. See, for example, Matthew Kahn, "Does Sprawl Reduce the Black/White Housing Consumption Gap?" *Housing Policy Debate* 12, no. 1 (2001): 77–86.

22. For geographer Richard Morrill the "three central pillars" of anti-sprawl rhetoric were that density is good, that transit is good, and that political fragmentation is bad ("Myths about Metropolis," in *Our Changing Cities*, ed. John Fraser Hart [Baltimore: Johns Hopkins University Press, 1991], 1–11). He argued that larger regional governments often result in the concentration of decision-making power in the hands of a technical elite that may favor much larger and more cost-intensive regional systems, where smaller local ones would actually serve the purposes better. He also argues that smaller governments can give minorities a larger say in decisions made by government. This is a variant of a classic thesis by economist Charles M. Tiebout, who advanced the theory that a proliferation of small local governments afforded citizens more choice in the kinds of services that they wanted or needed ("A Pure Theory of Local Expenditures," *Journal of Political Economy* 64 [October 1956]: 416–24).

23. There are arguments about the virtues of the local property-tax-based government in William Fischel, *The Homevoter Hypothesis* (Cambridge, MA: Harvard University Press, 2001). This is mirrored by the arguments from the political left in Richard A. Walker and Michael K Heiman, "Quiet Revolution for Whom?" *Annals of the Association of American Geographers* 71, no. 1 (March 1981): 76–83.

24. Jane Jacobs, *Death and Life of Great American Cities* (New York: Vintage Books, 1961), 410.

25. Myron Orfield, *Chicago Regional Report: A Report to the John D. and Catherine T. MacArthur Foundation* (Minneapolis: Metropolitan Area Program, 1996).

26. Anthony Downs, "Some Realities about Sprawl and Urban Decline," *Housing Policy Debate* 10, no. 4 (1999): 955–74.

27. For a simple but reliable study of the amount of cash subsidy to various kinds of transportation by the federal government, see U.S. Department of Transportation, Bureau of Transportation Statistics, "Federal Subsidies to Passenger Transportation" (December 2004). For a typical anti-sprawl argument on subsidies, see Gillham, *The Limitless City*, 126–30; or Vukan Vuchic, *Transportation for Livable Cities* (New Brunswick, NJ: Rutgers Center for Urban Policy Research, 2000). For an

opposing view, see Peter Gordon and Harry Richardson, "Are Compact Cities a Desirable Planning Goal?" *Journal of the American Planning Association* 63 (1999): 95–106. See also O'Toole, *The Vanishing Automobile*, 306–10, 380–83.

28. Figures for vehicle efficiency are taken from the General Transit Administration, *Transit and Urban Form* (Washington, DC: U.S. Department of Transportation, 1996). The average load of a transit bus in the United States in the same years was nine.

29. A summary of environmentalist assumptions and beliefs can be found in F. Kaid Benfield, Matthew D. Raimi, and Donald C. T. Chen,, *Once There Were Greenfields* (Washington, DC: National Resources Defense Council, 1999).

30. World Commission on Environment and Development, *Our Common Future* (Oxford: Oxford University Press, 1987), 8.

31. For an interesting analysis of some of the complexity of sustainability, see Daniel Mazmanian and Michael Kraft, *Toward Sustainable Communities: Transition and Transformations in Environmental Policy* (Cambridge, MA: MIT Press, 1999).

32. Some of the most powerful arguments about the need to preserve biodiversity have come from Harvard biologist Edward O. Wilson—for example, in his masterful books *The Diversity of Life* (Cambridge, MA: Harvard University Press, 1992), and *The Future of Life* (New York: Vintage Books, 2003).

33. To my mind, the most balanced account of the debates around species extinction, as around many environmental issues, can be found in Gregg Easterbrook's superb book, *A Moment on the Earth* (New York: Viking, 1995), chap. 30 "Species."

34. For a recent, popular summary of information on global warming, see "Global Warming," special issue of *National Geographic,* vol. 206, no. 3 (September 2004).For an account of the attempts by scientists to document the history of climate and create the global warming diagnosis, see Spencer R. Weart, *The Discovery of Global Warming* (Cambridge, MA: Harvard University Press, 2003). For some interesting alternative perspectives on this subject, see Easterbrook, *A Moment on the Earth,* chaps. 16 and 17.

35. For a skeptical view of the environmental alarmism, see Bjørn Lomborg's eye-popping but ultimately persuasive examination of the subject in *The Skeptical Environmentalist: Measuring the Real State of the World* (Cambridge: Cambridge University Press, 2001), 249–57. Although the savagely negative reviews of this book—particularly those in the November 9, 2001, issue of *Science* magazine, the January 2002, issue of *Scientific American,* and the January 1, 2002, issue of *Nature*— are at first daunting, on closer examination it seems clear that these reviewers do not really engage Lomborg on his own turf. They attempt to discredit him because he does not follow the conventions of academic scientific writing, because his treatment is "unbalanced," and because he attacks "straw men" when he discusses common perceptions of environmental problems rather than the pronouncements of the best authorities. But Lomborg never claimed to be a scientist or to be reporting new empirical evidence. Rather, he was trying to show how activists selectively used science for their own political purposes. He was not presenting a "balanced" picture because he was trying to counter the overwhelming weight of publication to date. In their overheated denunciations, the reviewers appear to confirm many of Lomborg's criticisms. A short but useful review of Lomborg's position, as well as some new material, can be found in another polemic against received opinion,

Johan Norberg's *In Defense of Global Capitalism* (Washington, DC: Cato Institute, 2003). See also the measured assessment by Easterbrook in *A Moment on the Earth*. Further information on global warming can be found in Bjørn Lomborg, ed., *Global Crises, Global Solution* (Cambridge: Cambridge University Press, 2004), which reports the results of the "Copenhagen Consensus" project to determine the most cost-effective measures for dealing with the world's next critical problems.

36. A great deal of the writing by environmentalists implicitly accepts the idea that man is separate from nature. For example, Barry Commoner writes, in *The Closing Circle: Nature, Man and Technology* (New York: Knopf, 1971): "The environmental crisis tells us that there is something seriously wrong with the way in which human beings have occupied their habitat, the earth. The fault must lie not with nature, but with man" (175).

37. James Howard Kunstler, *The Geography of Nowhere: The Rise and Decline of America's Man-Made Landscape* (New York: Simon & Schuster, 1993); John Miller, *Egotopia: Narcissism and the New American Landscape* (Tuscaloosa: University of Alabama Press, 1997).

38. Andres Duany, Elizabeth Plater-Zyberk, and Jeff Speck, *Suburban Nation: The Rise and the Decline of the American Dream* (New York: North Point Press, 2000). On a related movement to preserve rural land, see Randall Arendt, *Rural by Design* (Washington, DC: American Planning Association, 1994), and *Growing Greener* (Washington, DC: Island Press, 1997). See also Peter Calthorpe, *The Next American Metropolis: Ecology, Community and the American Dream* (New York: Princeton Architectural Press, 1993); Peter Calthorpe and William Fulton, *The Regional City* (Washington, DC: Island Press, 2001). A collection of statements about urban problems and the way they can be corrected can be found in Congress for the New Urbanism, *Charter of the New Urbanism* (New York: McGraw-Hill, 2000).

39. Even if more people walked and fewer drove, this might only prove that self-selection was at work, that the publicity generated by the designers and developers attracted people who didn't want to drive. On driving in New Urbanist communities, indeed on the entire question of the relationship between land use and automobile use, some of the best analyses have been done by Randall Crane. See his "Travel by Design," *Access*, no. 12 (Spring 1998), 2–7, "Cars and Drivers in the New Suburbs: Linking Access to Travel in Neotraditional Planning," *Journal of the American Planning Association* 62, no. 1 (Winter 1996): 51–65, and *The Impacts of Urban Form on Travel: A Critical Review*, Working Paper (Cambridge, MA: Lincoln Institute of Land Policy, 1999); and Marlon Boarnet and Randall Crane, *Travel by Design: The Influence of Urban Form on Travel* (New York: Oxford University Press, 2001). See also Ruth Steiner, "Traditional Shopping Centers, *Access*, no. 12 (Spring 1998), 8–13.

40. The "New Suburbanism" sobriquet comes from Alex Krieger, "Whose Urbanism?" *Architecture* 87 (November 1998): 73–76. For a reply by Andres Duany, see "Our Urbanism," *Architecture* 87 (December 1998): 37–40. For an interesting argument about the New Urbanism and its critics, see the Spring 2003 issue of *Markets and Morality* (vol. 6, no. 1), notably, Charles C. Bohl, "Controversy: To What Extent and in What Ways Should Governmental Bodies Regulate Urban Planning?" along with a dialog with Mark Pennington (211–60). Some good balanced comments on New Urbanism can be found in Kenneth Kolson, *Big Plans: The Allure and Folly of Urban Design* (Baltimore: Johns Hopkins University Press, 2001), chap. 7, "Two Cheers for Sprawl." Kolson persuasively argues that the New Urbanism is only the latest version of a long-standing desire by cultural elites to manage middle-class urban life.

41. The phrases "sensitive minority" and "vulgar mass" were used by Aaron Wildavsky, "Aesthetic Power or the Triumph of the Sensitive Minority over the Vulgar Mass," *Daedalus* 96 (1967): 1115-28.

42. On the tradition of intellectuals railing against the suburbs, see Elizabeth Wilson, "The Rhetoric of Urban Space," *New Left Review*, no. 209 (January–February 1995), 146-60.

43. Reyner Banham, *Los Angeles: Architecture of the Four Ecologies* (New York: Harper & Row, 1971).

44. Robert Venturi, Denise Scott Brown, and Steven Izenour, *Learning from Las Vegas: The Forgotten Symbolism of Architectural Form* (Cambridge, MA: MIT Press, 1977). This was the second edition of this publication but because of the high price of the original edition, this has been the one seen by most readers. Sprawl is discussed on xxi, 117-19. Venturi and Scott Brown continued their study of sprawl in "The Highway," *Modulus* 9 (1973): 6-14.

45. Houston has been the inspiration for an entire series of provocative reflections on the form of the contemporary city from individuals like Lars Lerup, *After the City*, rev. ed. (Cambridge: MIT Press, 2001); Albert Pope, *Ladders* (Houston: Rice University School of Architecture, 1996); and Stephen Fox, *Houston Architectural Guide* (Houston: Herring Press, 1990). For some spectacular evocations of Las Vegas, see David Hickey's essay on Liberace in *Air Guitar: Essays on Art and Democracy* (Los Angeles: Art Issues Press, 1997). On Phoenix, see Grady Gammage, Jr., *Phoenix in Perspective: Reflections on Developing the Desert* (Tempe: Arizona State University, Herberger Center, 1999).

46. Of the books produced by Koolhaas and various collaborators, the ones that deal most directly with sprawl are two huge volumes in the series Project on the City, the results of classes at the Harvard Design School, both edited by Chuihua Judy Chung, Jeffrey Inaba, Rem Koolhaas, and Zse Tsung Leong. The first, *The Harvard Design School Guide to Shopping* (Köln: Taschen; Cambridge, MA: Harvard Design School, 2001), was an exploration of the new spaces of retailing. The second, *Great Leap Forward* (Köln: Taschen; Cambridge, MA: Harvard Design School, 2001), was a study of urbanism in Shenzen, Guangzhou, and the Pearl River Delta region of China. See, particularly, the extravagant essay by Koolhaas, "Junkspace," in *Guide to Shopping*, 408-21. A somewhat similar point of view is found in a publication by the Belgian firm of Xaveer de Guyter, architects, in their book *After-Sprawl: Research for the Contemporary City* (Rotterdam: NAi Publishers, 2002). This book includes a spectacular set of urban diagrams clearly indicating the dispersal of European cities.

47. Aaron Betsky and Erik Adigard, *Architecture Must Burn* (Corte Madera: Gingko Press, 2000), sec. 1.0.

48. Thomas Sieverts, *Cities without Cities: An Interpretation of the Zwischenstadt* (London: Spon Press, 2003), 44-48. A book that appeared too late for me to read before finishing the manuscript for this book was Richard Ingersoll's *Sprawltown: Cercando la città in periferia* (Rome: Meltemi, 2004). However, in the drafts of chapters for an English-language edition generously sent to me by Ingersoll, it is clear that he is attempting to deal with various kinds of aesthetic response to sprawl.

49. On the work of American Farmland Trust, see their report, *Farming on the Edge: A New Look at the Importance and Vulnerability of Agriculture Near American Cities* (Washington, DC: American Farmland Trust), 1994.

50. On the history of the Sierra Club, see Michael P. Cohen, *The History of the Sierra Club, 1892–1970* (San Francisco: Sierra Club Books, 1988). For more recent history, there is interesting material in Hal K. Rothman, *Saving the Planet* (Chicago: Ivan R. Dee, 2000), 96-97.

51. For the Sierra Club's attitudes toward sprawl, see "The Dark Side of the American Dream: Costs and Consequences of Suburban Sprawl" (Sierra Club Sprawl Report, San Francisco, 1998), www.sierraclub.org/sprawl/report98/.

52. Benfield, Raimi, and Chen, *Once There Were Greenfields*. The Natural Resources Defense Council also published F. Kaid Benfield, Jutka Terris, and Nancy Vorsanger, *Solving Sprawl: Models of Smart Growth in Communities across America* (New York: Natural Resources Defense Council, 2001).

53. One of the most important aspects of Downs's work has been his concern about how suburbs have used various means to exclude poor residents. This was the subject of his classic work, *Opening up the Suburbs: A Strategy for Urban America* (New Haven, CT: Yale University Press, 1973).

54. In *New Visions for Metropolitan America* (Washington, DC: Brookings Institution, 1994), Downs described the "dominant vision" of the last half-century, which he characterized as "unlimited low-density sprawl." He then described alternative development patterns with more planning and higher densities and what results could be expected from each. The Brookings Institution has continued to published some of the most reliable studies on recent urban growth and sprawl, including a number by Downs—for example, *Stuck in Traffic: Coping with Peak Hour Traffic Congestion* (Washington, DC: Brookings Institution, 1992)—and a recent title by Robert E. Lang, *The Edgeless City: Exploring the Elusive Metropolis* (Washington, DC: Brookings Institution, 2003). Downs has continuously updated his views, every year becoming, it appears to me, less optimistic about the possibility of stopping sprawl and perhaps more skeptical of the advisability of so doing. For a recent assessment, see his remarks on smart growth in New Jersey in "The Impacts of Smart Growth upon the Economy." See also his "The Costs of Sprawl Revisited."

55. With the arrival of the National Trust into the anti-sprawl coalition came a new interest in using governmental agencies and the courts to deal with aesthetic issues. On this, see Kenneth Pearlman, "Aesthetic Regulation and the Courts," in *Environmental Aesthetics*, ed. Jack L. Nasar (Cambridge: Cambridge University Press, 1988), 476–92. Also on environmental aesthetics, see Arnold Berleant, *The Aesthetics of Environment* (Philadelphia: Temple University Press, 1992).

56. One particularly successful project of the National Trust for Historic Preservation starting in 1980 was the Main Street program, which attempted to revive old downtowns that had been hurt by strip competition by reversing the process of "modernization" that had, in the opinion of preservationists, degraded the streetscape. Using preservation, restoration, and new management techniques, preservationists hoped to revitalize both the built environment and the economy of these towns.

57. On the National Trust and Wal-Mart, see a book coauthored by Richard Moe, president of the National Trust, and Carter Wilkie, *Changing Places: Rebuilding Community in the Age of Sprawl* (New York: Henry Holt & Co., 1997); see also Constance Beaumont, *How Superstore Sprawl Can Harm Communities and What Citizens Can Do about It* (Washington, DC: National Trust for Historic Preservation, 1994), and *Better Models for Superstores—Alternatives to Big Box Sprawl* (Washington, DC: National Trust for Historic Preservation, 1997).

58. Bernard J. Frieden, *The Environmental Protection Hustle* (Cambridge, MA: MIT Press, 1979).

59. Edward Banfield, *The Unheavenly City The Nature and the Future of Our Urban Crisis* (Boston: Little, Brown & Co., 1968), 5–6.

60. *Beyond Sprawl: New Patterns of Growth to Fit the New California*. The text of this piece, which

was written by William Fulton, was distributed by the Bank of America. The text can be seen at the Web site of Radical Urban Theory at www.rut.com/misc/beyondSprawl.html.

61. Peter Gordon and Harry W. Richardson, *The Case for Suburban Development* (Los Angeles: Lusk Center Research Institute, School of Urban and Regional Planning, University of Southern California, 1995). This is also known as the "Beyond beyond Sprawl" report. In the wake of the unexpected publicity, Bank of America quietly backed away from original *Beyond Sprawl* publication.

62. This debate occurred in the *Journal of the American Planning Association* in a pair of articles in 1997 (vol. 63, no. 1). In "Is Los Angeles–Style Sprawl Desirable?" (107–28), Reid Ewing defended the mainstream position most commonly seen in professional planning literature. He argued that more planning at higher levels was needed to place limits on private-market activities in order to create a compact city that would be coordinated to allow good accessibility for everyone to jobs, recreation, and public open space. His ideal was a fairly high-density city with multiple higher-density nodes of activity. As indicated by his title, his object lesson in what not to do was Los Angeles. In their counterargument ("Are Compact Cities a Desirable Planning Goal?" 95–106), Peter Gordon and Harry Richardson questioned the basic assumptions of the anti-sprawl forces. Because they were economists by training, they were more likely to take a cost-benefit approach to any proposed actions rather than advocate something because of hard-to-measure aesthetic or social goals. They also represented a Libertarian approach that is inclined to believe that the market is a more efficient way than government to allocate most resources. They argued that sprawl had been the most effective mechanism for resolving many urban problems such as overcrowding or congestion and that the kinds of government regulations called for by people like Ewing were not only largely unnecessary but would also prove counterproductive. Among the most striking aspects of the Gordon-Richardson vs. Ewing debate that followed in the letters column of the journal in Spring 1997 (vol. 63, no. 2) was the basic confusion over the meaning of the term "sprawl." In fact, as Ned Levine, a planner in Bethesda, MD, pointed out, the compact city as described by Ewing, one that had fairly high densities and multiple centers, appeared in many ways to be fairly similar to the Los Angeles described by Gordon and Richardson. A recent restatement of the ideas of Gordon and Richardson can be found in their essay "Compactness or Sprawl: America's Future vs. the Present," in *Cities for the New Millennium,* ed. Marcial Echenique and Andrew Saint (London: Spon Press, 2001), 53–64.

63. For market-friendly solutions to the problems of sprawl, see, for example, Samuel Staley, *Sprawling America: In Defense of the Dynamic City,* Reason Public Policy Institute Policy Study 251 (Los Angeles: Reason Public Policy Institute, 1996); Jane S. Shaw and Ronald D. Utt, *A Guide to Smart Growth: Shattering Myths, Providing Solutions* (Washington, DC: Heritage Foundation and the Political Economy Research Center, 2000); Randal O'Toole, *The Vanishing Automobile and Other Myths: How Smart Growth Will Harm American Cities* (Bandon, OR: Thoreau Institute, 2001); Steven Hayward, "Suburban Legends," *National Review* 51, no. 5 (March 22, 1999): 35–38; and Marshall Kaplan, Todd Steelman, and Allan Wallis, *Sprawl and Growth Management: Problems, Experience and Opportunity* (Denver: University of Colorado, Institute for Policy Research and Implementation, 1990). On free-market environmentalism, see Terry L. Anderson and Donald R. Leal, *Enviro-Capitalists* (Lapham, MD: Bowman & Littlefield, 1997). In recent years, many market solutions—or example, schemes to trade emission rights or congestion pricing—have become popular even on the political left, as witness London mayor Ken Livingston's toll on vehicles entering central London.

64. See, for example, Greg Easterbrook, "Suburban Myth," *New Republic* 51 (March 15, 1999), 18–21. One of the best books that has been written about sprawl and land-use policies in a single city is Gammage, *Phoenix in Perspective.* A very good and, as usual, quite sensible essay linking smart growth to problems in housing affordability can be found in Anthony Downs, "Conflicts between Smart Growth and Housing Affordability" (paper presented at the Association of Collegiate Schools of Planning, Cleveland, November 8, 2001; available at www.anthonydowns.com). See also an article by planner Melvin Webber, who was a pioneer in recognizing new urban patterns, particularly on the West Coast: "The Joys of Spread-City," *Urban Design International* 3, no. 4 (1998): 201–6. For a good survey of problems and benefits of sprawl by authors who see many benefits, see Edward L. Glaeser and Matthew Kahn, "Sprawl and Urban Growth" (working paper no. 9733, National Bureau of Economic Research, Cambridge, MA, May 2003).

65. The term "smart growth" appears to have become popular through an initiative launched in 1994 by the American Planning Association, the U.S. Department of Housing and Urban Development (HUD), Henry M. Jackson Foundation, National Resource Defense Council (NRDC), and the Surface Transportation Policy Project (STPP). On this, see the American Planning Association (APA), *Growing Smart Legislative Guidebook: Model Statutes for Planning and the Management of Change,* phase I interim ed. (Chicago: APA, 1996). Perhaps the best summary to date of pro and con arguments over smart growth can be found in a largely favorable review of smart growth concepts by Karen A. Danielsen, Robert E. Lang, and William Fulton in an essay entitled "Retracting Suburbia: Smart Growth and the Future of Housing," *Housing Policy Debate* 10, no. 3 (1999): 513–40, with a telling rejoinder by Gregg Easterbrook (541–47).

66. For an excellent skeptical analysis of smart growth, see Anthony Downs, "What Does 'Smart Growth' Really Mean?" *Planning* 67, no. 4 (April 2001): 20–25. See also the comments by Douglas Porter ("Viewpoint," *Planning* 69, no. 10 [November 2003], 54), who suggested that smart growth and related terminology was, to a considerable degree, merely standard planning wisdom with a new name.

67. Among Web sites, one of the most interesting is www.sprawlwatch.org because this site, in its attempt to stamp out the heresies of those it accuses of being "pro-sprawl," provides a "Backgrounder on Pro-Sprawl Players and Messages," a useful source of information and bibliography for anyone who is publicly skeptical of the pro-sprawl crusade. I had not yet earned a place on the list as of late 2004.

68. A curious thing often happens when highly complex or technical issues like sprawl reach the general public through a magazine like *Time.* Instead of the complicated set of interlocking questions, each one of them hotly debated by the experts, a much condensed argument is presented, sometimes as a single, unified argument and sometimes in the form of a binary "debate." In a few details concerning measures to combat sprawl, the *Time* article "The Brawl over Sprawl" by Richard Lacayo (March 22, 1999, 44–48) presented some opposing opinions. In the larger issue of whether sprawl was a problem to begin with and caused the ills cataloged in the article, the authors simply accepted the propositions that they found in most of the popular anti-sprawl literature.

69. European Commission, *Green Paper on the Urban Environment* (Brussels: European Commission, 1990).

70. This is one of the key points of Sieverts, *Cities without Cities,* for example, xii–xiv. Sieverts

vividly describes himself and his fellow architects and urban designers as being in a situation much like the members of the guilds at the end of the ancien régime, trying to prop up an order that is in the process of irrevocable dissolution.

71. Patrick Troy, *The Perils of Consolidation: A Discussion of Australian Housing and Urban Development Policies* (Annandale: Federation Press, 1996). Some of the same ideas can be found in Michael Poulton, "Affordable Homes at an Affordable (Social) Price," in George Fallis et al., *Home Remedies: Rethinking Canadian Housing Policy* (Toronto: C. D. Howe Institute, 1995), 50–122.

72. On Japan, see André Sorensen, "Land Readjustment, Urban Planning and Urban Sprawl in the Tokyo Metropolitan Area," *Urban Studies* 36, no. 13 (1999): 2333–60; Michael Hebbert, "Urban Sprawl and Urban Planning in Japan," in *Planning for Cities and Regions in Japan*, ed. Philip Shapira, Ian Masser, and David W Edgington (Liverpool: Liverpool University Press, 1994).

73. On Israel, see E. Razin, "Policies to Control Urban Sprawl: Planning Regulations or Changes in the 'Rules of the Game'?" *Journal of the American Planning Association* 35, no.2 (1998): 321–40.

74. For negative reactions to the anti-sprawl campaign, see, for example, Kenneth Orski, "The Backlash against 'Smart Growth,'" *Innovation Briefs*, vol. 14, no. 6 (November–December 2003).

75. For an analysis of the anti-sprawl campaign from a free-market perspective, see Peter Gordon and Harry W. Richardson, "Defending Suburban Sprawl," *Public Interest* 139 (Spring 2000): 65–71.

76. Poulton, "Affordable Homes at an Affordable (Social) Price." A similar analysis can be found in Gregg Easterbrook *The Progress Paradox* (New York: Random House, 2003), 130. Economist William Fischel provides a good explanation of this kind of behavior by homeowners with his "homevoter hypothesis." As obvious as this idea sounds, it is remarkable how much it explains in Fischel's hands (*The Homevoter Hypothesis* [Cambridge, MA: Harvard University Press, 2001]).

77. A very good analysis of the politics of smart growth can be found in C. Kenneth Orski, "The Culture of Low Density" (remarks delivered to the Joint National Association of Regional Councils, Washington Policy Conference, Washington, DC, March 2001), www.demographia.com .db-orski.htm.

78. For some astute observations on the Progressive politics of the baby boom generation, see David Brooks, *Bobos in Paradise: The New Upper Class and How They Got There* (New York: Simon & Schuster, 2000).

79. Robert Freilich, *From Sprawl to Smart Growth: Successful Legal, Planning and Environmental Systems* (Chicago: American Bar Association, 1999), xvii. Freilich was one of the chief figures in the second campaign against sprawl and one of the architects of the famous growth management plan for Ramapo, New York.

80. An excellent general statement on this seeming contradiction can be found in Easterbrook, *The Progress Paradox.*

81. Charles Rubin, *The Green Crusade: Rethinking the Roots of Environmentalism* (New York: Free Press, 1994), 15.

82. Samuel P. Hays and Joel A. Tarr, eds., *Explorations in Environmental History: Essays* (Pittsburgh: University of Pittsburgh Press, 1998), 9–11.

83. Some readers will recognize in my formulation of the problems of sprawl as being, in part, a result of rising expectations an echo of the famous analysis by Edward Banfield of the "urban crisis" in his classic work *The Unheavenly City: The Nature and the Future of Our Urban Crisis* (Boston: Little, Brown & Co., 1968).

Chapter 11

1. On the history of London's sprawl, see Patrick Abercrombie, *Town and Country Planning* (London: Thornton Butterworth Ltd., 1933); Jules Lubbock, *The Tyranny of Taste: The Politics of Architecture and Design in Britain, 1550–1960* (New Haven, CT: Yale University Press, 1995), 25–32. On Paris, see the testimony in Norma Evenson, *Paris: A Century of Change, 1878–1978* (New Haven, CT: Yale University Press, 1979), 327.

2. *Oxford English Dictionary*, compact ed., s.v. "blight."

3. Lawrence Veiller, "Slum Clearance," in *Housing in America*, Proceedings of the Tenth National Conference on Housing (New York: National Housing Assoc., 1929), 75.

4. Ebenezer Howard, *Tomorrow: A Peaceful Path to Real Reform* (London: Swann Sonnenschein, 1898), reissued as *Garden Cities of Tomorrow* (London: S. Sonnenschein, 1902).

5. A good summary of Howard's ideas with their sources can be found in Peter Hall, *Cities of Tomorrow* (London: Basil-Blackwell Inc., 1988), 89–94. See also Alexander Garvin, *The American City: What Works, What Doesn't* (New York: McGraw-Hill, 1996), 315–20; and Kenneth Kolson, *Big Plans: The Allure and Folly of Urban Design* (Baltimore: Johns Hopkins University Press, 2001), who devotes an excellent chapter, "Two Cheers for Sprawl" (chap. 7), to the schemes from Howard through the New Urbanists to stop sprawl.

6. The profession of planning was born in the late nineteenth and early twentieth centuries, as specialists in Germany, France, Britain, and the United States started to organize themselves into a coherent professional group devoted to solving the major technical problems involved in providing water delivery, wastewater treatment, parks, and adequate transportation systems, as well as creating attractive communities (Anthony Sutcliffe, ed., *Towards the Planned City: Germany Britain, the United States and France, 1780–1914* [New York: St. Martin's Press, 1981]). Howard provided a dramatic political and social agenda. On the visions of Taut, see his *Die Auflösung der Städte; oder, Die Erde eine gute Wohnung* (Hagen: Folkmang Verlag, 1920). On Taut and other German anti-urbanists, see Thomas Sieverts, *Cities without Cities: An Interpretation of the Zwischenstadt* (London: Spon Press, 2003), xiv, 7, and passim. On the visions of Frank Lloyd Wright, see Wright's *The Disappearing City* (New York: W. F. Payson, 1932), *When Democracy Builds* (Chicago: University of Chicago Press, 1945), and *The Living City* (New York: Horizon House, 1958). There is an interesting analysis of Broadacre City in Robert Fishman, *Urban Utopias in the Twentieth Century: Ebenezer Howard, Frank Lloyd Wright, Le Corbusier* (New York: Basic Books, 1977). On the Russian disurbanists, see also the discussion of Moscow in chap. 12 of this book as well as Selim O. Khan-Magonedov, *Pioneers of Soviet Architecture* (New York: Rizzoli, 1983); and Catherine Cooke, "Extensive or Intensive Development? A Century of Debates and Experience in Moscow," in *Cities for the New Millennium*, ed. Marcial Echenique and Andrew Saint (London: Spon Press, 2001).

Chapter 12

1. On the campaign to stop ribbon development and establish growth boundaries, see Anthony King, *The Bungalow The Production of a Global Culture* (Boston: Routledge & Kegan Paul, 1984), 186–89; Peter Hall, *Cities of Tomorrow* (London: Basil-Blackwell, Inc., 1988), 39.

2. Sir Patrick Abercrombie, *Greater London Plan, 1944* (London: HMSO, 1945).

3. Abercrombie used the word "sprawl" several times, both as noun and as verb. While alarm over sprawl in the text was somewhat measured, the illustrations told a different story. Using what would become a standard technique, Abercrombie chose for one of his illustrations of sprawl (between pages 22 and 23) an aerial photograph of a new housing estate still under construction and for this reason clearly raw and without any softening landscape. To this picture he supplied this deliberately inflammatory caption: "Sprawl and ribbon development: the beginnings of another formless suburb eat into London's precious Green Belt." The book jacket went even further, displaying a map of the London area with areas of sprawl picked out in bright red.

4. On the uses of planning to protect the affluent, see Colin Ward, "Green Challenge to Planners," *Town and Country Planning* 55 (October 1996), 262–63.

5. On the intellectual origins of the London plan, see Peter Hall et al., eds., *The Containment of Urban England* (London: PEP, 1973), 1:106–13.

6. On Milton Keynes and its relation to American social science, there has been the interesting work by British historian Mark Clapson, for example, his book, with Jeff Rooker, *A Social History of Milton Keynes: Middle England/Edge City* (London: Frank Cass, 2004).

7. After the text of this book was essentially complete, this traffic congestion had become so great in London that the left-wing mayor, Ken Livingston, taking a page from the Libertarian's handbook, introduced a market mechanism solution, charging a fee for all vehicles entering central London.

8. The most comprehensive attempt to evaluate the British postwar planning system can be found in Hall et al., eds., *The Containment of Urban England*, vol. 2. For a more recent study of the important question of how much the planning system raised land prices and what would have happened without any planning system at all, see Paul Cheshire and Stephen Sheppard, "British Planning Policy and Access to Housing: Some Empirical Estimates," *Urban Studies* 26 (1989): 469–85.

9. Hall, *Cities of Tomorrow*, 306.

10. For a highly skeptical view from the mid-1950s, see H. Myles Wright, "The Next Thirty Years: Notes on Some Probable Trends in Civic Design," *Town Planning Review* 27 (1956): 103–23.

11. Ian Nairn, *Outrage* (London: Architectural Press, 1955), a reprint of *Architectural Review*, special issue no. 119 (June 1955), 865.

12. A description of the laws aiding the construction of single-family houses in the suburbs and then the postwar repudiation of these policies can be found in Henri Raymond et al., *L'habitat Pavillonnaire*, 2d ed. (Paris: Centre de Recherche d'Urbanisme, 1971). On the former see, esp., 44–45.

13. On the shift from private housing to publicly funded housing, see Jean Bastié, *La croissance de la banlieue Parisienne* (Paris: Presse universitaires de France, 1964).

14. The Parisian regional plan, *Plan d'Aménagement et d'Organisation de la Région Parisienne* (PADOG) was approved in 1960. A much more ambitious scheme, the *Schéma Directeur d'Aménagement et d'Urbanisme de la Région de Paris* was produced in 1965 and approved in 1971. For a discussion of postwar regional development, see Norma Evenson, *Paris: A Century of Change, 1878–1978* (New Haven, CT: Yale University Press, 1979), 336–61.

15. For an overview of land-use planning in the second campaign against sprawl, see Frank J. Popper, "Understanding American Land Use Regulation since 1970: A Revisionist Interpretation," *Journal of the American Planning Association* 54, no. 3 (Summer 1988): 291–301. An excellent summary of growth-control measures developed during the 1960s and 1970s can be found in the volumes

issued by the Urban Land Institute starting in 1975: Randall W. Scott, ed., *Management and Control of Growth* (Washington, DC: Urban Land Institute, 1975–).

16. For a typical statement on the evils of the "fragmentation of local authority," see Robert Wood, *1400 Governments: The Political Economy of the New York Metropolitan Region Prepared for the Regional Plan of New York* (Cambridge, MA: Harvard University Press, 1961).

17. A skeptical view of the efforts by "experts" to push land-use decision making to higher levels of government can be found in Richard Babcock, *The Zoning Game* (Madison: University of Wisconsin Press, 1966).

18. On the "quiet revolution," see Fred P. Bosselman and David L. Callies, *The Quiet Revolution in Land Use Control* (Washington, DC: Superintendent of Documents, 1972).

19. Richard A. Walker and Michael K. Heiman, "Quiet Revolution for Whom?" *Annals of the Association of American Geographers* 71, no. 1 (March 1981): 68–69.

20. On the report of the Task Force on Land and Urban Growth, see chap. 9.

21. For the story of national land-use policy from the mainstream liberal side, see Noreen Lyday, *The Law of the Land: Debating National Land Use Legislation, 1970–75* (Washington, DC: Urban Institute, 1976). For a challenging view from a point of view further to the left, see Sidney Plotkin, *Keep Out: The Struggle for Land Use Control* (Berkeley: University of California Press, 1987), 149–73; and Walker and Heiman, "Quiet Revolution for Whom?"

22. On the conference organized for *Fortune* by William Whyte, see the discussion in chap. 9.

23. Editors of *Fortune* magazine, *The Exploding Metropolis* (Garden City, NY: Doubleday, 1958), 131–40.

24. On the Stockholm model, see Peter Hall's splendid "The Social Democratic Utopia," chap. 27 of his magisterial *Cities in Civilization* (New York: Pantheon Books, 1998), 842–87. The Stockholm system is laid out in Stockholm Stadsplanekontor, *Generalplan för Stockholm* (Stockholm: K. L. Beckmans Boktryckeri, 1952), which has an English summary.

25. On the influence of Stockholm, see Hall, "The Social Democratic Utopia"; and Stockholm Stadsplanekontor, *Generalplan för Stockholm*. A typical product at the end of this era is David Popenoe, *The Suburban Environment: Sweden and the United States* (Chicago: University of Chicago Press, 1977), which compares Vällingby and Levittown.

26. National Capital Regional Planning Council, *A Policies Plan for the Year 2000* ([Washington, DC]: National Capitol Planning Commission, 1961).

27. Maryland–National Capitol Park and Planning Commission, *On Wedges and Corridors* (Silver Spring, MD: Maryland–National Capitol Park and Planning Commission, 1964). Also see Mel Scott, *American City Planning since 1890* (Berkeley: University of California, Press, 1969), 573–80.

28. Many American planners were very heavily influenced by the well-known plans of Fritz Schumacher in Hamburg and the postwar "Finger Plan" for Copenhagen. See, for example, Bo Larsson and Ole Thomassen, "Urban Planning in Denmark," in *Planning and Urban Growth in the Nordic Countries*, ed. Thomas Hall (London: Spon Press, 1991), 30–32,

29. For a good, succinct summary of efforts at Reston and Columbia, see Alexander Garvin, *The American City: What Works, What Doesn't*, 2d ed. (New York: McGraw Hill, 2002), 399–401. Robert E. Simon bought 7,400 acres or 11.56 square miles in 1961 and planned a settlement of 75,000 people, meaning that there would be approximately ten people per acre or nearly 6,500 people per

square mile. This density was already less than that of many conventional suburbs, and by 2001 the town of Reston still only had a population of 56,407 people on 17.4 square miles. In the case of Columbia, the initial land purchase of 15,600 acres was intended for 110,000 people or about 4,500 per square mile. In 2000 population of 88,254 occupied twenty-eight square miles. In each case, the gross density of just over 3,000 people per square mile today is well within the average range for American densities and extremely low by any historical standards.

30. Federal funding for new towns was authorized in Title IV of the *Housing and Urban Development Act of 1968* (S 1123, 90th Cong., 2d sess.) and Title VII of the *Housing and Urban Development Act of 1970* (HR 91-1784, 91st Cong, 2d sess.).

31. On the Woodlands, see Ann Forsyth, "Ian McHarg's Woodlands: A Second Look," *Planning* 89, no. 8 (August–September 2003), 10–13, as well as in her book *Reforming Suburbia: The Planned Communities of Irvine, The Woodlands and Columbia* (Berkeley: University of California Press, 2005), which was not yet published at the time of this writing.

32. According to Alexander Garvin, the new towns were oversold. Any land-use policy that was touted as useful in reducing inefficiency, conserving resources, providing good housing, increasing choices, and helping disadvantaged citizens all at the same time was almost inevitably going to fall short (*The American City*, 405–6).

33. Jane Jacobs believed that new towns would draw resources away from efforts at reviving town centers (*Death and Life of Great American Cities* [New York: Vintage Books, 1961], 21). See also Richard B. Peiser and Alain C. Chang, "Is It Possible to Build Financially Successful New Towns? The Milton Keynes Experience," *Urban Studies* 36, no. 10 (1999): 1679–1703.

34. Mark Baldassare, *Trouble in Paradise: The Suburban Transformation in America* (New York: Columbia University Press, 1986), 18–21, 72–100.

35. For a summary of the Boulder experience written during the second campaign against sprawl, see William Reilly, *The Use of Land: A Citizen's Policy Guide to Urban Growth* (New York: Thomas Y. Crowell Co., 1973), 57–61. For a recent history of the Boulder system, see Joseph N. de Raismes III et al., "Growth Management in Boulder, Colorado: A Case Study," on the Web page of the city of Boulder, Office of the City Attorney. For an optimistic evaluation of the Boulder experience, see Robert Freilich, *From Sprawl to Smart Growth* (Chicago: American Bar Association, 1999), 195–97; see also Rolf Pendall, Jonathan Martin, and William Fulton, "Holding the Line: Urban Containment in the United States" (August 2003), 18–20, a discussion paper prepared for the Brookings Institution, available on the Web sites of the Solimar Institute and the Brookings Institution; and Amalia Lorentz and Kirsten Shaw, "Are You Ready to Bet on Smart Growth?" *Planning* 66, no. 1 (January 2000): 4.

36. Ironically enough, the move to have municipal improvement be financed by municipal governments was a major plank in "Progressive" reform efforts earlier in the century.

37. On impact and other fees, see Charles E. Connerly, "The Social Implications of Planning Fees," *Journal of the American Planning Association* 54, no. 1 (1988): 75–79; Douglas R. Porter, "The Rights and Wrongs of Impact Fees," *Urban Land* 45, no. 7 (July 1986): 16–19.

38. For a recent study in the Chicago area, see Brett M. Baden and Don L. Coursey, "An Examination of the Effects of Impact Fees on Chicago's Suburbs" (working paper series 99.20, Irving B. Harris Graduate School of Public Policy Studies, University of Chicago, 2005).

39. Boulder County Planning Director Vince Porecca suggested that by making itself more attrac-

tive Boulder was increasing the growth pressure on the entire area but deflecting the growth outside its own boundaries, according to William Reilly (*The Use of Land*, 61).

40. On Petaluma and Ramapo and growth management, see Garvin, *The American City*, 453–56. For an extended discussion of Ramapo by one of the chief players, see Freilich, *From Sprawl to Smart Growth*, 39–106.

41. On the concept of NIMBY, see *"Not in My Backyard": Removing Barriers to Affordable Housing: Report to President Bush and Secretary Kemp* (Washington, DC: U.S. Department of Housing and Urban Development, 1991).

42. On zoning, see William Fischel, *The Economics of Zoning Laws: A Property Rights Approach to American Land Use Controls* (Baltimore: Johns Hopkins University Press, 1985).

43. William H. Whyte, *Cluster Development* (New York: American Conservation Association, 1964). See also Walker and Heiman, "Quiet Revolution for Whom?"

44. The major intellectual assault on regulatory takings was launched by Richard A. Epstein in his *Takings: Private Property and the Power of Eminent Domain* (Cambridge, MA: Harvard University Press, 1989).

45. On environmental impact statements and their abuse, see Bernard J. Frieden, *The Environmental Protection Hustle* (Cambridge, MA: MIT Press, 1972); see also Garvin, *The American City*, 456–60.

46. For some figures on highway capacity, population, and congestion, see Oliver Gillham, *The Limitless City* (Washington, DC: Island Press, 2002), 95.

47. An attempt to alert the nation to the problem of underfunded infrastructure can be found in Pat Choate and Susan Walter, *America in Ruins: Beyond the Public Works Pork Barrel* (Washington, DC: Council of State Planning Agencies, 1981).

48. For a classic study of the way transit projections were overstated, see Don Pickrell, *Urban Rail Transit Projects: Forecast versus Actual Ridership and Costs* (Washington, DC: U.S. Department of Transportation, Urban Mass Transportation Administration, 1989).

49. Transit ridership, in the last few years, has risen faster than automobile travel. However, the figures for transit are so low that at least to date this trend has not been very meaningful.

50. Reilly, *The Use of Land*, 33.

51. Walker and Heiman, "Quiet Revolution for Whom?"; Bernard J. Frieden, *The Environmental Protection Hustle*, 32–36; Baldassare, *Trouble in Paradise*, 18–21; Christopher Leo et al., "Is Urban Sprawl Back on the Political Agenda? Local Growth Control, Regional Growth Management Policies and Politics," *Urban Affairs Review* 34, no. 2 (November 1998): 189.

52. For a discussion of Stalinist-era planning in Moscow, see Maurice Frank Parkins, *City Planning in Soviet Russia* (Chicago: University of Chicago Press, 1953); James Bater, *The Soviet City: Explorations in Urban Analysis* (Beverly Hills, CA: Sage Publications, 1980); and R. A. French, and F. E. Ian Hamilton, *The Socialist City: Spatial Structure and Urban Policy* (Chichester: John Wiley & Sons, 1979). Also on Moscow, see Peter Hall, *The World Cities* (New York: McGraw Hill, l966), 158–81; R. A. French, "Moscow: The Soviet Metropolis," in *Metropolis 1890–1940*, ed. Anthony Sutcliffe (Chicago: University of Chicago Press, 1984); and Catherine Cooke, "Extensive or Intensive Development? A Century of Debates and Experience in Moscow," in *Cities for the New Millennium*, ed. Marcial Echenique and Andrew Saint (London: Spon Press, 2001).

53. *Moscow: General Plan for the Reconstruction of the City* (General'nyi plan rekonstruktsii goroda Moskvy) ([Moscow] Union of Soviet Architects, 1935).

54. For an excellent analysis of Russian development and planning since the collapse of the Soviet Union, see Blair Ruble, *Money Sings: The Changing Politics of Urban Space in Post-Soviet Yarslavl* (Washington, DC: Woodrow Wilson Press; Cambridge: Cambridge University Press, 1995); and Grigory Ioffe and Tatyana Nefedova, *The Environs of Russian Cities* (Lewiston, NY: Edward Mellens Press, 2000).

Chapter 13

1. The population in 1965 was 1.85 million. By the year 2000, the population had fallen to under 1.7 million.

2. Freie und Hansestadt Hamburg, *Hamburg City + State*, 8th ed. (Hamburg: Staatliche Pressestelle der Freie und Hansestadt Hamburg, 1999), 6.

3. The price paid by European societies to maintain their nineteenth-century downtowns is very well laid out by Pietro S. Nivola in his admirable short book *Laws of the Landscape: How Policies Shape Cities in Europe and America* (Washington, DC: Brookings Institution, 1999), 38, 88–89.

4. For data on the number of rooms in houses in Europe and in North America, see table 7.1 of "Trends in Europe and North America" on the Web site of the United Nations Economic Commission for Europe.

5. For Paris, see Yvonne Bernard, *La France au logis: Étude sociologique des pratiques domestiques* (Liege: P. Mardaga, 1992), 27–32; and Norma Evenson, *Paris: A Century of Change, 1878–1978* (New Haven, CT: Yale University Press, 1979), 249–55.

6. Christian Gerondeau, *Transport in Europe* (Boston: Artec House, 1997), 223–27, 254; Genevieve Giuliano, "Urban Travel Patterns," in *Modern Transport Geography*, ed. Brian Hoyle and Richard Knowles (New York: John Wiley, 1998); U.S. Department of Transportation, Bureau of Transportation Statistics, *G-7 Countries: Transportation Highlights* (Washington DC: Bureau of Transportation Statistics, 1999).

7. Gerondeau, *Transport in Europe*, 222, fig. 3.

8. For good and balanced reviews of British policies over a number of years, see the work of Michael Breheny, a professor of geography at the University of Reading, for example, "Density and Sustainable Cities: The UK Experience" in *Cities for the New Millennium*, ed. Marcial Echenique and Andrew Saint (London: Spon Press, 2001), 39–51. One of Breheny's most interesting observations, following a Town and Country Planning Report titled *The People: Where Will They Work?* concerns the way jobs have moved in massive numbers from the large cities to what Breheny calls small towns and the country but, in my analysis, would be better classified as exurbia.

9. Richard Rogers and Richard Burdett, "Let's Cram More into the City," in *Cities for the New Millennium*, ed. Echenique and Saint. Rogers has been one of the most conspicuous anti-sprawl critics in England in recent years through his work with the Urban Task Force, whose report *Towards an Urban Renaissance: Final Report of the Urban Task Force* (London: Spon Press) was issued in 1999. Rogers has also generated opposition. Jules Lubbock in article "Planning Is the Problem" in the online journal *openDemocracy* (April 7, 2001), has called Richard Roger's new urbanism "shallow and authoritarian. Its impulse to confine people in high-density settlements has disastrous social

and economic effects." Lubbock argues that Britain has too much planning and not enough build-ing in the countryside. He states that three-quarters of the population are needlessly jammed into 7 percent of the land.

10. On growth management systems since the 1960s, see Robert H. Freilich, *From Sprawl to Smart Growth: Successful Legal, Planning and Environmental Systems* (Chicago: American Bar Association, 1999); Christopher Leo et al., "Is Urban Sprawl Back on the Political Agenda? Local Growth Control, Regional Growth Management Policies and Politics," *Urban Affairs Review* 34, no. 2 (November 1998): 189. For an inventory of recent developments, see also Samuel Staley, Jefferson G. Edgens, and Gerard Mildner, "A Line in the Land: Urban Growth Boundaries, Smart Growth and Housing Affordability," Reason Public Policy Institute, policy study no. 263, http://www.riip.org/urban/ps263.html.

11. Brent Walth, *Fire at Eden's Gate: Tom McCall and the Oregon Story* (Portland: Oregon Historical Society Press, 1994), 356.

12. Ibid., 314.

13. For a good history of the Portland system, see Carl Abbott, Deborah Howe, and Sy Adler, *Planning the Oregon Way: A Twenty Year Evaluation* (Corvallis: Oregon State University Press, 1994).

14. On the way Los Angeles and an increasing number of American cities came to be denser since the 1950s, see chap. 5.

15. Portland Metro, 2040 Regional Framework Plan, on Portland Metro Web site. See also the concise summary, *The Nature of 2040: The Region's 50-Year Plan for Managing Growth*, also on Metro Web site.

16. A useful study comparing Cedar Hills, a postwar suburban development, with Orenco Station, a new urbanist community built at a rail stop, can be found in Thomas Harvey and Martha A. Works, "Suburban Morphology and Portland's Urban Growth Boundary," in *Suburban Form an International Perspective*, Kiril Stanilov and Brenda Case Scheer (New York: Routledge, 2004).

17. For an introduction to the Portland system, see Abbott, Howe, and Adler, *Planning the Oregon Way*; Gerrit Knaap and Arthur C. Nelson, *The Regulated Landscape: Lessons from Land Use Planning in Oregon* (Cambridge, MA: Lincoln Institute of Land Policy, 1992). For pro and con views, see *Housing Policy Debate*, vol. 8, no. 1 (1997), on Portland, with an article by Carl Abbott ("The Portland Region: Where City and Suburbs Talk to Each Other—and Often Agree"); and "Comment," the response by Henry R. Richmond and William A Fischel. This publication is available on the Fannie Mae Foundation Web site. Summaries of major issues can be found in Gerrit J. Knaap, "The Urban Growth Boundary in Metropolitan Portland, Oregon: Research, Rhetoric , and Reality" (paper presented at the Workshop on Urban Growth Management Policies in the United States, Japan and Korea, in Seoul, Korea, June 23–24, 2000, with a summary in *Public Investment*, a newsletter of the American Planning Association [December 2000]); and Arthur C. Nelson and Terry Moore, "Assessing Growth Management Policy Implementation: Case Study of the United States' Leading Growth Management State," *Land Use Policy* 13, no. 4 (1996): 241–59. A good analysis of the political alliance involved in the Portland system can be found in Christopher Leo, "Regional Growth Management Regime: The Case of Portland, Oregon," *Journal of Urban Affairs* 20, no. 4 (1998): 363–94. See also Leo et al., "Is Urban Sprawl Back?" 189; the discussion of Portland in Peter Calthorpe and William Fulton, *The Regional City* (Washington, DC: Island Press, 2001); and two recent works by Yan Song and Gerrit-Jan Knaap, "Measuring Urban Form: Is Portland Winning the

War on Sprawl?" *Journal of the American Planning Association* 70, no. 2 (Spring 2004): 209–25; and Gerrit-Jan Knaap, Yan Song, and Zorica Nedovic-Budic, "Measuring Patterns of Urban Development: New Intelligence for the War on Sprawl" (paper posted on the Web site for the National Center for Smart Growth, ca. 2004). In these last two essays the authors show that, using a number of different indicators, like the connectivity of street intersections or the distance from houses to retail areas, Portland can perhaps be said to have turned a corner in 1990, is now performing better on these measures than several places without a similar growth management system, and could be said to be "winning the war on sprawl." It may be that this will turn out to be an accurate assessment, but it is not yet clear whether a similar analysis for other places wouldn't obscure the picture, whether these trends are due to planning or to changes in the market, and whether satisfying these criteria really does constitute defeating sprawl.

18. The most comprehensive attack on the Portland system can be found in Randal O'Toole, *The Vanishing Automobile and Other Myths* (Bandon, OR: Thoreau Institute, 2001). Also see Gerard Mildner, Kenneth Dueker, and Anthony Rufolo, *Impact of the Urban Growth Boundary on Metropolitan Housing Markets* (Portland: Center for Urban Studies, Portland State University, 1997); Gerard Mildner, *Growth Management in the Portland Region and the Housing Boom of the 1990s* (Urban Futures working paper no. 98-1, Portland State University Center for Urban Studies, May 1988), with an excellent analysis of the reasons the Portland consensus might fall apart, and "Regionalism and the Growth Management Movement," in *Smarter Growth: Market Based Strategies for Land Use Planning in the Twenty-First Century,* ed. Randall Holcombe and Samuel Staley (Westport, CT: Greenwood Press, 2001), 113–30; John Charles, "The Dark Side of Growth Controls: Some Lessons from Oregon" (Goldwater Institute, Arizona Issue Analysis no. 150, May 1998; available on the Goldwater Institute Web site); Samuel Staley and Gerard Mildner, "Urban Growth Boundaries and Housing Affordability: Lessons from Portland" (policy brief no. 11, Reason Public Policy Institute, Los Angeles, October 1999); Richard Carson, "A Failure of Fairness: Planning in the Pacific Northwest," *Texas Planning Review* (September–October 1999); John A. Charles, "Lessons from the Portland Experience," in *A Guide to Smart Growth: Shattering Myths, Providing Solutions,* ed. Jane S. Shaw and Ronald D. Utt (Washington, DC: Heritage Foundation; Bozeman, MT: Political Economy Research Center, 2000); Charles, a former Portland planning true believer and former head of the Oregon Environmental Council, explains his disenchantment in "Ditching the Doctrine," *Oregonian,* December 8, 2002. Andres Duany, the standard bearer of the New Urbanist movement and an individual who might be expected to be positive in his assessment of the Portland experiment, had a surprisingly large list of negative things to say about this venture in a widely distributed Web posting in 2000 partly quoted in Charles, "Lessons from the Portland Experience," 133 and reproduced in full on the Web site of Duany's firm, www.dpz.com. Among the organizations fighting the Portland planning system are Oregonians in Action and ORTEM ("Metro" spelled backward).

19. Most of the early enlargements were very small. In 1998, the council added 3,527 acres and in 1999 it added another 377 acres (Knaap, "The Urban Growth Boundary in Metropolitan Portland").

20. Pressure to remove local control from land-use decisions is a major theme in O'Toole, *The Vanishing Automobile,* 61–67. In most places in the country, zoning provides the maximum that can be built in any given area. In the Portland area, Title I of chap. 3.07.140, the "Urban Growth Management Functional Plan" of the Portland Metro Code (effective January 6, 2005) requires cities to adopt regulations that require minimal residential densities. The code can be found on Metro's Web site

at www.metro-region.org. For a typical story about opposition to the densification efforts, see Kara Briggs, "Frustration Pours out over Housing Infill," *Oregonian*, April 10, 2003.

21. Although he clearly exaggerated for effect, Richard Carson, former planning director for Metro, has written, "Portland is no longer the Mecca of good planning and is on its way to becoming the new Beirut" ("Why Would Someone Want Planning Job?" *Oregonian*, November 29, 1999). Voters in some municipalities, for example, in suburban Milwaukie, have revolted and have voted out of office public officials who agreed to upzone. For an interesting narrative on the resistance of residents of the Oak Grove neighborhood, see O'Toole, *The Vanishing Automobile*, 9–16. See also Brent Hunsberger, "Portland's Desire for Density Stirs Up Residents' Worries," *Oregonian*, December 15, 1998.

22. "Oregon: Two Sides of the Antisprawl Line," *New York Times*, April 22, 2001, real estate sec., 41; Kim Murphy, "Despite Careful Urban Planning, Portland Area Feels Growing Pains," *Los Angeles Times*, April 1, 2001.

23. Northwest Environment Watch, "Sprawl and Smart Growth in Metropolitan Portland Comparing Portland, Oregon, with Vancouver, Washington during the 1990s" (www.northwestwatch.org, Executive Summary).

24. For a general discussion of this issue, see the recent and apparently quite reasonable analysis by Rolf Pendall, Jonathan Martin, and William Fulton, "Holding the Line: Urban Containment in the United States" (discussion paper, Brookings Institution, Washington, DC, August 2002). See also Arthur C. Nelson, Rolf Pendall, Casey J. Dawkins, and Gerrit J. Knaap, "The Link between Growth Management and Housing Affordability: The Academic Evidence" (discussion paper, Brookings Institution Center on Urban and Metropolitan Policy, Washington, DC, February 2002). The authors believe that where zoning and early growth control measures were exclusionary, Portland's growth management system is inclusionary and for this reason has not raised prices more than elsewhere. Arthur C. Nelson, in his publication "Economic Development and Smart Growth" (American Planning Association, Economic Development Division, News and Views, October 1999), makes the same argument and compares Portland with Atlanta, concluding that Portland has performed better in a whole series of comparisons. The same is true for Justin Philips and Eban Goodstein, "Growth Management and Housing Prices: The Case of Portland Oregon," *Contemporary Economic Policy* 18, no. 3 (July 2000): 344–45. Their conclusions are hotly contested by Wendell Cox, "American Dream Boundaries: Urban Containment and Its Consequences" (issue analysis, Georgia Public Policy Foundation, Atlanta, 2001, www.gppf.org), who argues exactly the opposite (with rebuttal to Cox by John Fregonese and Lynn Peterson, "Correcting the Record"); and Randall J. Pozdena, *Smart Growth and Its Effects on Housing Markets: The New Segregation* (Washington DC: National Center for Public Policy Research, 2002). If the results are inconclusive it may well be because it is so difficult to isolate a single variable like the urban growth system in the performance of cities that are so different in size, government structure, and recent history and because the time frames are so narrow. Some of the problems are demonstrated very well in Edward L. Glaeser and Joseph Gyourko, "The Impact of Zoning on Housing Affordability" (discussion paper no. 1948, Harvard Institute of Economic Research, Cambridge, MA, March 2002). Although they were concerned primarily with zoning, their analysis shows how difficult it is to isolate variables or to measure the actual impact of regulations as opposed to what they do in principle.

25. What appears to be a convincing demonstration of the effect of regulations on housing prices

can be found in Edward L. Glaeser and Joseph Gyourko, "The Impact of Building Restrictions on Housing Affordability," *Federal Reserve Bank of New York Economic Policy Review* 9, no. 2 (June 2003): 21–39.

26. On the effect of regulations on housing prices in California cities, see Glaeser and Gyourko, "The Impact of Zoning on Housing Affordability." For summaries of costs in Portland compared to other places, see the analyses by Knaap in *Public Investment News* (December 2001); and Staley and Mildner, "Urban Growth Boundaries and Housing Affordability." Virginia Postrel, in her essay "Economic Scene: Where It's Easier to Buy a Home," *New York Times,* March 28, 2002, has suggested that the differences correspond to the political cleavage between liberal coastal areas and more conservative ones between.

27. For a description of the often contradictory positions of the Sierra Club, see Bernard Frieden, *The Environmental Protection Hustle* (Cambridge: MIT Press, 1979), 9.

28. On the adverse effect of the rail system on bus ridership, see O'Toole, *The Vanishing Automobile,* 95–99. According to Peter Gordon and Harry Richardson, "Compactness or Sprawl: America's Future vs. the Present," in *Cities for the New Millennium,* ed. Echenique and Saint, 59, the taxpayer subsidy for the Portland light rail system, at 97 percent, was the highest in the country. This piece provides an excellent review of the reasons that public transportation systems are likely to have only a minimal impact on the overall metropolitan pattern

29. On the declining share of jobs in the central business district in American cities, including Portland, see Peter Gordon and Harry W. Richardson, "The Geography of Transportation and Land Use," in *Smarter Growth: Market-Based Strategies for Land-Use Planning in the Twenty-first Century,* ed. Randall Holcombe and Samual Stanley (Westport, CT: Greenwood Press, 2001), 27–58. Randal O'Toole has compared figures on congestion since 1982 for places like Portland and Minneapolis–Saint Paul, which tried to divert substantial sums away from road projects and into transit, with places like Houston, where the main strategy was to build new roads. He concludes that congestion has gotten worse faster in the former than the latter ("Increased Congestion and Proposed Solutions," *Environment and Climate News* [July 2001], 4–5, available on the Web Site of the Heartland Institute, www.heartland.org).

30. O'Toole, *The Vanishing Automobile,* 119. According to O'Toole, even with all of the efforts at creating transit and discouraging driving, Metro predicts that the share of riders using transit will only jump to something like 6.4 percent in the region by 2040, meaning that the vast majority of newcomers to the area will drive on roads that are already overcrowded

31. On Portland and farming, see Arthur C. Nelson, "Preserving Prime Farmland in the Face of Urbanization: Lessons from Portland," *Journal of the American Planning Association* 58, no. 4 (Autumn 1992): 473; Knaap and Nelson, *The Regulated Landscape,* 125–59; and Jeffrey Kline and Ralph Alig, "Does Land Use Planning Slow the Conversion of Forest and Farm Lands?" *Growth and Change* 30, no. 1 (1999): 3–22.

32. Charles, The Dark Side of Growth Controls,'' 8.

33. It is certainly true that the original impetus for farmland protection came from farmers in rural areas, but there are comparatively few of these farmers in Oregon, and it has been the urban voters of the Willamette Valley who have provided the votes to maintain the system over the years. On this, see Charles, "Lessons from the Portland Experience," 121.

34. As with Contra Costa County outside of San Francisco, by far the largest category of agri-

cultural production in Clackamas County, for example, is "specialty crops," meaning ornamental plants, Christmas trees, and sod. In Clackamas County in 1998, specialty crops generated a full $179 million of a total of $262.4 million in farm revenue. The next highest category was vegetables at $22 million, according to Clackamas County Web site.

35. Charles, "Lessons from the Portland Experience," 121, has noted that the boundaries included within them a great deal of prime agricultural land that will be developed simply because it is within the growth boundary and they excluded from development an even larger amount of nearby land that was of marginal use for agricultural production solely because it didn't contribute to the creation of proper urban form.

36. The original legislation creating the Oregon growth system included a provision to compensate landowners outside the boundaries financially, but legislators never followed through with a bill to authorize the money.

37. "It's the land of the gentry revolting against the rabble from the city ruining their views," according to one scholar who had studied the situation.

38. Robin Franzen and Brent Hunsberger, in "Preserving Farms or Abetting Hobbyists?" (*Oregonian*, December 14, 1998), cite a Farm Bureau survey that shows that 17,000 of Oregon's 37,500 farms occupied less than fifty acres and produced less than $10,000 worth of farm income. Also by the same authors: "Have We Outgrown Our Approach to Growth? Oregon's Land-Use Rules Have City Folks Feeling Too Tightly Packed and Farmers Feeling Beset by Urban Sprawl," *Oregonian*, December 13, 1998.

39. A good analysis of the private and public conservation and preservation initiatives on Nantucket can be found in Warren Boeschenstein, *Historic American Towns along the Atlantic Coast* (Baltimore: Johns Hopkins University Press, 1999), 42–43.

40. A survey in the late 1980s showed that land just inside the growth boundary could sell for six times the price of land just outside the boundary (Mildner, "Regionalism and the Growth Management Movement," 128). On the unfairness of this windfall for some people and heavy loss for others, see Carson, "A Failure of Fairness," 11–12.

41. On the advantages of smart growth for the affluent, see the comments by Richard Morrill, "Impact of Government Regulations and Fees on Housing Costs" (Washington Research Council, e-briefs, May 2001, www.researchcouncil.org). An economic analysis of the redistributive effects of land-use regulations can be found in Samuel R. Staley, "Zoning, Smart Growth and Regulatory Taxation," in *Politics, Taxation and the Rule of Law: The Power to Tax in Constitutional Perspective,* ed. Donald P. Racheter and Richard E. Wagner (Boston: Kluwer Academic Publishers, 2002), 203–24.

42. This description, which parallels my characterization of the Portland system in practice as an incumbents' club was used by Robert Lang and Steven Hornburg, "Editor's Introduction: Planning Portland Style: Pitfalls and Possibilities," *Housing Policy Debate* 8, no. 1 (1997): 1–10.

43. For a passionate argument about the inequities of the Portland system, see John A. Charles, "Ditching the Doctrine" *Oregonian*, December 8, 2002.

44. The Houston region, for example, had a population not much larger than that of Portland after World War II, with Houston at 701,000 people and Portland with 513,000. Between 1950 and 1990 the Portland urbanized area grew to 1,173,000, an increase of 128 percent. The Houston urbanized area, during the same years, in contrast, grew to 2,902,000 or about 314 percent

45. The need for accurate information on land use has led Portland public agencies to develop a

wide variety of new analytical tools. See Gerrit Knaap, Richard Bolen, and Ethan Seltzer, "Metro's Regional Land Information System: The Virtual Key to Portland's Growth Management Success" (working paper, Lincoln Institute of Land Policy, Cambridge, MA, 2003).

46. Haya E. Nasser, "Anti-sprawl Fervor Meets Backlash," *USA Today*, August 25, 2002, news, 3A. Kenneth Orski, "The Backlash against Smart Growth," *Innovation Briefs* 14, no. 6 (November–December 2003). For a good analysis of the reactions to Governor Parris Glendening's program in Maryland, see Peter Shoriskey, "Investing in Sprawl: The Limits of Smart Growth," *Washington Post*, August 10, 2004, A01. In November 2004, after this manuscript went to the publisher, Oregon voters passed Proposition 37, a measure that requires Oregon governments to compensate property owners when regulations reduce property values. Although the effects of this measure are uncertain and it is not clear that voters understood completely the effects of their action, it is certain that the passage of the measure by a wide margin represents a potential major setback for anti-sprawl reformers in Portland and elsewhere.

Some Conclusions

1. For a well-informed and reasonable guess at future urban patterns and sprawl, see Peter Hall and Ulrich Pfeiffer, *Urban Future 21* (London: Spon Press, 2000). On the effect of new digital technologies on urban form, see also the work of Joel Kotkin, for example, *The New Geography: How the Digital Revolution Is Reshaping the American Landscape* (New York: Random House, 2000); and that of William Mitchell, for example, *City of Bits: Space, Place and the Infobahn* (Cambridge, MA: MIT Press, 1997).

BIBLIOGRAPHIC ESSAY

The notes sections of this book contain an extensive bibliography, a good deal of which is technical in nature or difficult to find in most libraries. I have not included most of that literature in this short bibliographic essay. Instead, I have tried to gather, here, a short list of easily accessible works in English that allow some further exploration of this vast topic.

Descriptions of Sprawl

Although the literature on sprawl is extensive, so far most of it has been largely unsatisfactory because observers have tended to rush to judgment before trying to understand or even describe it. Certainly one of the most successful attempts at a description to date is a great classic in geographic literature written nearly a half century ago: Jean Gottmann's *Megalopolis: The Urbanized Northeast Seaboard of the United States* (New York: Twentieth Century Fund, 1961). Gottmann's was a pioneering effort to understand the urban landscape as a large interlocking system rather than as a set of discrete cities surrounded by countryside. More recently, a fascinating attempt to describe some aspects of American sprawl is Joel Garreau's *Edge City* (New York: Doubleday, 1991). Although Garreau, a writer for the *Washington Post,* was looking only at one specific kind of development at the urban periphery, and many of his conclusions are problematic, he had the advantage over most other writers on the topic of being willing to go out to look and listen. His report on what he saw is still very much worth reading. The best European book to date on sprawl, particularly as it affects the historic cities of Western Europe, is *Cities without Cities: An Interpretation of the Zwischenstadt* (London: Spon Press, 2003) by Thomas Sieverts, an architect and planner, former professor at the University of Darmstadt, and head of a planning firm in Bonn. What I cite here is the English language edition of a German book that first appeared in 1997 and attracted widespread attention. Although critical of sprawl, Sieverts, like Garreau, was willing to take a close look at actual settlement patterns on the ground and believed that architects and planners had to understand it before trying to deal with some of its deficiencies. A splendid effort to compare American and European urban areas and the policies that made them can be found in Pietro Nivola, *Laws of the Landscape: How Policies Shape Cities in Europe and America* (Washington, DC: Brookings Institution, 1999).

The Sprawl Debate

Perhaps the best single volume dedicated to presenting the different points of view on sprawl is a recent volume entitled *Cities for the New Millennium* (London: Spon Press, 2001), edited by Marcial Echenique and Andrew Saint, both faculty members at the University of Cambridge. It presents the voices of critics of sprawl, such as British architect Sir Richard Rogers, skeptics of smart growth, such as University of Southern California professors of planning Harry Richardson and Peter Gordon, and more even-handed observers like the late Michael Breheny, a planner and professor of geography at the University of Reading who, although an opponent of sprawl, was able to present a balanced picture of the costs and benefits of anti-sprawl measures. Oliver Gillham's *The Limitless City* (Washington, DC: Island Press, 2002) is also useful and represents an attempt to give a balanced assessment of the sprawl debate in the United States. However, his presentation of some dubious statistical analyses, frequent reduction of arguments to simplified paraphrases and his conclusions that come down squarely in every case on the side of the anti-sprawlers, robs the book of much of its potential value.

Anti-sprawl Tracts

The majority of literature on sprawl consists of polemics against it. Perhaps the best place to survey this literature is in the two great American studies on the costs of sprawl. The first of these, produced by the Real Estate Research Corporation of Chicago, was titled *The Costs of Sprawl: Environmental and Economic Costs of Alternative Residential Development Patterns at the Urban Fringe,* 3 vols.

(Washington, DC: Government Printing Office, 1974). Volume 2, the literature review, summarized most of what had been written up until that point. This work has been updated and expanded in Robert Burchell et al., *Costs of Sprawl Revisited* (Washington, DC: Transportation Research Board, National Research Council, 1998), and *Costs of Sprawl—2000* (Washington, DC: Transportation Research Board, National Research Council, 2002). The classic argument against sprawl on grounds of energy efficiency was Peter Newman and Jeffrey Kenworthy, *Cities and Automobile Dependence: An International Sourcebook* (Aldershot: Gower Publishing Co., 1989). This book was later expanded and updated by Jeffrey Kenworthy and Felix Laube with Peter Newman, *An International Sourcebook of Automobile Dependence in Cities, 1960–1990* (Boulder: University of Colorado Press, 1999). A highly influential attack on the social problems caused by sprawl can be found in Myron Orfield, *Metropolitics: A Regime Agenda for Community and Stability* (Washington, DC: Brookings Institution Press; Cambridge, MA: Lincoln Institute of Land Policy, 1997). The environmental case has been laid out by F. Kaid Benfield et al., *Once There Were Greenfields* (Washington, DC: National Resources Defense Council, 1999). Some telling criticisms of sprawl on aesthetic objections can be found in Andres Duany, Elizabeth Plater-Zyberk, and Jeff Speck, *Suburban Nation: The Rise and the Decline of the American Dream* (New York: North Point Press, 2000).

There has been much less literature on the other side of the debate, and it is more difficult to find. In the United States, much of this literature has come from individuals with Libertarian affiliations. Perhaps the most scholarly and coherent body of work has come from University of Southern California professor of planning Peter Gordon and various associates, notably Harry Richardson. In a series of articles, Gordon and Richardson did a great deal to undermine the statistical arguments of the anti-sprawlers, particularly on transportation issues. Unfortunately, aside from a booklet produced in the 1990s, these authors have produced no book-length treatment. For a highly personal and pungent attack on the principles of smart growth, particularly as practiced in Portland, Oregon, see Randal O'Toole, *The Vanishing Automobile and Other Myths* (Bandon, OR: Thoreau Institute, 2001), as well as the material up on the Web site of the Thoreau Institute (www.ti.org). Another good place to go for a refutation of smart growth assumptions is Samuel Staley, *The Sprawling of America: In Defense of the Dynamic City*, Policy Study no. 251 (Washington, DC: Reason Public Policy Institute, 1996).

History of Suburbs and Sprawl

Two valuable books on urban development generally are the work of Peter Hall: his massive compendium *Cities in Civilization* (New York: Pantheon Books, 1998) and his *Cities of Tomorrow: An Intellectual History of Urban Planning Design in the Twentieth Century* (London: Basil Blackwell, 1988). Although there is a very large literature that deals primarily with city centers, the literature on suburban development is much thinner. For the United States, there is Kenneth Jackson's *Crabgrass Frontier: The Suburbanization of the United States* (Oxford: Oxford University Press, 1985); Robert Fishman, *Bourgeois Utopias: The Rise and Fall of Suburbia* (New York: Basic Books, 1987); and Dolores Hayden, *Building Suburbia: Green Fields and Urban Growth, 1820–2000* (New York: Pantheon Books, 2003). Although there is a great deal of valuable information in each of them, each tends to have a jaundiced view of recent middle-class suburbia. Despite a similar disdain for middle- and working-class suburbs by much of the British social and intellectual elite, English historians on the whole have done better in chronicling them. H. J. Dyos set a high standard in 1966 with his *Victorian Suburb: A Study of the Growth of Camberwell* (Leicester: Leicester University Press), a case study in South London up to World War I. This was followed by Alan A. Jackson's *Semi-Detached London: Suburban Development, Life and Transport, 1900–39* (London: George Allen & Unwin Ltd., 1972), which looked at several case studies during the interwar years, and David Thorn's *Suburbia* (London: Paladin, 1972). An excellent introduction to the postwar working-class suburb can be found in Mark Clapson's *Invincible Green Suburbs, Brave New Towns* (Manchester: Manchester University Press, 1998). A good corrective for many misconceptions about suburbs can be found in the work of geographer Richard Harris—for example, his book with Peter J. Larkham entitled *Changing Suburbs: Foundation, Form and Function* (London Spon Press, 1999). One of the first books to attempt a history of sprawl is Owen Gutfreund, *Highways and the Reshaping of the American Landscape* (London: Oxford University Press, 2004).

INDEX

Note: Italicized page numbers indicate figures.

Abercrombie, Patrick, 173, *174*, 175–76, 266n3
Abrams, Charles, 251n2
academics and professionals: on anti-sprawl
    campaign, 254n4; anti-suburban orientation
    of, 123; backlash from, 121; "diversity" focus of,
    143–44; elite support for, 118; self-interests of,
    163; on social problems and sprawl, 125–26,
    144. *See also* elites; planning professionals
aesthetics: anti-sprawl arguments about, 132–35,
    150–51; elites' imposition of, 134–35, 254n38;
    farmland concerns and, 142; of landscape,
    118–19, 133–34; L.A.'s possibilities for, 153–54;
    Portland's planning system and, 213
affluence: aesthetics issues and, 150–51; environ-
    mental concerns and, 126–29, 150; expansion
    of, 36, *86*, 89, 93, 164, 218; industrial produc-
    tion of, 26; measurement of, *110*; postwar rise
    of, 42–43, 121, 172; sprawl linked to, 109–12.
    See also housing, affluent
affluent cities: automobile's dominance in, 141;
    decreased densities in, 18–19; focus on, 11–12;
    London as, 24–25; population and land area of,
    51; twentieth-century changes in, 12–13
affluent people: as anti-highway, 193; as ben-
    eficiaries of slow-growth policies, 189, 195;
    choices of, 111; European planning's effects
    on, 179–80; in exurbia, 87, 89–91; job loca-
    tions of, 56–57; mobility demands of, 131–32;
    outward movement of, 34; population densities
    controlled by, 57–58; return to city center,
    53–54; rural areas as preserve of, 175–76,
    214–15; suburbanization of, 45; as worried
    about sprawl, 164–66. *See also* elites
African-Americans, 97–98
agricultural land: abandonment of, 89; anti-sprawl
    arguments about, 141–43; conversion of, 6,
    119, 275n35; as "natural" (or not), 133–34;
    Portland's planning system and, 212–15; shift
    to forest, 142, 255n12
agricultural production: changes in, 24; disconnec-
    tion from, 1–2; subsidies for, 142–43, 212
airplane travel, 132
airport areas, *92*, 92–93
Akron (Ohio), 88
Alaska: population density of, 240n10
alienation, 125, 144
American Farmland Trust, 155
American Housing Survey, 245n54
American Planning Association, 263n65
Amsterdam (Netherlands), 52
amusement parks, 71, *72*
annexations, 145, 238n8
anti-sprawl campaigns: aesthetic and symbolic
    objections in, 132–35, 150–51; on automobile
    use, 2–3, 127, 129–32, 140–41, 192; on costs
    of sprawl, 122–23, *124*, 125, 138–40; economic
    downturn linked to, 161, 189, 195; on environ-
    mental issues, 126–28, 148–50; on farmland
    and open space, 141–43; governmental
    intervention juxtaposed to, 99–100; historical
    context of, 115–16; illogical targets of, 69;
    impetus for, 8–11; on land use, 135–36; "limits

Main Street program (National Trust), 261n56
Mall of America (Bloomington, Minn.), 71
Malthus, Thomas, 128
Manchester (England), 29, 91, 236n15
Manhattan (N.Y.), 4, 27, 55, 233n8
Manila (Philippines), 27
marginalized groups, 21–22
Marin County (Calif.), 217
Marsh, Benjamin, 99, 100
Marshall Field's, 243n37
Maryland: anti-sprawl efforts in, 3; garden city in,
    171, 186; planning success in, 185–86, 276n46;
    population densities of, 62, 267–68n29
Maryland–National Capitol Park and Planning
    Commission, 182, 183
Massachusetts, planning efforts in, 192, 215, 217.
    See also Boston (Mass.)
Massachusetts Institute of Technology, 128
master-planned communities. See planned
    developments
McCall, Tom, 203, 204
McHarg, Ian, 134
McMansions, 88–89, 151, 214
megalopolis concept, 49–50, 94, 277
Melbourne (Australia), 107
Merton Park (South London), 34
Mesopotamian times, 18
Metro (D.C.), 185–86, 194
Metro (Metropolitan Service District). See Portland
    (Oreg.)
metropolitan area definitions, measures in, 60,
    240n10
Mexico City (Mexico), population and land area
    of, 51
Miami–Dade County (Fla.): population densities
    of, 63; population pattern of, 231n1; postwar
    growth of, 43; regional government of, 145
Michigan, exurban areas of, 30. See also Detroit
    (Mich.)
middle class: access to suburbia and exurbia, 115,
    116, 117–18; aristocratic models for, 28; elites'
    disdain for, 125–26, 134–35, 151, 254n38; in
    exurbs, 34–35, 89; increased wealth of, 86;
    outward movement of, 33–35, 74; postwar

demands of, 177, 180; as vulgar mass, 153. See
    also automobile; choices; housing, middle-class
Milan (Italy), 73
military considerations, crowding and, 23
Miller, John, 151
Milton Keynes (England), 177
Milwaukee (Wisc.), 62, 94
Minneapolis–Saint Paul (Minn.): mall and amuse-
    ment park near, 71; minority population of, 97;
    population densities of, 62; Portland compared
    with, 274n29; regional government of, 145
Minnesota. See Minneapolis–Saint Paul (Minn.)
minority groups: affordable suburban housing
    for, 64; better housing for, 48; gentrification
    fostered by, 56; opportunities for, 218; outward
    movement of, 45, 74, 97–98; sprawl's effects
    on, 145, 257nn21–22
Missouri. See Kansas City (Mo.); Saint Louis (Mo.)
Mitchell, Joni, 132
mixed-use developments, 151–53, 190
mobile (or manufactured) homes, 58, 241n17,
    246n63
mobility: automobile's role in, 129–30; decentral-
    ization linked to, 108–9; demand for, 131–32;
    opportunities for, 218; postwar increase in, 180;
    rights and choices in, 110
Montpellier (France), 80
Morrill, Richard, 257n22
mortgages, self-amortizing, 102
Moscow (Soviet era), 195–98
Moses, Robert, 253n23
Muir, John, 30
multicentered urban regions, 52
multinucleated cities, 39–40, 48–49, 94
Mumford, Lewis, 94, 119, 134–35
Munich (Germany), 74, 76

Nairn, Ian, 178–79
Nantucket Island (Mass.), 192, 215, 217
Napa Valley (Calif.), 217
Naperville (Ill.), 64
Naples (Italy), 77
Napoléon III, 35
National Association of Home Builders, 159

Saint Louis (Mo.): city center crisis in, 47; decentralization of, 57, 107; population densities of, 62
Salt Lake City (Utah), 210
San Antonio (Tex.), 62
San Bernardino County (Calif.), 67–68
San Diego city and county (Calif.): aerial view of, 80; freeways and travel times in, 253n25; in metropolitan area definitions, 60; population densities in, 63, 67–68
San Francisco and Bay area (Calif.): architectural heritage of, 135; BART system of, 194; city center(s) of, 52–53, 146; decentralized planning in, 211; freeways in, 192–93; gentrification in, 48, 56, 240–41n13; land prices in, 210; population densities of, 63, 211; Portland compared with, 210
San Jose (Calif.), 43, 52, 63
Santa Ana (Calif.), 67
Santa Monica (Calif.), 217
São Paulo (Brazil), 79
satellite cities: concept of, 182–83; in Moscow plan, 196–97
satellite downtowns, 71–72
scattered (or noncontinuous) development, 67, 125
Schaumburg (Ill.), 71
schools, 57, 138–39
Schumacher, Fritz, 267n28
Scotland, postwar population of, 42
Seaside (Fla.), 151, 152
seasonal exurban territories, 30
"seasonal suburban," use of term, 233–34n12
Seattle (Wash.), 62
security, 23, 25
Seeger, Pete, 135
segregation, 98, 145, 187
"sensitive minority," use of term, 153
septic systems, 88–89
settlement patterns: assumptions about, 125; comparison of, 201; components of, 93–94; critique of, 134; galactic metropolis metaphor for, 83, 94–95; problems of various, 10–11; research needed on, 149; sprawl as preferred, 17

sewage treatment: cost of, 139; in developing world, 150; fees for, 188; methods for, 88–89, 128; population threshold for providing, 61; in Rome (early), 22
Sharp, Thomas, 118–19, 151, 202
shopping centers and malls: as city center competition, 52, 243n37; expanded activities in and around, 71, 72; as intensified downtowns, 72–73; postwar British, 178; restrictions on, 200–201; scapegoating of, 47
Siegan, Bernard, 249n22
Sierra Club, 127, 155, 159, 211
Sieverts, Thomas: on human clustering, 109; on peripheral beauties, 154; on planning debates, 263–64n70; on sprawl, 277–78; on Zwischenstadt, 75, 244n43
Silver Spring (Md.), 185
Simon, Julian, 252–53n20
Simon, Robert E., 267–68n29
Singapore, 160
Skokie (Ill.), 243n37
Small, Kenneth A., 231n1
Smart Growth America, 156
smart growth movement: backlash against, 218–19; blamed for economic downturn, 161, 189, 195; groups supporting, 159; housing costs and, 263n64; on increased population density of city centers, 57–58; influence on, 171; New Urbanism and, 152; use of term, 3, 8, 263n65. See also regional growth management system
Smith, Neil, 235n7
smog, 116. See also pollution
Snell, Bradford, 100
social class: in anti-sprawl arguments, 115, 116, 117–18, 151; attack on automobile use and, 130–32. See also affluent people; aristocracy; elites; middle class; poor people; working class
social order: North American vs. European, 28–29; physical landscape as reflective of, 118–19
social problems: anti-sprawl arguments about, 125–26, 143–48; decline of, 164; radical dispersal to reduce, 170–72. See also racism; segregation